Richard Strauss

The Staging of His Operas and Ballets

Rudolf Hartmann

Richard Strauss

The Staging of His Operas and Ballets

PHAIDON · OXFORD

Copyright © 1980 by Office du Livre, Fribourg (Switzerland)

First published in German by Office du Livre S.A., Fribourg, 1980,
as *Die Bühnenwerke von der Uraufführung bis heute*

First published in the U.S.A. by Oxford University Press, Inc., 1981

This edition published 1982 by Phaidon Press Ltd., Littlegate House,
St. Ebbe's Street, Oxford, OX1 1SQ

English translation by Graham Davies

British Library Cataloguing in Publication Data

   Hartmann, Rudolf
     Richard Strauss: the staging of his operas
     and ballets.
     1. Strauss, Richard—Performances
     2. Opera—Production and direction
     3. Dance production
     I. Title II. Richard Strauss: Die Bühnenwerke
     von der Uraufführung bis heute. *English*
     782.1'092'4   ML50.S93

     ISBN 0-7148-2254-X

This book was printed in Germany by Freiburger Graphische Betriebe,
Freiburg im Breisgau
Filmsetting: Febel AG, Basle
Photoengraving: Cooperativa lavoratori grafici, Verona
Binding: Burkhardt AG, Zurich

Design: Franz Stadelmann
Production: Emma Staffelbach

Printed in Germany.

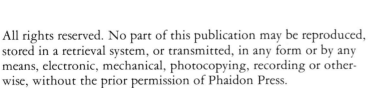

84- 125

Table of Contents

Foreword

When the Office du Livre, Fribourg, asked me to write a book on Richard Strauss, I hesitated because of the extensive specialized literature that already exists on the subject. I feared that many potential readers might exclaim: 'what, yet another book on Strauss?' Then I decided that I could not resist the challenge to discuss, with lavish illustrations, the origin and content of all the works which Strauss wrote for the stage, as well as the circumstances attending their first and subsequent performances throughout the world up to the present day. I recalled a letter that I received from Richard Strauss in 1948, part of which is reproduced at the end of this book. It was the composer's own invitation, coupled with that of M. Jean Hirschen of Office du Livre, which eventually persuaded me to undertake this formidable task.

I have dealt here with all the stage works by Richard Strauss from *Guntram* to *Capriccio*—in all, fifteen operas and two ballets, written over a period that extends for more than half a century, from 1892 to 1942.

As far as possible I have tried to let the composer and his fellow artists tell the story of how these works came into being, because their authentic words give the most reliable account of their genesis. My own experiences and opinions are culled from personal knowledge of many performances of these works, and also—particularly as far as the later ones are concerned—from a number of conversations with their creators.

Contemporary events are referred to wherever necessary to enable the reader to find his way through the material, or wherever they had a direct influence on Strauss's work.

Retracing the steps taken by Strauss and his later librettists, from *Guntram* to *Capriccio,* almost tangibly feeling the closeness of their personality and minds, and following up every clue that would help towards an understanding of their works, has been a most valuable experience for which I feel deeply indebted.

Munich, May 1980   Rudolf Hartmann

This votive tablet in rustic style depicts Strauss's villa in Garmisch. Beneath it is the epitaph for *Guntram.* An idyllic brook runs along the foot of the little hill where it stands.

Guntram

In the Austrian and Bavarian mountains it has long been a popular custom to put up a commemorative plaque, called a *Marterl,* to those who have suffered a painful accidental death.

One such *Marterl* can be found in the grounds of Richard Strauss's villa in Garmisch. It commemorates the composer's first stage work. The inscription reads as follows:

> Here rests
> the honourable and virtuous youth
> Guntram,
> Minnesinger,
> who was brutally slain
> by the symphonic orchestra
> of his own father.
> May he rest in peace.

Guntram received its first performance on 10 May 1894 at the Grossherzogliches Hoftheater at Weimar.

Contemporary reports show that it was given four times with only moderate success, and a production at the Munich Hoftheater (16 November 1895), which had been arranged with great difficulty, only ran for one evening. Some years later (9 October 1901), the Neues Deutsches Theater in Prague staged the work for the first time, with rehearsals directed by the courageous conductor Leo Blech, and with Strauss himself conducting. Several years afterwards, in 1910, a further attempt was made to revive the work in Frankfurt, but it was no more than a vain act of love.

It is probable that Strauss himself drew up the text for the *Marterl* with characteristic Bavarian humour in the years prior to the First World War, and raised the original plaque in the grounds of his villa at that time. To this day, however, it has not been possible for Strauss's family to verify this.

Following *Salome,* and *Elektra,* Strauss was approaching the world-wide success of *Der Rosenkavalier,* and it is likely that with the epi-taph on the *Marterl* he intended to take his final leave of this, his 'first attempt'. However, *Guntram* failed to depart in the spirit of eternal peace intended for it. That was not all. Almost symbolically the *Marterl* plaque changed its position in the grounds more than once, and for a time disappeared completely, only to reappear at what is likely to be its final resting place, a beautiful spot where it can be seen from the house. The 'first-born' which had caused the composer such anguish and pain continued to haunt him. In 1934 a radio performance by Hans Rosbaud induced Strauss, almost fifty years after the first conception of the work, to begin a revision and an abridgement of *Guntram,* above all in its orchestration. This substantially eased the singers' task and had a beneficial effect on the intelligibility of the libretto when the opera was revived at the Deutsches Theater in Weimar on 29 October 1940.

The Staatsoper in Berlin followed Weimar's example on 15 June 1942 with a new production of *Guntram,* incorporating the best of casts, costumes and settings. A few months later, on 28 October, Strauss's last work, *Capriccio,* was first performed in Munich.

In his *Recollections*[1] Strauss himself passed judgement on the Weimar and Berlin performances and—with the benefit of decades of hindsight—wrote the following on the significance of *Guntram* in the context of his work as a whole:

> Commenting on my work, it gives me great satisfaction to mention that in Berlin (under Heger) and in Weimar (under Sixt) *Guntram*—which for a number of reasons had lain untouched for over fifty years—was applauded as the important first stepping-stone of my dramatic achievements and correctly appreciated as such. Certainly, the libretto is no masterpiece (and is by no means perfect in terms of language). But this apprentice piece by a fledgling Wagnerian, who

Weimar.

Großherzogl. Hof-Theater.

Donnerstag den 10. Mai 1894.

Mit aufgehobenem Abonnement,

zum Vortheil des Chorpensionsfonds:

Zum ersten Mal:

Guntram.

In drei Aufzügen.

Dichtung und Musik von Richard Strauß.

In Scene gesetzt von Herrn Regisseur F. Wiedey.

Personen:

Der alte Herzog	Hr. Karl Bucha.
Freihild, seine Tochter	Frl. de Ahna.
Herzog Robert, ihr Gemahl	Hr. Schwarz.
Guntram } Sänger	Hr. Zeller.
Friedhold } Sänger	Hr. Wiedey.
Der Narr des Herzogs	Hr. Gießen.
Eine alte Frau } arme Leute	Frl. Tibelti.
Ein alter Mann } arme Leute	Hr. Lutz.
Zwei jüngere Männer } arme Leute	Hr. Barth. Hr. Hermann Bucha.
Drei Vasallen	Hr. Fischer. Hr. Schusthérr. Hr. Hennig.
Ein Bote	Hr. Hermann Bucha.
Vier Minnesänger	Hr. v. Szpinger. Hr. Knößler. Hr. Glitsch. Hr. Weyrauch.

Vasallen des Herzogs, Minnesänger, Mönche, Knechte und Reisige.

Die Handlung spielt in Deutschland um die Mitte des dreizehnten Jahrhunderts.

Textbücher sind an der Kasse für 80 Pfg. zu haben.

Grossherzogliches Hoftheater, Weimar, 1894
The programme for the première is not particularly attractive—the event was for charity. But the young composer himself conducted and his fiancée, Pauline de Ahna, sang the female lead. Set and costumes, following those of *Tannhäuser* and *Lohengrin,* were in conventional style. The producer was himself one of the leading singers. No mention is made of a designer; the set probably depended on items that could be found in stock.
Producer: Ferdinand Wiedey.
Conductor: Richard Strauss.

was sensing his way to independence, did lead to much fresher, more melodious, lush-sounding music . . . all in all: it is still . . . no worse than the libretto of the famous *Trovatore.*

Following the rejection of tradition—

my life determines
the law of my spirit;
my God speaks
to me through myself!

Guntram, Act III

—the way was clear for unimpeded, independent creativity.[1]

These words of the master convey a sense of commitment and clarify the meaning and significance of his first stage work in a far better manner than does the comprehensive literature on Strauss, where the numerous available assessments and analyses of *Guntram* are contradictory and confusing. All manner of opinions have been aired, from uninhibited enthusiasm to ironically casual references to a 'sin' of the composer's youth. The libretto, which Strauss himself refers to as incomplete in its somewhat awkward imitation of Wagnerian language, has repeatedly evoked disparaging comments and irreverent quotation. But that leaves the music, and here commentators are virtually unanimous that—despite a certain bias towards Wagnerian style—Strauss was searching for a new direction and, in part, had even succeeded in making his own distinctive voice heard.

In this context it is worth drawing attention to a review in the *Münchner Neueste Nachrichten* of the Munich première of *Guntram* by Oskar Merz. Despite several critical objections to the

Königliches Hof- und Nationaltheater, Munich, 1895
Strauss left Weimar for Munich,
which now became his artistic
centre. Here his work was performed, despite a good deal of resistance. Again he conducted, and
Pauline de Ahna, now his wife,
once again sang the main part of
Freihild. The chief producer, Anton Fuchs, besides directing sang
the role of Friedhold. As in Weimar, there was no designer and
the sets appear to have been constructed from what was available.
Producer: Anton Fuchs.
Conductor: Richard Strauss.

work, the reviewer noticed the young composer's great talent and encouraged him.

How did *Guntram* come about? Let Strauss
himself tell the story: 'The subject was suggested
by Alexander Ritter*. I am indebted to him for
the discovery of my dramatic vocation. Without
his encouragement and co-operation it would
hardly have occured to me to write an opera,
overawed as I was by Richard Wagner's gigantic
work, since there were no suitable librettists, or
rather ... they did not stimulate me.'[2]

Quite by chance, Strauss had read in the
Viennese *Neue Freie Presse* (most likely in 1887)
an article about certain medieval Austrian secret
societies which had dedicated themselves to attaining eternal peace for Mankind; an ideal imbued with a belief in the Good of Man, and in
Art as the saving grace of the human spirit.
From the summer of 1887 onwards Strauss
began to consider the possibility of an opera
along these lines. Alexander Ritter supported
his young friend's decision to work on this
material, and helped him to shape the libretto.
Strauss—on the Wagnerian model—wrote this
himself, even though from the outset he did not
place all that much faith in his own poetic ability. The encouragement he received from Ritter
and other friends enabled him to complete the
difficult task he had set himself between 1888
and 1892, and then, in a surprisingly short space
of time he set the libretto to music. Strauss recalled later that in 1892 he was sent on a journey
to Egypt to cure a lung ailment he had contract-
ed, and that he used the trip—generously
financed by his uncle Georg Pschorr—to compose the music and draw up the instrumentation
for his *Guntram* libretto: 'On the way out I
spent the month of November in Corfu, Olym-
pia and Athens, a stay which was to determine
my whole attitude towards Greek civilization
and especially towards the art of the fourth and
fifth centuries, B.C. In Luxor I scored the first
act of *Guntram*.'[3] For the liberally educated
Strauss, the great cultural flowering of the
Periclean age was to become an ever more deeply
felt ideal. But neither his visits to Luxor, Cairo,
Sicily, nor the Bavarian alps around Marquartstein (where *Guntram* was completed), were

---

* Alexander Ritter, more than thirty years
older than Strauss, was violinist in the Meinin-
gen Orchestra under Hans von Bülow. He composed operas himself, and later lived in Munich.
His influence on the young Strauss was significant, above all in introducing him Wagner's
work.

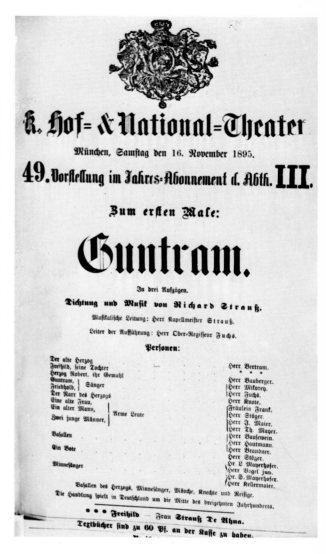

able to distract him from composing the music
for his medieval German subject. On the contrary, it would appear that the new and unfamiliar impressions fuelled his imagination.
The great contrast between his surroundings
and the world of his fantasy provided a rich
foundation for his creative imagination.

Let us follow Strauss in his struggle to write
the libretto. On 6 September 1888 he wrote to
his parents: '...have already completed the *an-
dante* of the violin sonata, and have written the
first draft of my opera libretto, which I believe will
be very good. The draft is good, and may the
poetic development of it not cause me any insur-
mountable difficulties!!!'

On 28 November 1889 he reported from
Weimar: 'Today I again began work on my libretto, and I am "kneading" away at it; so much
so that beads of anxious perspiration wet my
brow, but I will beat it yet.'

Königliches Hof- und National-
theater, Munich, 1895
This scene from Act I as presented
at the Munich première on 16
November 1895 shows a typical
multi-purpose forest landscape.
The focal points of the action
were then added as required.
Producer: Anton Fuchs.
Conductor: Richard Strauss.

This typical 'knights' hall', with
its Romanesque elements, was
used for Act II of the same production. Similar scenery was designed by the well-known studio-
workshops (e. g. Brückner at
Coburg) attached to every theatre
at that time.

Confirmation of his completion of a provisional version is contained in a letter from his father on 6 October 1890. This was soon followed by another letter containing suggested alterations and critical comments. Strauss himself was not satisfied and continued to work on the final shaping of the libretto. His serious illness (pleurisy) in 1891 caused a long interruption. Not until October of the same year was Strauss able to report to his father that he had resumed work on Act III, and only on 18 March 1892 was he able to inform his mother that he had completed the first version. Then Strauss immediately started to compose the music. He drafted the overture, and on 19 October 1892 could report that Act II was already finished. On 5 September 1893 in Marquartstein he noted: 'Score of Act III completed.'

Strauss's second version of the third Act led to a complete estrangement from his old friend and mentor, Alexander Ritter. It was characteristic of the unswerving determination of the young composer that he should adhere firmly to his own ideas—which he felt were correct—despite his great regret over the difficulties that were arising with Ritter. Many decades later Strauss referred to these events in his *Recollec-*

tions, and the way he described them is very illuminating:

I am indebted to Ritter for suggesting the *Guntram* text, although it became the cause of our estrangement. When during my stay in Egypt I became familiar with the works of Nietzsche, whose polemic against Christianity was particularly to my liking, the antipathy which I had always felt against a religion which relieves the faithful of responsibility for their actions (by means of confession) was confirmed and strengthened. Ritter could never quite forgive me for the renunciation of society (Third Act, Guntram-Friedhold scene) when Guntram judges himself and abrogates the right of the community to punish him.[4]

Strauss tried repeatedly to repair the broken bridges between himself and his old friend but, despite his affection for him, was unable to do so: 'After all, only what you have experienced for yourself has true meaning. I am really sorry that my dear, good Ritter gets excited over this, and I am really a little embarrassed as to how I can uphold my convictions (which I cannot throw aside) while at the same time not hurting him.'

The former Grand Ducal Court Theatre in Weimar was rebuilt in art nouveau style in 1907, and after 1918 was given the name Deutsches Nationaltheater (German National Theatre). The architect was Max Littmann of Munich, who had also drawn up the plans for the Prinzregententheater. The Goethe-Schiller monument stands in the foreground.

Here it is important to remember the overwhelming impression which Strauss's encounter with Antiquity made on him, and its decisive influence on the development of his creative personality. The path he had begun to tread was thereafter pursued with consistent purpose. Although not yet perceived as such by the young composer, it was to take him well beyond his immediate difficulties with *Guntram* and on towards the discovery of his own individual voice. But Strauss had first to circumvent and overcome the influence of Richard Wagner, whom he passionately admired but who also inhibited him in his own development. *Guntram* was the first and ultimately frustrating attempt in this direction. But after the next opera, *Feuersnot,* a satirical piece necessary for Strauss's inner liberation, the explosive originality of *Salome* suddenly erupted. If *Guntram,* the first of Strauss's fifteen operas, is seen in this light, it takes on a pre-eminence and significance far beyond the inconsequentiality of a youthful sin. Richard Specht recognized this in a study of the composer published in 1921: '...*Guntram* was a liberation from doctrine, the rejection of everything which ran counter to his own artistic self-determination, a commitment to his inner dictates, and at the same time a farewell to the world of Richard Wagner...' The same author also recognized, with critical discernment, that the libretto had its weakness and that the musical style was in part heavily Wagnerian; but he looked beyond these failings: '*Guntram* is the gateway through which Strauss, the epigone, could stride forward along the path towards his own fulfilment... Strauss buried his work. But did he disown it? That I do not believe.' With these words Specht anticipated the revival of *Guntram* in 1940–2. In the first volume of his major Strauss biography (1976), Willi Schuh talks of the 'significance accruing to the work in terms of Strauss's intellectual development at that time, a significance that cannot be measured against the modest success of this first opera, which moves all too powerfully within Wagnerian parameters. This significance must correspond to the role the work played at the time.' This is surely a just assessment of *Guntram*.

The plot of the piece, which is set in medieval times, is simple despite the sweeping, hymn-like songs of peace and the horrifying portrayals of war. As a member of a secret order of knights sworn to the noblest ideals, and bound to the Christian ethic, the Minnesänger Guntram is sent to a dukedom whose people are suffering under the arbitrary cruelty of its rulers. The young duchess, Freihild, attempts to alleviate these sufferings but, despairing of her lack of success, determines to kill herself. Guntram saves her and is invited to the court by her father, the old duke. A magnificent banquet—including an entertainment by Minnesängers—gives Guntram the opportunity to hymn the ideals of peace, to evoke the horrors of impending war, and to appeal on behalf of the long-suffering people. His song wins the enthusiastic approval of the young duchess, and her father, too, is moved by Guntram's words. But his son-in-law, a man without feeling and the cause of the people's misery, reacts with ridicule and scorn. He threatens Guntram with his sword (most probably out of jealousy, because he recognizes his wife's warm feelings for the stranger). Guntram, compelled to defend himself, kills the son-in-law. The old duke, enraged by the death of his heir has Guntram arrested and condemned to death. In the loneliness of the dungeon, Guntram recognizes his guilt and realizes that he could not justify his behaviour before the order of his fellow knights. He knows that he must work out his own salvation. Neither the love of Duchess Freihild—which opens the doors of his dungeon—nor the earnest warnings of his mentor Friedhold, sent with the order to bring him before their court, can divert Guntram from his purpose. Bidding farewell to all, he departs to face his fate alone, ready to give himself up but also to be true to himself.

The points where this plot bears on Strauss's own life are clearly recognizable. Guntram's zeal and dilemmas were very much those of the composer. The hero's mentor, Friedhold, is identifiable with Alexander Ritter, the traditionally minded friend who was alienated and dismayed by the amended Act III, with its renunciation of Christian values.

Almost half a century later, under the impact of world political events and the attendant dangers of war, Strauss wrote a second opera devoted to the pursuit of peaceful ideals—*Friedenstag* ('Armistice Day'). Based on a text by Joseph Gregor, it glorified the Peace of Westphalia which had followed the terrible Thirty Years' War. This cannot help but make one wonder whether ominous turns in world events at the time *Guntram* was written did not also help to shape that opera's pacifist philosophy. It seems unlikely that that article in the *Neue Freie Presse* about medieval secret societies was the sole spur to the composition of *Guntram*. The German Emperor Wilhelm I had died at the beginning of 1888 (9 March), his son Friedrich III succeeding to the throne for only a few months (he died on 15 June of the same year), and *his* son

Staatsoper, Berlin, 1941–2
A scene from Act I in the production at the Berlin Staatsoper in 1941–2. After almost 50 years Strauss had produced a revised version of the work. Guntram was sung by the famous tenor Franz Völker and Freihild by the soprano Hilde Scheppan. The gestures are typical of the old 'Wagnerian' style.

Staatsoper Berlin, 1941–2
Act II of the Berlin production in
1941–2: a beautiful proportioned
Romanesque hall, created by the
designer Emil Preetorius, whose
work at the Bayreuth festivals was
well known. Robert Heger conducted; the producer was Wolf
Völker. Paul Sixt also staged the
revised version in Weimar in
1940 with new stage designs by
Moritz Schmidt.

succeeded to the title of Emperor as Wilhelm II on the same day.

Comments in the world's press on the likely repercussions in Germany—and in Europe as a whole—were not reassuring. There are reasonable grounds to assume that Richard Strauss was strongly affected by this, and that it had its effect on the conception of *Guntram*. Strauss was stimulated by those works of his idol, Richard Wagner, which are steeped in the ideals of chivalry—*Lohengrin, Tannhäuser* and *Parsifal*.

The early productions of *Guntram* followed the style of Wagnerian Romanticism. Above all the setting and the production of the all-important second Act were modelled on those generally adopted for *Tannhäuser*.

The revivals of the opera in 1940–2 likewise showed only minor changes in the settings and a more concentrated style of production. The affinity with the atmosphere of *Lohengrin* or *Tannhäuser* remained as before. In his *Recollections* Strauss recalls the opera's very first performance: '*Guntram* scored a "succès d'estime", but after a few futile attempts to revive it in Frankfurt and Prague by making extensive cuts it vanished completely from the stage, and with it disappeared for the next six years my courage in writing for the theatre.'[5]

Elsewhere Strauss mentions other early dramatic projects, for example *Eulenspiegel* (which later became a tone-poem) and *Schildbürger,* which remained unfulfilled. Not even his acute disappointment with the failure of *Guntram* could prevent him planning new works. An inextinguishable passion for the stage had been aroused in the thirty-year-old composer, who was already famous for his songs and the tone-poems 'Aus Italien', 'Don Juan', 'Macbeth', and 'Tod und Verklärung'. Deep down, he knew he could also succeed in opera. The example of his hero Wagner must surely have driven him on, for by about the same age Wagner had already written *Rienzi, Der fliegende Holländer,* and *Tannhäuser.*

Guntram fulfilled the purpose prescribed for it. It was a stepping stone towards his future fulfilment, paving the way for all the other stage works that were to emerge during Strauss's long creative life. Strauss recognized this and never forgot either the inadequacy of his first libretto or the way in which the heavy orchestration drowned the singers.

When Strauss went to Weimar in 1940 to hear the revived and newly re-published *Guntram* after almost fifty years, he invited me to join him. We stayed at the famous Elephant Hotel and attended the first night together. I was struck by Strauss's taciturnity and his air of deep contemplation. He followed the performance with the greatest concentration, and as usual was most warmly applauded at the end. But he avoided the large reception held afterwards and left with me without saying a word. We walked to the Goethe-Schiller monument, where he stood for a long time in silence. Then I heard him half mumble to himself: 'Yes, yes, these two . . . the language . . .' Then without a further word he returned to the hotel.

When he came to begin work on his last stage work, *Capriccio,* which immortalizes the perennial conflict in opera between the claims of words and of music, Strauss's first concern was with the libretto. He searched in vain for someone to work with. Clemens Krauss, the conductor and theatre director in Munich who shortly became that person, remembered asking: 'Dr. Strauss, why don't you write the libretto yourself?', to which the composer quickly replied, 'No, no, I can't do that. Unfortunately I've no poetic talent.' 'But you wrote *Intermezzo* yourself, didn't you?' 'Yes, but that was something different. That was something I had experienced myself, and in many ways it was everyday language. The new work [the title *Capriccio* had not yet been decided on] needs a text of crystalline clarity. And that I can't manage.'

The choice of Clemens Krauss as collaborator proved to be a particularly happy one. But so far as I am aware, Strauss never took advantage of his close relationship with Krauss to ask for a performance of *Guntram* in Munich after the second attempt to put it on in Weimar and Berlin. The chapter on *Guntram* seemed truly closed. The *Marterl* underlines the point: 'May he rest in peace.'

Feuersnot

After the failure of *Guntram* I had lost the courage to write for the stage. Then I came across the Flemish legend, *The Quenched Fires of Audenarde,* which gave me the idea of writing, with personal motives, a little intermezzo against the theatre. To wreak some vengeance on my dear native town, where I, little Richard the third (there is no 'second', Hans von Bülow once said), had just like the great Richard the first thirty years before, had such unpleasant experiences...[1]

This was how decades later Richard Strauss recorded the origin of his opera *Feuersnot* ('Fire-Famine'), and his need to overcome the bitter disappointment of what was—as he himself conceded—the failure of *Guntram.*

No longer wanting to write a libretto himself, he found a librettist in Ernst von Wolzogen, a man of caustic wit, who also had a grudge against Munich because of the failure of his plans for a cabaret. The setting of the Flemish saga was transposed to the banks of the river Isar, in the heart of Munich, and encompassed the old Sendlingergasse; Strauss would get his own back on the narrow-minded, philistine attitudes of the respectable bourgeoisie.

Strauss possessed an inborn sense of humour which produced a flood of musical ideas for this material. He was delighted to compose music full of melodies, portraying the petit bourgeois world, upon which he poured a great deal of scorn, but which he also loved—with its attitude to life at once self-righteous and affirmative. He had himself been born in the heart of Munich, at Altheimereck and had grown up near the Sendlingergasse. The names and exact characterizations of the burghers—Jörg Pöschel (narrow and self-important), Kunz Gilgenstock (cheerful and good-natured), etc.—may well be based on figures from Strauss's youth, characters which Wolzogen was happy to adapt. There are folklorish songs; there is the magic of midsummer night, *Johannisnacht,* and its close asso-

ciations with *Die Meistersinger;* and the summer solstice, with its mythical associations, filled with the atmosphere of girls and young men in love, desirable and desiring. All this, however, is little more than the background against which one Kunrad, a deeply offended man, settles his account with the burghers. Kunrad is Strauss, and his one-time Master, the great Richard (Wagner), is the other figure whom the citizens of Munich have also badly abused.

This is the plot: the midsummer night festival is being celebrated according to ancient custom in early medieval Munich. There is dancing; young people are cheerful, carefree and gay. Children go from house to house, asking for wood and gathering logs from every quarter for the great bonfire to be kindled in front of the Sendlinger Gate. Only one house in the foreground remains dark and silent, withdrawn from the general hubbub of the festivities. The children impatient pound on the door of the almost sinister abode, shouting and mocking, until its occupant finally reveals himself. He is Kunrad, a strange individual who has recently returned home and has won a curious reputation in the malicious gossip of the Sendlingergasse. The house is a legacy from his Master, Reichhart (Richard), and there Kunrad is to cultivate what he has learned, developing his knowledge by virtue of his own talents. Kunrad observes the children singing and the happy people like a man who just woken up. Lost in his work, he had missed the most beautiful day of the year, and now—in an exuberant mood—he determines to make up for the omission. He gives the children all the available wood in the house, helping them collect it, and at first sight falls in love with Diemut, the beautiful daughter of the burgomaster. With carefree abandon, out of sheer love of life, he kisses the surprised girl in full view of everyone—an act which earns him the crusty disapproval of the burghers. The maiden, believing herself humiliated and de-

Königliches Opernhaus, Dresden, 1901
The programme for the Dresden première is significant because *Feuersnot* was the first of the long series of Strauss premières at the same theatre. Ernst von Schuch, the conductor, became an enthusiastic advocate of Strauss's work. Maximilian Moris was the producer; the set was designed by Emil Rieck, who worked from historical sources.

graded, bursts into tears, swearing revenge which she plots with three of her playmates. The crowd, and the children carrying the wood, disappear through the Sendlinger Gate in the background and shortly afterwards the glow of the midsummer night bonfire can be seen. Diemut appears on the high balcony of the burgomaster's house and pretends to engage Kunrad below in a lovers' dialogue. She persuades him to let her pull him up to the balcony in a large basket. Kunrad, head over heels in love, readily accepts. But when the basket is only halfway up to the balcony, Kunrad is wickedly left hanging in mid-air and is ridiculed by the vengeful Diemut. Her three friends—followed later by the townspeople—return. In his unhappy position Kunrad becomes the object of general derision, and

Diemut is celebrated as a cunning and superior opponent. Anger wells up in Kunrad. With the help of the great Master, whom he invokes, Kunrad punishes the mocking citizens by extinguishing all the fires, which he extols as symbols of life and love. Darkness descends suddenly and the people are paralysed with horror. At this critical moment, they turn on the mayor's daughter, reproaching and berating her, knowing that fire and light will only return if she gives herself to her suitor, Kunrad. In a long address Kunrad points out all the failings of the faint-hearted townspeople and indicates the new paths they can follow in the future, including the penance he demands of Diemut. In the darkness Kunrad has by now swung himself up to the balcony; Diemut ultimately takes him into her room, and, amidst the lamentations of the people, light suddenly appears from within the house; the lights of the city and the mighty midsummer night bonfire are rekindled and jubilation erupts among the citizens in celebration of Diemut's deed and her acceptance of love.

Ernst von Wolzogen enthusiastically seized upon the idea of the opera and on 23 March 1899 wrote to Strauss:

> ... I now have the following idea: *Feuersnot*—one act—setting: old Munich in the semi-legendary era of the Renaissance. The young hero is himself a magician; the grand old Master—his mentor, once expelled by the people of Munich—never appears in person. At the close, to save the town from fire, the wicked maiden is forced to sacrifice her maidenhead to the young magician at the urgent insistence of the Council and the citizenry. Then, when love is united with the magic of genius, light will dawn on even the most incorrigible philistine!... As for the language, I am thinking of a drily humorous, somewhat archaic style, with dialect nuances...

The style of the language—with its unmistakable plain-speaking, especially in the closing scene—later gave rise to moralistic objections which prevented the work being performed. Strauss was working in Berlin at the time and was counting firmly on a première at the Berlin Hof-Oper. Various excuses were made until the composer lost patience and wrote the following letter to the theatre directorate in Berlin:

> As I believe you also will be interested in coming to a conclusion over my opera *Feuersnot,* permit me most humbly to send you the following final resumé. In the course of negotiations you have repeatedly declared that the conditions I have laid down, in relation to the première of the work, cannot be fulfilled by the general directorate of the Königliche Schauspiele in Berlin. Furthermore, you declared only this morning that you would have to forego any performance of the work if you did not acquire the very first performance.
>
> To my regret, I am less able today than at any other time in the past to undertake modifications to the contract, because (particularly since this morning's somewhat heated debate) I have become convinced that it is urgent that my work has those guarantees which I feel are necessary for its first performance at the Berlin Opera House. Therefore, may I permit myself a final word in this matter, and humbly inform you that—once and for all—I gratefully and politely decline both the honour of a première of *Feuersnot* and the distinction of ever seeing any of my dramatic works performed at the Berlin Opera House...

Königliches Opernhaus, Dresden, 1901
Emil Rieck's design of 1901 was freely based on earlier models and endeavours to do justice to the action in the piece. The houses reveal no sense of the irony which Ernst von Wolzogen had in mind.

Königliches Opernhaus, Berlin, 1902
The first time the names of the ensemble appeared in the programme was at the Berlin première of 1902. The producer was the Royal Opera's chief producer, Georg Droescher; the sets were by the technical director Brandt and the 'Royal theatre artist' Quaglio. As in Dresden, Strauss had to conduct the second part of the evening as well; in both cases this involved a ballet: in Dresden, Delibes's *Coppélia,* and in Berlin *Javotte* by Saint-Saëns.

Strauss could allow himself the luxury of such self-confidence because he was already certain of requests for a first performance of *Feuersnot* from Dresden and Vienna. Gustav Mahler had shown lively interest, and so had Ernst von Schuch, who with *Feuersnot* began a series of nine premières of Strauss's works at the Dresden Opera House.

Even here things did not always go smoothly, as is shown by an amusing letter about the fees that were to be asked. Strauss wrote to Schuch: '... 1500 marks is also a bit much! Oh, the theatre! May the Devil take the task of composing operas!... If things won't work out, then I shall proceed to Mahler in Vienna, who will do everything if I offer him a first performance. I shall rechristen myself Riccardo Straussino and

have my work published by Sonzogno, and then you'll agree to everything!'

The reference to an Italian publisher and to the italianization of his own name shows that theatre managements were then as now running blindly after the 'foreign sound' in opera.

The first performance in Dresden was given on 21 November 1901, but only after some revisions to the libretto had been undertaken there too.

A year later Berlin followed suit—despite the anger Strauss had expressed earlier. There were seven repeat performances, but then the run was ended because of objections from the Empress. Wolzogen's care-free, cabaret-style language had evoked displeasure because Diemut's sacrifice of her virginity in the final scene was referred to as

Lirumlarumlei (an untranslatable term suggesting 'much ado about nothing'). In a letter to Strauss the librettist irreverently gave vent to his anger: '. . . I can well believe that H. M. does not wish to know anything further of *Lirumlarumlei*—particularly after having 7 nippers. But I cannot believe that Siegfried Meyer [Wolzogen means Wilhelm II]—for all his Siegesallee [Victory avenue]!—would say he does not need a composer-conductor.'

Munich—the city for which this epigrammatic opera had been written—did not put on a first performance until 23 December 1905. In the meantime Strauss had learned from experience, and for the benefit of the producer, Anton Fuchs, wrote precise stage directions which he sent from Berlin. Until then productions had shown up the difficulties set by the demands made on the choirs (of children) and by the need to make the libretto clearly intelligible despite often massive orchestration, Strauss's instructions contributed greatly to clarity in production. Here are extracts from these stage directions:

During the waltz twilight has fallen, and night has arrived by figure 94.

Figure 106 moon on Diemut's balcony.

At figure 121 the moon disappears completely, so that by figure 123 complete darkness sets in.

Figure 131 utterly dark

Figure 140 the moon, in the meantime moved back a little, re-appears slowly from the clouds so that the lovers, Kunrad in the basket,

Diemut in the sky-light and later on the balcony again, are at least lit up a little (not brightly).

Figure 148 the moon disappears entirely: from the entrance of the chorus onwards some light is provided again by the torches and lanterns of the people.

After figure 159 *absolute blackness*

Page 131 from Talbeck's 'Wer hat's gewusst' onwards, move the forward ramp up a little so that the faces can be seen. The children after

Königliches Opernhaus, Berlin, 1902

The costumes, designed by Heinrich Leffler of Vienna, are remarkable both for their stylistic unity and simplicity, and their individual quality.

figure 161 move across the front of the stage until [by] figure 163

they are on the other side, and from figures 163 to 172, while

they start to sing, the children creep round behind the people so that by their entrance [at] figure 172 they are back where they started from.

For two reasons *Feuersnot* failed to gain a permanent place in the repertoire of the opera houses of the day: first, the work made very high demands, especially musical ones, upon any theatre, particularly one of medium size; and second, one-act operas were not popular with either theatre directors or audiences. Bizarre double bills became the practice; the evening was often filled out with a ballet, until Strauss himself took matters in hand and 'completed' the evening's programme with *Josephslegende* (1914). However, this did not really improve *Feuersnot's* situation. The plot demands complicated stage machinery and that almost inevitably means a long interval between one work and the next, leading to an over-long evening programme. Time, too, has dealt other blows to regular productions of the work. As with any contemporary polemic, Kunrad's address, the mainstay of the work, has lost its interest because the events to which it refers (and the witty allusions to names like Strauss, Wagner and Wolzogen) are so far removed from us.

This is a pity, because the musical substance of the work is fresh and alive. It is still possible to delight in the Wagner quotations, in the old Munich songs interwoven into the music, and in the joyous waltzes which Strauss employed for the first time—among them a slow waltz anticipating *Der Rosenkavalier*. What a pleasure it is to hear this unconstrained, inventive music and to marvel at the masterly treatment of the orchestra. What a pity, too, it is that it is so hard to free the libretto from the dust it has gathered over the years.

Until the end of his life Strauss was much concerned about the fate of *Feuersnot,* perhaps because he perceived its significance in relation to his work as a whole. Even in the last entry in his diary, dated 19 June 1949, Strauss was still thinking about his first one-act work: 'One forgets that this work, by no means perfect (particularly in terms of the uneven orchestral treat-

ment), nevertheless marks a new subjective style in the essence of old opera—above all at the beginning of the century. It is a prelude!'

In terms of the music, that is probably the right emphasis to place on *Feuersnot:* it was a prelude. With that comment Strauss recalled his difficulties in freeing himself from the Wagnerian model. In an earlier diary entry (according to Willi Schuh, for 4 February 1945) Strauss considered the development of opera as a whole, and of his own work. He wrote of *Feuersnot:*

The new elements (at least compared with the normal opera tradition, with its knights, bandits, gypsies, Turks, Sicilian peasants, troubadours and court jesters) were initially to be found in the new genre of dialect opera; in the courage of the author to express a personal, polemical commitment; in the slightly satirical character of this new form; and musically the new element was found in the rejection of the splendid organ-like sound of four horns from Wagnerian opera—which was still evident in *Guntram.* This applied particularly to my more varied treatment of the woodwind section, which became a decisive factor in the somewhat brash sound I later applied in the instrumentation.

There has always been criticism of the fusion of styles in *Feuersnot:* harmless jest mixed with Kunrad's admonishing speech. I concede that objection; without this mixture, though, the whole thing would have been too simplistic, and anyway, the Kunrad address was the important thing for me; the rest of the plot was an amusing accessory; nevertheless, people must have recognized the courage of a previously unsuccessful operatic composer [Strauss was thinking here of *Guntram*] in giving his own countrymen a small lecture on the way they had behaved towards Richard Wagner. I do not think I need to emphasize that the slightly scornful passages reminiscent of the great Master's often somewhat bombastic lyricism are not an oversight on the part of the librettist.

Whatever the case, *Guntram* and *Feuersnot* are two natural and necessary building-blocks in relation to dramatic style, to the orchestral treatment, and to all the experiences culled from the performances and from personal enmities, from which grew the evil child *Salome;* she was the first beautiful representative of all those female forms whose finely diverse psychology was to inform the neurotic counterpoint and the diffuse colours of my later scores: from Salome's kiss and Clytaemnestra's dreams, to Danae's Golden Nights,

Bayerische Staatsoper, Munich, 1930
Leo Pasetti's design for the new production of 1930 in Munich gave the houses, with their exaggerated high gables, a magical quality which was heightened in the half-light and in the flickering glow of the torches.
Producer: Alois Hoffmann.
Conductor: Hans Knappertsbusch.

Städtische Oper, Berlin, 1931
There is a similar sense of movement in the unified structure of the set for the Städtische Oper, Berlin, 1931, designed by Emil Preetorius.
Producer: Hans Niedecken-Gebhard.
Conductor: Paul Breisach.

Helen's Draught of Recollection, Ariadne's metamorphosis, and the embrace of Apollo and Daphne!

From the germ of *Feuersnot* emerged also the 'confessions' of the *Ariadne* prelude, the *Intermezzo* experiment, and the *Capriccio* last will and testament! . . .

Here, the composer outlined perhaps better than anyone else the significance of *Feuersnot* and its place in relation to his entire work. Strauss's assessment of the work, a clear critical appraisal, was nevertheless broad and generous. He again countered the objections raised to Kunrad's long address:

As to Kunrad's superfluous speech of admonition I will say this: that all those who piously listened to the longest of arias in the old operas (*horribile dictu*—Handel!) and who slept for years through the 'unbearable' Wotan story (with only the occasional angry interruption) because the Master placed it, by way of caution, neither at the beginning nor at the end of an act—all these people should be the first to keep their mouth shut.

With this rugged Bavarian comment, which sounds almost like a closing sentence from Kunrad's address, Strauss concluded his defence of the *Feuersnot* he loved so much.

Both the composer and the librettist suspected that a libretto with a time-bound polemic as its nucleus would be in danger of aging rapidly. 'An amusing accessory', was how Strauss described the plot arranged around Kunrad's address. Through their instructions for the set and for the direction of the cast, Wolzogen and Strauss tried to liberate the work from too transient an association and to allow it to float freely and timelessly.

The instructions for the location of the action read: 'in Munich, in the timelessness of fable . . .' A production could thus be shaped purely by imagination. Moreover the more detailed comments on the scenery stated that houses in the street (presumed to be the Sendlingergasse) should look 'as grotesque as possible'. Wolzogen, too, made similar remarks on several occasions; and Strauss repeatedly stressed the cheerfulness of the whole affair. He wanted lightness and humour in the singer's portrayal of Kunrad. Both sought to raise the work into the sphere of timelessness—a difficult task, owing to the polemic.

Parallels to *Die Meistersinger* constantly suggest themselves: comedy characters, the joyful revelry of midsummer's night against the background of serious efforts to grapple with fun-

Bayerische Staatsoper, Munich, 1958
The grotesque appearance of the houses (which is part of the action) was emphasized by Max Bignens in his set for this production. The Sendlinger Gate became perhaps a shade too significant. But on the whole the set, with its different levels, provided an effective background for the action.
Producer: Herbert Graf.
Conductor: Meinhard von Zallinger.

damental questions of art, together with the substantial part played by 'the people'. These parallels also reveal the basic differences. With Wagner, the plot has real historical foundations, and is given timeless validity through the convincing power and presence of the leading figure, Hans Sachs. Sachs's closing monologue universalizes the action of the opera.

Despite his strenuous efforts the librettist of *Feuersnot* has not succeeded in achieving universality. The final scene gives no indication that Kunrad's admonition achieves a cleansing effect; the dominant event is a love scene, brought somewhat embarrassingly to the fore. The people, the scorned bourgeoisie, celebrate not from enthusiasm for artistic creativity, but because the fire and the light have returned, following the unsettling period of darkness. The

symbolism which illuminates the action of *Die Meistersinger* fails to achieve the same for *Feuersnot*.

So *Feuersnot* failed to gain a permanent place in the repertoire, despite the fact that it was initially produced on over thirty stages; most notably it was a sensational success in Vienna under Gustav Mahler.

Performed together with *Josephslegende, Feuersnot* experienced a brief revival, but thereafter performances became infrequent and productions were limited to special occasions, such as anniversaries and birthdays.

The stage-designers for the first productions of *Feuersnot* tended to overlook the author's demands for a free interpretation of the Bürgerstrasse which would have given a grotesque quality to the houses that were an integral part

Volksoper, Vienna, 1964
This design by Otto Werner Meyer for the production at the Vienna Volksoper in 1964, celebrating the hundredth birthday of Richard Strauss, is very close in character to Act II of *Die Meistersinger*. The use of banners, and distaffs for the women and girls, underlined the parallels with the midsummer's night in *Die Meistersinger*.
Producer: Adolf Rott.
Conductor: Peter Maag.

Bayerische Staatsoper, Munich, 1980
Günther Schneider-Siemssen from Vienna designed the set for the 1980 Munich festival. The sketch shows the playful and comic transformation of the Sendlingergasse, just as Wolzogen had conceived it, which had at first looked just like a normal street scene. Producer: Giancarlo del Monaco. Conductor: Gustav Kuhn.

of the action. Instead the designers created more or less historically accurate reproductions of the Sendlingergasse on the stage. In addition—from the Dresden first performance onwards—in many cases the proscenium arch was too low, so Kunrad's suspension lost much of its point.

However, in later productions stage-sets gradually began to free themselves from historical associations, in some cases very skilfully. In similar fashion, costume designers allowed themselves to be influenced by the imaginative qualities of the music. But the problematic issues of the main theme in the libretto remained, and so dust gradually gathered on it.

Despite these failings, the importance of *Feuersnot* to Strauss's work should not be forgotten. Let us hope that from time to time good productions will keep it alive in the minds of the opera-going public.

The production problems of *Feuersnot* are still to be solved. To solve them would be more valuable than the attempts occasionally made to rewrite the libretti of operas which owe their success to their music rather than, or even despite, their dramatic work.

Salome

A clarinet flurry introduces the scene: 'A grand terrace in the palace of Herod...' Immediately we hear the voice of Narraboth uttering effusive words of love praising the beauty of the Princess Salome. A few bored soldiers are standing on the moonlit terrace; Herodias' page has stolen away from the banquet table inside the palace to see his friend, the Syrian captain of the guard who is himself passionately enthralled by Salome. He is concerned about him: 'Something terrible will occur.'

Herod, Salome, Herodias: these names begin to interweave with one another like the dark-coloured threads of an oriental carpet which, interspersed with shimmering silver strands, contain mysterious and multiple meanings—as does everything which the sultry air of this strange evening holds in store by way of encounters, rumours, confused talk about religion, political antagonisms and personal passions.

'The tetrarch is drunk', comments one of the soldiers observing the banquet. But who is this 'tetrarch', this ruler of a quarter, to take the literal Greek meaning? According to the evidence the term 'tetrarch' originates from northern Greece. In Thessaly, centuries before Christ, four different tribes were represented by elected chiefs who had religious and judicial but not political powers. In time the Greek term 'tetrarch' entered Roman administrative terminology. It was used for the first time by the Romans in connection with the Palestinian territories when they appointed the Idumaean Herod as governor. Herod I (the Great) ruled the entire land of Palestine with its four provinces of Judea, Samaria, Galilee and Perea. He later also acquired the title of king, but the Romans reserved the right to appoint or confirm the tetrarch.

The family history of the Herod clan is cruel and bloody. Herod I was not a Jew and not much loved by his people. Concerned about the security of his throne he had his wife, Mariamne, and three of his sons murdered. When he died, the Romans divided his kingdom among three of his other sons: Herod Antipas, the youngest, received Galilee and Perea, and was tetrarch there at the time of Christ. He had kidnapped his second wife, Herodias, from his elder half-brother. Legend has it that he imprisoned his troublesome brother for twelve years, after which he had him strangled.

This tale is told by the soldiers in Oscar Wilde's drama. Other accounts and sagas give the name of this unhappy man as Herod Philippus.

This, however, is just one of many confusions which occur in the sources, which are frequently imprecise. 'Herod' should be taken as the family name of the whole clan. The individual sons each had additional names, for example Herod Archelaos, Herod Philippus, Herod Antipas and so on.

Herod Philippus was never a prisoner of his brother Antipas. He was regarded as an exception among the Herod family, since his rule over the eastern provinces was mild and beneficent. Herodias' first husband was another step-brother who lived in Rome and showed no interest in acquiring the position of tetrarch. There is credible evidence of his existence and on that basis he would have been the father of Princess Salome. Together with his eldest brother, Herod Archelaos, who inherited the Jewish provinces Judea and Samaria, there were therefore four living brothers, three of whom succeeded to the domains left to them, and were confirmed by the Romans, while the fourth brother declined his position. After Archelaos was deposed, the Romans themselves took over the administration of the two most important provinces, Judea with Jerusalem, and Samaria. The might of Rome was represented by a procurator.

The night on the terrace has a special significance: Herod Antipas is celebrating his birthday

This historical map of Palestine at the time of Christ is from a Dutch atlas of 1750 and shows the geography of the tragedy of *Salome:* its actual location, Macherus, to the east of the Dead Sea; Jerusalem, the Judaean capital; the city of Tiberias, built by Herod Antipas on the lake of Genesareth (Galilee); and Caesarea, the official seat of the Roman procurator on the Mediterranean coast. (From the map collection of the Bavarian State Library, Munich, reproduced by kind permission.)

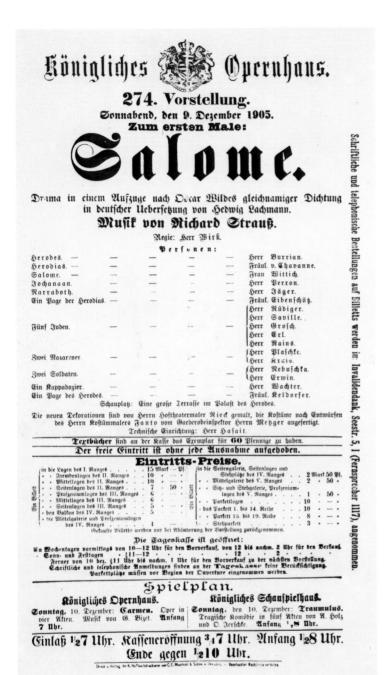

Königliches Opernhaus, Dresden,
1905
The programme for the Dresden
première on 9 December 1905,
with the names of the company's
leading singers. The producer,
stage-designer, costume-designer
and technician were also named,
but not the conductor. This was
the *Generalmusikdirektor,* Ernst
von Schuch, who from the outset
was closely associated with
Strauss's stage works.
Producer: Willi Wirk.
Sets: Ernst Rieck.
Costumes: Leonhard Fanto.

amid a crowd of honoured guests: a colourful mixture of Egyptians (Arabs), Jews, Greeks and the real rulers, the mighty Romans, represented by a proconsul, or perhaps even by the procurator himself, whose seat was at Caesarea on the Mediterranean. At the time of our story the procurator was Pontius Pilate. All these characters remain enveloped, as it were, in a veil of mystery, whose relationship to their confusing and variegated milieu can only be guessed at. But the scene of the action can be exactly ascertained: the fortification of Machaerus in Perea, to the east of the Dead Sea. There, as well as huge secret stocks of weapons and other war supplies, Herod Antipas had a kind of palace, which dated from the days of his father, for himself and his court. The times seemed too full of danger for him to feel safe in his new capital of Tiberias on the Lake of Gennesaret (Galilee), which he had re-named in honour of the Roman emperor Tiberius.

It seems worth noting that the ferment and unrest in the country arose from motives similar to those which today, almost two thousand

Königliches Opernhaus, Dresden, 1905
The design for the première by the court theatre artist, Emil Rieck, was strongly historical, with a marked architectural emphasis. The acting area was strangely restricted, and the whole set offered few opportunities for developing the atmospheric features (such as the clouds and the moon) as part of the action. However, we should remember that stage technology in 1905 had its limitations.
The original oil sketch, which can be seen in the Munich Theatre Museum, shows the palace on the right. Later photographs of the stage show it on the left, probably at the request of the producer who needed more room for the terrace.
Producer: Willi Wirk.
Conductor: Ernst von Schuch.

years later, agitate the Middle East. To this day the differences between Arabs and Jews have remained; their cause lies, now as then, in competing political and religious ideologies. Then it was the military might of Rome that intervened; now it is the western world, led by the United States; but basically the problems have remained the same.

It is from this milieu, heightened by legend, prophecy, incomprehensible miracles and the appearance of new mysterious personalities, that a strange creature emerges whose existence and tragic life have been mentioned through the centuries, from the Bible to Oscar Wilde, Gustave Flaubert and Richard Strauss: 'Salome, the daughter of Herodias, Princess of Judea'. She was the step-daughter of Herod and the child of her mother's previous marriage, which we have already mentioned. Her step-father and the men in his entourage are bewitched by the unusual beauty of this young girl, who lived a life of great luxury, and had been educated in Rome, then the centre of the western world.

The princess, who in the words of the infatuated Narraboth has feet 'like white doves', leaves the banquet table and runs out on to the terrace. She is sickened by the drunken assembly and the

argumentative discussions she cannot understand. Wrapped in her cloak, she flees from the lustful leers of her step-father, Herod. In the moonlight she calms herself, and then suddenly becomes aware of the distant echoing voice of the prophet John, the Baptist (Jokanaan), who is kept imprisoned by the tetrarch in a cistern on the terrace. Salome knows this from soldiers' conversation. She is curious and demands to see the prisoner of whom, as she says, even Herod is afraid. By skilful flirtation and promises she succeeds in persuading Narraboth to contravene the tetrarch's strict command and to let Jokanaan out of the cistern.

Thus the drama begins. In its course the two main characters will have no close relationship to one another at all, although their encounter will lead to a tragic fate for them both. The voice of Jokanaan, and subsequently his physical presence, awaken intense erotic desire in Salome. Having remained pure and chaste in a court filled with vice of all kinds, she is consumed with blind passion and seeks only to yield to the power of her desires.

She encounters in Jokanaan an equally powerful passion, but one governed by cold fanaticism. He is driven by his own obsession, and is insensitive to anything which could distract him from it or destroy it. Jokanaan shows no pity for the girl's inner turmoil and nothing he says shows any understanding of her plight or any desire to help her. For her part Salome does not even notice the suicide of the desperately jealous Narraboth, so numbed with despair and loneliness is she after Jokanaan has returned to the cistern.

The drama is approaching its climax, but the crescendo is first interrupted by the entrance of Herod. He is drunk and, besotted with lust, is looking for Salome. His birthday celebration allows him the subterfuge of inviting his guests to spend a little time on the terrace and to enjoy the Sicilian wine given him as a present by the Emperor Tiberius, a wine 'as red as blood'.

The presence of the group of guests, who spend their time observing one another, casts light on the complex historical background sketched above. Two Nazarenes who attach themselves to the group bring a new shade of colour into the sombre setting: they report on the miracles of Jesus in Galilee, at which Herod, ever unsure of himself, is gripped by profound anxiety. Intermittently the voice of Jokanaan can be heard from the cistern uttering scornful accusations against Herodias. She is consumed with rage and demands that he be handed over to the Jews, who have long desired to get this herald of a new religion into their clutches.

Herod turns down all such requests. He is tired and exhausted. He asks Salome to dance for him, but she refuses until, in his drunken state, he swears that he will fulfil any wish she might have. The music now prefigures the tragic outcome of the plot: it expresses the ominous thoughts of the scorned and wounded Salome who declares that she will dance. The climax of the work approaches.

Richard Strauss first became acquainted with Oscar Wilde's drama in 1903, when he saw a performance directed by Max Reinhardt in Berlin. He was impressed by the sensational acting, above all by Gertrud Eysoldt in the title role. In search of new creative material Strauss at once felt that the play cried out for musical treatment. A young Viennese poet, Anton Lindner, set down a few initial scenes, but these failed to inspire Strauss. In his *Recollections* he commented that he suddenly decided to compose his music to the words of Oscar Wilde's prose poem and that this released a tempestuous flow of ideas. From the line 'How beautiful the princess Sal-

Königliches Opernhaus, Dresden, 1905
The setting for Salome's dance shows an obvious concern to incorporate authentic details. The figures at the palace entrance almost overpower the principal performers and there is little evidence of any attempt to contrast the groups of Romans, Egyptians, Jews, etc.
Producer: Willi Wirk.
Conductor: Ernst von Schuch.

Metropolitan Opera, New York, 1907
James Fox, the stage-designer for the first Met. production, followed the Dresden model in adopting a historical approach and recreating a palace of the Herodian era.
Producer: Anton Schertel.
Conductor: Alfred Hertz.

ome is tonight' onward, his thoughts developed without interruption.

According to Strauss's own record he began writing the music for *Salome* on 27 November 1904 and finished it on 20 June 1905. As far as Strauss was concerned the only possible venue for the first performance was Dresden, where Ernst von Schuch had been an enthusiastic supporter of his stage works ever since *Feuersnot*. The première, which was eagerly awaited, took place on 9 December 1905 and the opera quickly became world-famous. Ernst Roth, for many years head of the London music publishers, Boosey and Hawkes, wrote in 1954: 'With his incredibly steady hand and cool technical mastery, Richard Strauss had written the most exciting music ever heard in a theatre up to that time.'

Despite moralistic objections to *Salome,* its victorious progress could not be halted. In quick succession major opera-houses throughout the world added it to their repertoire. Strauss himself wrote: 'The first performance in Dresden was, as usual, a success but the critics, gathered together in the Bellevue Hotel after the performance, shook their heads and agreed that the piece would perhaps be performed by a few of

the largest theatres but would soon disappear.' [Strauss was thinking here of the unusually large orchestration prescribed in the score—approximately 105 musicians]. Three weeks later it had been accepted by, I think, ten theatres and had been a sensational success in Breslau with an orchestra only seventy strong. There was a hullaballoo in the papers; the churches objected—the first performance in the Vienna State Opera did not take place until October 1918, after an embarrassing exchange of letters with Archbishop Piffl—and so did puritans in New York, where the opera had to be taken out of the repertoire at the instigation of a certain Mr. Morgan. The German Kaiser [Wilhelm II] only permitted the performance of the opera after Hülsen [head of the Court Opera in Berlin] had had the bright idea of signifying the advent of the Magi at the end by the appearance of the Morning Star.[1]

Actually the birth of Christ, accompanied by the comet, had occurred some thirty years earlier. This derisory anachronism apparently mollified the reservations entertained by the Imperial court. But the very preparations for the première in Dresden revealed all kinds of unexpected difficulties, which Strauss recalled with amusement in his *Recollections:* 'During the casting rehearsals the extravagant Frau Wittich went on strike. She had been entrusted with the part of the sixteen-year-old princess with the voice of Isolde. 'One just does not write a thing like that, Herr Strauss: either one thing or the other', choosing thus to voice her complaint about the very taxing role and the huge orchestra. She indignantly protested in the manner to be expected from the wife of a Saxon burgomaster: 'I won't do it. I'm a decent woman'; thereby the producer, Wirk, who was all for 'perversity and outrage', was reduced to desperation and despair.'[2] Later Professor Willi Wirk was associated for many years with the Nationaltheater in Munich. He taught extensively, and was the author's mentor.

Strauss commented several times on the demands that were to be made of the singers. He also warned against exaggeration, which regularly insinuated itself into productions and for many years seemed impossible to remove:

> ...The capers cut in later performances by exotic variety stars, indulging in snake-line movements and waving Jokanaan's head about in the air, went beyond all bounds of decency and good taste. Anyone who has been in the East and who has observed the decorum with which women there behave, will appreciate that Salome, being a chaste virgin and an oriental princess, must be played with the simplest and most restrained of gestures, unless her defeat by the miracle of a great world is to excite only disgust and terror instead of sympathy ... Generally speaking, the acting of the singer should, in contrast with the excessive turmoil of the music, be limited to the utmost simplicity: Herod in particular must remember, amidst the comings and goings of the hysterical crowd, that he should endeavour, oriental parvenu though he is, to preserve his dignity and composure before his Roman guests, in imitation of the greater Caesar in Rome, notwithstanding all momentary erotic misdemeanour. Turmoil on and in front of the stage simultaneously—that would be too much. The orchestra alone is quite adequate.[3]

Strauss here emphasized Herod's position as surrogate of the Roman emperor and accentuated the importance of the group of Roman guests.

Producers in recent times have increasingly sought to turn the colourless minor roles into more vigorously delineated characters. Perhaps the best casting arrangement is to create figures

Bayerische Staatsoper, Munich, 1922
Leo Pasetti's design placed a characteristically strong emphasis on visual elements and successfully freed the production from narrow historical limitations. His design was the first to make full use of the directions for the moon and clouds. The scene shows Salome's dance in vigorous colours. However, the effect of his brilliant design was somewhat dulled by the technical imperfections—especially in lighting—of the time. Pasetti's work for Wagner's operas, too, was well ahead of its time.
Producer: Willi Wirk.
Conductor: Hans Knappertsbusch.

Charles Ricketts's design, from the early 1920s, was one that sought to free stage design from the purely historical, but did not fully succeed. The painter and stage-designer Charles Ricketts belonged to the circle of artists who followed the ideas espoused by the Swiss genius Adolphe Appia and opened up new avenues of stage design (Gordon Craig, Norman bel Geddes among others).

Nationaltheater, Mannheim,
circa 1925
Closely linked to Expressionism,
but remarkable for the concentric
arrangement around the cistern. A
decisive attempt to find a freer
form.
Producer: Francesco Sioli.
Conductor: Erich Orthmann.
Sets: Heinz Grete.

Städtische Bühnen, Frankfurt-am-Main, 1927
A very simplified form, Expressionist in style. The idea of a 'snail-like' progression towards the cistern is expressive and inspired other productions long afterwards.
Producer: Lothar Wallerstein.
Conductor: Clemens Krauss.
Sets: Ludwig Sievert.

Bayerische Staatsoper, Munich, 1937
In the 1937 production Salome was sung by Hildegarde Ranczak, Herod by Julius Pölzer and Herodias by Karin Branzell. The setting was much simplified, devoid of irritating architectural details and concentrated on the *dramatis personae*. The figure of the Roman consul occupies a dominant position next to Herodias.
Producer: Rudolf Hartmann.
Conductor: Clemens Krauss. Sets and costumes: Ludwig Sievert.

Bayerische Staatsoper, Munich, 1937
The major scene between Salome and Jokanaan: Hildegarde Ran-czak as Salome and Hans Hotter as Jokanaan, both singers who performed their roles with great conviction.
Producer: Rudolf Hartmann.
Conductor: Clemens Krauss. Sets and costumes: Ludwig Sievert.

that illustrate the social and political tensions and to fill these parts with excellent character actors, even if they have nothing actually to say.

But back to the terrace: Herod is now very drunk, and prone to hysterical outbursts brought on by the hallucinations that plague him. Herodias by contrast is quietly scornful. The reactions of the guests vary from mocking amusement to barely concealed disgust. Meanwhile Salome is being helped by her servants to prepare for the Dance of the Seven Veils, the start of which she announces with the words: 'I am ready, tetrarch'.

And now the dance. Strauss composed the music for this after completing the rest of the work. Willi Schuh records that it was written and orchestrated in a fortnight in the middle of August 1905. We can only speculate as to why it was later on that Strauss inserted this extensive and complex section, which he himself described as central to the opera. Was it supposed to be the symphonic summation of the entire work, like overtures in certain earlier operas, which were often composed last of all? Or was it more than that; for instance, did it express the clarification of Salome's confused feelings and wishes,

the development of a playful adolescent to a fully-grown woman with passions and desires?

As Strauss looked back in later years he increasingly demanded a sense of respect and decency during the dance scene; at times his instructions had gone a little too far and conflicted with his music. Nevertheless, he was right when he criticized the wild 'sexual acrobatics' of some Salomes as inappropriate and showing a lack of understanding of the dramatic situation.

With a few movements of her body Salome begins a dance which she had often danced before. But this time her intention is to make a fool of the tetrarch by giving much freer expression to her dance than on previous occasions. For this reason she deviates now and then from the prepared pattern of her dance. Her impatience becomes apparent and she has to force herself to follow the usual form of the dance until at length she shows herself fully naked for a few moments to Herod, who by now is beside himself.

Since the first performance of *Salome,* this major scene has caused problems for producers. At first, one way out of the dilemma was to use a double in the part of Salome for the dance.

Then at the close, with the group of servants gathered round to conceal Salome, the singer would resume her place. But this was not very successful. The difference between the singer and the dancer could not be concealed, particularly since the singers were often ladies of mature proportions, so that they bore no resemblance whatever to a nubile dancer. Because of this, the work lost credibility, and the dance—usually choreographed as a ballet—remained an 'insert', which made it difficult for the audience to re-identify with the main figure of Salome.

So it was natural for singers of the part to try to do the whole scene themselves. Some were succcessful, particularly when Strauss, in 1930 or thereabouts, made changes in the orchestra-tion to allow the part to be sung by lighter voices, and therefore slimmer sopranos. But even these efforts were not wholly satisfactory. The dance scene is a long one, and the singers could not disguise a certain amateurishness in their dancing. Also, the major physical effort in-volved inevitably a deleterious effect on the de-manding vocal scena which follows. Some of the younger singers who played Salome did achieve near-perfect portrayals, for instance Maria Cebo-tari (at the festival in Zurich in June 1948, a year before her early death), Lisa della Casa and oth-ers. One experiment in Frankfurt that also worked successfully returned to the substitution of a double for the singer during the dance scene. The singer, Maria Kouba, whose figure

Städtische Bühnen, Essen, 1950
An interesting solution, using a round stage and with surrealistic influences. A return to the 'snail' used earlier by Sievert.
Producer: Hans Hartleb.
Conductor: Gustav König.
Sets: Paul Haferung.

◁ Royal Opera House, Covent Garden, London, 1949
Sets by Salvador Dali: an interesting idea, to use a famous painter to design the set. Earlier experiments in this direction had involved, among others, Max Slevogt *(Don Giovanni),* and Utrillo, who had once worked on a magically characteristic *Louise* by Charpentier at the Opéra-Comique in Paris. Such set-designs (a more recent example is Chagall's set for the New York *Magic Flute)* have all had great individual charm, but are often unsatisfactory in that they are not readily adaptable to constantly changing spatial requirements, something which is essential in the theatre.
Dali's set—a circular path leads round the cistern—indicates the central point (the cistern itself). The adjoining terrace is also circular. The additional feature of the central entrance seems rather modish.
Producer: Peter Brook.
Conductor: Karl Rankl.

was admirably suited to the part, danced the first section of the scene herself, and then at an opportune moment slipped off-stage unnoticed, leaving the dancer, whose figure was very similar to her own, to continue the scene. At the close, by another skilful substitution, the singer once more took her place on stage. Their different facial features, a potential distraction, were disguised by their wearing oriental masks which left only the eyes visible.

The costumes for the Dance of the Seven Veils are extremely important, and in my opinion this problem has yet to be solved satisfactorily. The exact sequence in which the individual veils are discarded is not established by the music, and this leaves the matter to the choreographer. Strauss once (probably in the 1920s) made a note about this which was discovered by Willi Schuh and published in the *Basler Theater-zeitung.*

With the permission of the author I reproduce the note here:

The presentation of Salome's 'Dance of the Seven Veils'. Quite slow, 3/4: begins with a

swaying movement on the spot. 3rd crotchet after D, Salome takes off the first veil and adopts the pose shown in Moreau's picture of Salome printed on page 12 of *La Danse* [by] G. Vuillier. 3rd bar before E, 3rd crotchet: a few lively paces towards Herod.

One bar before E, back again in three steps. E: three-bar interval with swaying movements.

4th bar after E, a swirling movement, Salome turns rapidly round and round.

F: beginning of calm dance movement, at this point only the slightest suggestion.

H: Salome quickly removes the second veil. 3rd bar after H a few (four) enticing steps. Very measured: three threatening, creeping steps towards the cistern where Jokanaan sits imprisoned.

Poco accelerando, A major: with a few charming, enticing movements she again turns to Herod.

The earlier musical time is resumed: three bars before K, she recoils softly; the terrified pose is relinquished in the next bar.

K: for four bars she remains still (with the swaying of the beginning).

Six bars after K (G sharp minor): very alluring, gentle movement.

M: Movement of passionate enticement directed towards Jokanaan.

Somewhat more lively: two bars before N (F major): highly erect pose, much as in 'Idyll' (*La Danse,* page 17), again relaxing more calmly out of this pose.

Three bars before O she moves on into a light, graceful evasive movement.—Second bar (after O): as the third on the 3rd quarter (dominant of A Major), two graceful, courting gestures which break off abruptly.

P: Salome tears off the third veil vigorously.

C sharp minor 'the first measure of musical time is resumed': start of a separate dance utilizing poses such as (*La Danse,* page II *Bacchante,* page 2 *Egyptian women* (!!!??), page 59 *Danseuse à l'écharpe,* pages 224 & 225 *Japanese Dancers,* page 315 *Le Paradis de Mahomet,* page 319 *Fête de Nuit à Laghouat,* pages 321 and 322 *Bayadères.*

C sharp major: a much more lively display of all her female charms (!) before Herod.

Staatsoper, Berlin, 1942
Ludwig Sievert and Irmingard Prestel: this very stylish sketch of Salome is close to the art nouveau of Aubrey Beardsley.

Bayerische Staatsoper, Munich, 1955
The stage-designer had the idea of forgoing all architectural details and using a magnificent mosaic to cover the whole of the huge terrace (which gravitates towards the cistern). This gave great power to the groups of singers, each with distinct costumes, standing against the night sky with its strange, misty moon. Only the light, spilling through an entrance, identified the palace as such.
The producer thus had full freedom to move the characters around as the action demanded. The mosaic floor was a fruitful idea that was repeated in other productions.
Birgit Nilsson sang the role of Salome for the first time.
Producer: Rudolf Hartmann
Conductor: Joseph Keilberth.
Sets: Helmut Jürgens.

Städtische Oper, Berlin, 1951
A very personal design, with the cistern skilfully placed in the corner of the terrace; the wind-catching sail dominates.
Producer: Heinz Tietjen.
Conductor: Arthur Rother.
Sets: Josef Fenneker.

SALOME · Hein Heckroth 61

Städtische Bühnen, Frankfurt-
am-Main, 1961
The idea of a transparent protective awning has been developed to
the point where it dominates the
set. There is also generous development of the 'snail–like' staircase leading to the cistern. The
Frankfurt set was later used in
several European cities (Paris,
Milan, Brussels).
Producer: Rudolf Hartmann.
Conductor: Georg Solti.
Sets: Hein Heckroth.

Teatro Colón, Buenos Aires, 1965
The main motif of this well-pro-
portioned setting is the mosaic
floor, adopted from the earlier
design by Helmut Jürgens. A
beautiful, imaginative solution.
Producer: Ernst Poettgen.
Conductor: Georges Sebastian.
Sets: Roberto Oswald.

Deutsche Oper am Rhein, Düssel-
dorf, 1968
The ornamentation is art nouveau
and the conception surrealistic.
There is no focus on the cistern.
An interesting attempt, but one
which produced no further de-
velopments.
Producer: Wolf Völker.
Conductor: Günther Wich.
Sets: Max Bignens.

From V onwards, a return to more abrupt
movements and calmer poses.
6th bar after W: lively dance rhythm (round
dance)
fatigue
she pulls herself together again,
Y: pulls off the 5th veil.
Furioso and close as marked in the piano passage.   Richard Strauss

The progressive unveiling of Salome's body
before Herod and Salome's intentions in showing more and more of herself to the tetrarch
form the main motif of the scene, which should
reach its climax with Salome standing complete-

ly naked. Therefore the costume for the dance
should be made in such a way that sensuality can
be built up effectively, by degrees, from the start
of the light, swaying belly-dance: first the arms
are bared, then the legs, the breasts and finally
the whole body. Veils tucked at random into the
belt of the skirt (something often seen) do not
achieve this effect. The figure of the naked girl
stands visible for a few seconds in the moonlight, then disappears like an alluring vision as
Salome runs quickly forward and throws herself
before Herod and is covered with her cloak by
her servants: this is the moment when the substitution of the singer for the dancer could take
place. The reactions to the dance of the guests

must be incorporated as a carefully thought-out mime, centring on the stirrings of jealousy within Herodias and the growing sensual excitement of the tetrarch.

The drama is rapidly approaching its close. Salome, asked by Herod what she desires, answers: the head of Jokanaan 'on a silver charger'. She remains adamant despite alternative offers by the appalled Herod, who has sworn to fulfil her wish.

Here the drama deviates freely from the traditional story, which has it that Salome first asks her mother, Herodias, and that the latter, in her hatred for Jokanaan, orders her unwitting daughter to ask for his head. That in the opera Salome herself asks for this gruesome wish to be fulfilled, thereby surprising even her mother, is a natural development of the young princess's unrequited passion; through the prophet's terrible death she believes she will find satisfaction. According to Oscar Wilde, Salome is wounded to the core by Jokanaan's scorn and inattention. A similarly free poetic interpretation of the legend forms the conclusion, where the drama

Bayerische Staatsoper, Munich, 1968
Design for *Salome* by Rudolf Heinrich. The ideas are spirited, a little disordered still, perhaps, but in the performance (cf. the next two illustrations) they led to the most beautiful results. A good example of this kind of progressive work.
Producer: Günther Rennert.
Conductor: Joseph Keilberth.

Bayerische Staatsoper, Munich,
1968
An impressive solution showing
further progress from the particular to the universal. The 'obstinate' circular lines point compell-
ingly towards the cistern; the
moon and clouds (exemplary
projections in strong colours) to a
certain extent reflect the events on
stage—a fruitful development in
keeping with the sense of the
drama.
Producer: Günther Rennert.
Conductor: Joseph Keilberth.
Sets: Rudolf Heinrich.

is violently resolved by Herod's order that the
princess be put to death.

The previous scene, where Salome kisses the
head of Jokanaan, approaches the limits of what
is bearable. Here the intensity of Strauss's music
once again has a purifying impact and triumphs
over the depraved realism of the events depicted
on stage. Herod's laconic order, 'kill this woman!' relaxes the tension, allows the audience
the relief of feeling pity for the young creature,
for the 'errant dove'.

When the soldiers with their shields carry out
the execution order and the girl's head, as if on
a silver charger, again becomes visible, the face
pale, the eyes opened wide—with an expression

of final understanding and almost animal fear—
—the following and beautiful poetic words are
fulfilled:

Denn das Geheimnis der Liebe ist grösser
    als das Geheimnis des Todes.

('For the secret of love is greater
    than the secret of death.')

Through his music for *Salome* Richard Strauss
found himself. With unerring certainty and in
the shortest of periods (seven months) he finally
detached himself from Richard Wagner and
thereby opened the door to the future for musical drama in the early twentieth century. With

47

the genius of his one-act dramas he established an unshakable basis for his work; he had overcome the difficulties facing him at the start of his career of writing for the stage. The composer was forty-one years old when *Salome* erupted into the world, to become a source of inspiration which continues to the present day. The experience and technical mastery which Strauss had gained gave him certainty and enabled him to fashion such difficult material. The years of experimental searching were past.

The earliest designs for *Salome* were models of historical accuracy: buildings and costumes were true to the period, tending perhaps to be too representational and dull. The weighty voices cast in the various roles lent performances a Wagnerian atmosphere with which contradicted the new Impressionist quality of the musical language. *Salome* is not an architectonic piece; its expressive force lies wholly in its colouration. It was in this direction that its design developed, and so too did the ambience of the action. It was no longer confined to a single location; every element in the production was drawn in—the moon, the night sky, the light from the palace, and by constant changes moulded to fit the mood of each scene. Modern stagings, where the decor has taken its inspiration directly from the music, have succeeded in an obtrusive realism and achieved a superbly refined impressionistic

Bayerische Staatsoper, Munich, 1968
An impressive shot of the entire set, showing the manner in which singers are deployed.
Producer: Günther Rennert.
Conductor: Joseph Keilberth.
Sets: Rudolf Heinrich.

48

Salzburg Festival, 1977
The very broad stage is made
more intimate by the movable
platforms. The shimmering structure of the palace is heavily emphasized, but the focal point is the
cistern. The sky allowed for projections (moon, clouds), which
were used to great effect in keeping with the action. The whole
set took a further step towards
intensifying and deepening the
work's spiritual atmosphere.
Producer and conductor: Herbert
von Karajan. Sets: Günther
Schneider-Siemssen.

atmosphere. Thereby, given good casting, the success of *Salome* has been assured.

The sets developed over the decades give us valuable insight into the intentions of producers and stage-designers, particularly where they show increasing awareness of work's colour. Nowadays, it is common practice to classify *Salome* as belonging to the world of art nouveau, but this is a restrictive interpretation. It attaches too little significance to the Impressionist qual-ity of the music and the multi-faceted hues of the text.

The illustrations are presented here in chronological order where possible and show a clear development from settings faithful to time and space to free imaginative ones that compel our attention to the timeless dramatic fate of the main characters, which thereby comes within the range of our own experience. This develop-ment has not been entirely consistent, but its main characteristic has been liberation from the particular, oriental milieu into a setting of uni-versal significance.

The producers' demands, too, have changed over the years, influencing the work of stage-designers. However these changes have remain-ed marginal to the central development of the opera's stage potential.

The character of Salome has increasingly ap-proximated to that which Strauss himself de-scribed: a magnetically alluring young girl, familiar with good and evil, erotically aware yet still a virgin. Salome, whose childish emotions have been hurt, finds only one way out of the labyrinth of her feelings, which leads her, too, to death. The producer's task has become in-creasingly interesting as he has had to wrestle to interpret the characters of the adolescent Sal-ome, the half-mad Herod and the profoundly corrupt Herodias. What was originally present-ed as a decorative play in an 'oriental' milieu has increasingly become a drama of the human soul.

Elektra

When I first saw Hofmannsthal's inspired play at the Kleines Theater in Berlin with Gertrud Eysoldt, I immediately recognized, of course, what a magnificent operatic libretto it might be (after the alteration I made in the Orestes scene it has actually become one) and, just as previously with *Salome,* I appreciated the tremendous increase in musical tension to the very end: in *Elektra,* after the recognition scene, which could only be completely realized in music, the release in dance—in *Salome,* after the dance (the heart of the plot), the dreadful apotheosis of the end. Both operas offered wonderful points of musical attack:

Salome: the contrasts; the court of Herod, Jokanaan, the Jews, the Nazarenes.
Elektra: the possessed goddess of vengeance contrasted with the radiant character of her mortal sister.
Salome: the three seduction songs of Salome, Herod's three persuasive speeches, Salome's ostinato *Ich will den Kopf des Jokanaan* ('I want the head of Jokanaan').
Elektra: the first monologue; the unending climaxes in the scene between Elektra and Chrysothemis and in that between Elektra and Clytaemnestra.

But at first I was put off by the idea that both subjects were very similar in psycholgocial content, so that I doubted whether I should have the power to exhaust this subject also. But the wish to contrast this possessed, exalted Greece of the sixth century with Winckelmann's Latinized version and Goethe's humanism outweighed these doubts, and *Elektra* became even more intense in the unity of structure and in the force of its climaxes. I am almost tempted to say it is to *Salome* what the more accomplished and stylistically more uniform *Lohengrin* is to its inspired forerunner *Tannhäuser.* Both operas are unique in my life's works, in them I penetrated to the uttermost limits of harmony, psychological polyphony (Clytaemnestra's Dream) and of the receptivity of modern ears.[1]

Thus Strauss's own summary of the origins of his opera *Elektra.*

In 1900, at the start of the new century, Strauss and Hofmannsthal met in Paris, having first met the year before in Berlin-Pankow, at the home of the poet Richard Dehmel. In his first letter to Strauss, Hofmannsthal referred to a conversation they had had at that time and offered the composer a finished ballet *scenario (Triumph der Zeit*; 'Triumph of Time') to set to music. But for the moment no association was established between composer and playwright. In a second letter Hofmannsthal urged Strauss to reply to his offer, but the composer could not warm to the ballet material.

In 1903 Hofmannsthal's play *Elektra* was published, freely based on Sophocles, and it was a significant success for the poet. It was again Max Reinhardt who produced it in Berlin and again Gertrud Eysoldt who took the title role. Strauss saw the performance and began to consider putting music to the drama, but hesitated. Hofmannsthal provided the necessary driving force: '... How goes it with you and *Elektra?* ... The more I thought about the idea, the more possible it seemed to me...'[2] (written in 1906). Strauss confirmed that he continued to feel the greatest enthusiasm for *Elektra;* but this was still outweighed by his reservations about its similarity with *Salome.* He evaded the issue, therefore; instead, he commented on the projected opera *Semiramis* and made suggestions about other matters: '...Have you got an entertaining Renaissance subject for me? A really wild Cesare Borgia or Savonarola would be the answer to my prayers!'[3]

This gold mask was found by Heinrich Schliemann during his excavations. He called it the 'mask of Agamemnon', after the king of Mycenae who destroyed Troy and, on his return to Mycenae, was killed by his wife Clytaemnestra. The mask was actually made several centuries before Agamemnon lived. The dignified solemn expression makes it an appropriate introduction to *Elektra.* This mask is in the National Museum, Athens.

Once again it was Hofmannsthal who would not be diverted from the issue, and he endeavoured to allay the composer's doubts about *Elektra*: '... the similarities with the *Salome* plot seem to me, on closer consideration, to dwindle to nothing. (Both are one-act plays; each has a woman's name for a title; both take place in classical Antiquity, and both parts were originally created in Berlin by Gertrud Eysoldt; that, I feel, is all the similarity adds up to.) ... I cannot, on the other hand, discern within the foreseeable future ... a chance of producing any other literary work ... In the far distance the vision of a *Semiramis* theme emerges rather like a mirage ... You spoke of some plot to be taken from the Renaissance ...'[4]

Hofmannsthal described this whole epoch as decidedly unsuitable and concluded his lengthy explanation by saying that everything pointed to *Elektra*. Again Strauss made another suggestion: *Saul and David*. Hofmannsthal turned it down and finally, in June 1906, Strauss wrote from Marquartstein: 'I am already busy on the first scene of *Elektra*, but I'm still making rather heavy weather of it ...'[5]

Things were now actually under way, but yet again his thoughts strayed to other subjects: 'How about a subject from the French Revolution for a change? Do you know Büchner's *Dantons Tod*? Sardou's *Ninth Thermidor* ...'[6]

Yet work on *Elektra* continued steadily; one of the finest artistic collaborations had begun. On 20 February 1908 Strauss wrote to his librettist: '... *Elektra* is making vigorous headway ...'[7]

At Strauss's request, Hofmannsthal re-shaped and re-wrote passages of the work because the composer had demanded exact explanations of the scenes; and for the final scene Hofmannsthal's explanation consisted of a basic outline of the various entrances and appearances of the characters. Each stimulated the other's creativity. At the same time, however, each was involved in other projects. *Semiramis* was discussed on repeated occasions and the idea of a comedy opera came to the surface. But on 25 January 1909 *Elektra* received its first performance, directed by Ernst von Schuch, in Dresden.

In his *Recollections* Strauss wrote: 'The first performance was a *succès d'éstime*, but as usual I did not learn this until later. Angelo Neumann [a famous theatre director in Prague] even wired to Prague: 'failure'. Many now consider *Elektra* the acme of my work. Others give their vote to *Die Frau ohne Schatten*. The majority swears by *Der Rosenkavalier*. One must be content to have achieved so much as a German composer.'[8]

Königliches Opernhaus.

23. Vorstellung.

Montag, den 25. Januar 1909.

Richard Strauß-Woche.

1. Abend.

Uraufführung:

Elektra.

Tragödie in einem Aufzuge von Hugo von Hofmannsthal.
Musik von Richard Strauß.

Regie: Georg Toller.

Musikalische Leitung: Ernst von Schuch.

Personen:

Klytämnestra.	—	—	—	Ernestine Schumann-Heinck.
Elektra, } ihre Töchter.	—	—	—	Annie Krull.
Chrysothemis, }				Margarethe Siems.
Aegisth.	—	—	—	Johannes Sembach.
Orest.	—	—	—	Karl Perron.
Der Pfleger des Orest.	—	—	—	Julius Puttlitz.
Die Vertraute.	—	—	—	Gertrud Sachse.
Die Schleppträgerin.	—	—	—	Elisabeth Boehm-van Endert.
Ein junger Diener.	—	—	—	Fritz Soot.
Ein alter Diener.	—	—	—	Franz Nebuschka.
Die Aufseherin.	—	—	—	Riza Eibenschütz.
Fünf Mägde.	—	—	—	Franciska Bender-Schäfer. Magdalene Seebe. Irma Tervani. Anna Zoder. Minnie Nast.

Dienerinnen und Diener. — Schauplatz der Handlung: Mykene.

Die Dekorationen sind vom Hoftheatermaler Rieck entworfen und angefertigt, die Kostüme nach Entwürfen des Professors Fanto vom Garderobe-Oberinspektor Metzger ausgeführt. Dekorative Einrichtung vom Oberinspektor Hasait.

Textbücher sind an der Kasse das Exemplar für 1 Mark zu haben.

Beurlaubt: Herr Rüdiger.

Der freie Eintritt ist ohne jede Ausnahme aufgehoben.

Gekaufte Billetts werden nur bei Abänderung der Vorstellung zurückgenommen.

Spielplan.

Königliches Opernhaus.

Dienstag, 26. Januar. Richard Strauß-Woche. 2. Abend: Salome. Drama in einem Aufzuge. Musik von Strauß. Anfang 8 Uhr. Mittwoch, 27. Januar. Richard Strauß-Woche. 3. Abend: Feuersnot. Singgedicht in einem Akt. Musik von R. Strauß. Symphonia domestica von Strauß. Anfang 8 Uhr.

Königliches Schauspielhaus.

Dienstag, 26. Januar: Die Rabensteinerin. Schauspiel in vier Akten von E. v. Wildenbruch. Anfang 1/2 8 Uhr. Mittwoch, den 27. Januar: Die glücklichste Zeit. Lustspiel in drei Akten von Auernheimer. Anfang 1/2 8 Uhr.

Einlaß 7 Uhr. Kasseneröffnung 1/2 8 Uhr. Anfang 8 Uhr.

Ende 3/4 10 Uhr.

Königliches Opernhaus, Dresden, 1909
Elektra (Anni Krull) and Aegisthus (Johannes Sembach). A scene obviously arranged for the photographer, showing some details of the set.
Producer: Georg Toller.
Conductor: Ernst von Schuch.
Sets: Emil Rieck.
Costumes: Leonhard Fanto.

In spite of the aloof and reserved reaction to *Elektra* of the public and the press, which contrasted with the reception given to *Salome,* the major theatres quickly followed the Dresden production with their own performances: Berlin (under Leo Blech) on 15 February 1909, Vienna on 24 March of the same year, and then Milan, London, Prague, Budapest, Frankfurt, Munich and so forth. Once *Der Rosenkavalier* had appeared, and also during the First World War, interest in *Elektra* subsided; even in the following years performances of the work were comparatively rare. *Elektra* has only relatively recently acquired a firm place in the repertory and at festivals. It would seem that in the course of time conductors and singers have learned from and 'cut their teeth' on the particular style of this work, and that they have had increasing success in mastering the work's monumental structure, with its balance of word and sound. Today it is impossible to imagine *Elektra* being absent from the basic repertoire; and every good performance of *Elektra* is an artistic event.

In contrast to the situation today we must bear in mind the impression which the original performance made on the musical world in 1909. The sequence of *Salome* and *Elektra* suggested that Richard Strauss had pointed the way to the future of musical drama. There was as yet no inkling of the later, surprising transition towards the style of *Der Rosenkavalier*. In this sense *Salome* and *Elektra*—no matter how contrasted they may be—constitute an impressive foundation to Strauss's dramatic work; they represent a chapter complete in itself, with no sequel.

The composer himself gave the reasons for this in his own writings: if he had continued to use the musical language of *Elektra,* especially when writing for full orchestra, he felt that he would be threatening tonality itself, the mode of musical expression he most loved and admired. The radical change indicated by the style of *Der Rosenkavalier* was taken greatly amiss in many quarters. Strauss was accused of being a traitor (he, the former vanguard of the 'new sound' in music) and was denounced as an opportunist to whom public approval was more important than deeper musical exploration. The composer himself remained little affected by such criticism and scorn. He adhered unswervingly to the course he had chosen, finding in his long life the strength for many successful stylistic variations within his œuvre. A close examination of his work reveals as many pointers to new musical directions as those of *Salome* and *Elektra,* albeit without their explosive power.

◁ Königliches Opernhaus, Dresden, 1909
Strauss's third Dresden première was *Elektra*, on 25 January 1909. It was the first evening of a Richard Strauss week at the Königliches Opernhaus, with Georg Toller as senior director. Ernst von Schuch conducted. The cast contained world famous names; the sets were by the experienced court theatre artist, Emil Rieck, to whom reference has already been made; the costumes were designed by Leonhard Fanto.

Elektra was the second of Strauss's operas to have the name of a woman as its title, and more such titles would follow. He never tired of trying to capture and portray the mystery of Woman. *Elektra* is the first of Strauss's operas set in Greek Antiquity, an era rich in important female characters whose lives and fates have always provided inspiration for poetry, music and the fine arts.

A powerful yet understated motif signifying Agamemnon raises the curtain on the drama of *Elektra*. We see towering edifices of dressed stone like Mycenaean structures—hard, uncompromising, terrifyingly gloomy, doomladen architecture.

Salome presented the vibrant colour of Impressionist painting, and in the same measure *Elektra*'s architectonic character, with its contrast of light and shade, is unmistakably Cubist in its rigid, merciless forms.

Hofoper, Vienna, 1909
Design by Alfred Roller for the
first performance in Vienna. The
set gives good emphasis to the
focal points: the gate, well, entrances from without, access to
the palace. The narrow opening to
the sky *(right)* helps to soften the
overall impression of architectural
severity.
Producer: Wilhelm von Wymetal.
Conductor: Hugo Reichenberger.

Opernhaus, Cologne, 1909
Design by Hans Wildermann. An
attempt at stylization with the addition of trees. Not entirely convincing in the way the main focal
points are arranged.
Producer: Max Martersteig.
Conductor: Otto Lohse.

THE OPERA THAT WILL "ELEKTRIFY" LONDON.

TO SING THE MOST ARDUOUS SCORE EVER WRITTEN: CHARACTERS IN STRAUSS'S "ELEKTRA,"
TO BE PRODUCED FOR THE FIRST TIME AT COVENT GARDEN ON SATURDAY.

ΕΛΕΚΤΡΑ

Royal Opera House, Covent Garden, London, 1910
Advance publicity for the London première on 18 August 1910, with pictures of some of the singers.
Producer: Willi Wirk.
Conductor: Thomas Beecham.

In the inner courtyard of this complex the maids gossip about their ladies and masters while they draw water from the well. The elder of the king's two daughters has given cause for malicious comment: Elektra, scorned yet feared as an unearthly soothsayer, has been filled since the murder of her father Agamemnon with a terrible desire for revenge. She has only one aim: to wreak an equally cruel vengeance on the murderers of her father—her mother Clytaemnestra, and the latter's lover, Aegisthus. Though a royal princess, Elektra leads the miserable life of an outcast, suffering hunger and torment; her fanatical will alone keeps her alive. She yearns passionately for the return of her brother Orestes who, she intends, shall carry out the act of revenge on Clytaemnestra and Aegisthus with the same axe which killed her father and which she has hidden.

Her vision of the desired hour of revenge leads to this cruelly passionate and grandiose outburst:

Vater! Agamemnon, dein Tag wird kommen.
Von den Sternen stürzt alle Zeit herab,
So wird das Blut aus hundert Kehlen stürzen in dein Grab!
So wie aus umgeworfenen Krügen wirds aus den gebundenen Mördern fliessen,
Und in einem Schwall, in einem geschwollenen Bach
Wird ihres Lebens Leben aus ihnen stürzen...

('Father, Agamemnon, your day will come.
All Time surges from the stars to us below,
So will the blood from one hundred throats surge and flow into your grave.
As from upturned jugs will it flood from the fast-bound murderers
And in a deluge, in a bursting stream
Will the life of their life surge from them...')

Elektra then becomes intoxicated with a series of bloody sacrificial visions, each one of greater ferocity. The final one is of a feast that will be a triumphant apogee of hatred; the crowning glory of this feast is to be a frenzied dance before

55

her brothers and sisters in honour of her revenged father. 'Agamemnon, Agamemnon...'

The appearance of her sister Chrysothemis forces her back to reality. Elektra does not want to speak to her; she despises her sister's adherence to the concept of happiness on earth. Chrysothemis wants to escape from the mysterious and sinister palace; all she seeks is the fulfilment of her own desires: 'I wish to have children ... I am a woman, and I desire a woman's fate!'

Elektra turns her away. Suddenly the palace is filled with noise heralding the approach of Queen Clytaemnestra; Chrysothemis flees after first warning Elektra about their mother: 'Go today, this hour, go from her path!' Elektra stays, utterly unshakable: 'As never before, I desire to talk to my mother.'

Tense, motionless, she awaits her mother's arrival. The dialogue which then develops between the two women is, in its poetic and musical structure, one of the grandest scenes in all musical drama.

Elektra triumphs, achieving total victory over her mother, who collapses in fear, truly hurled to the ground by her daughter's terrifying prophecies. Elektra invokes the figure of her distant brother Orestes, heralds his coming, and springs at her hated mother with a description of her inevitable death: 'He hunts you out; screaming, you flee before him. But he, he is behind you, driving you through the house!'

Clytaemnestra, paralysed by fear, is forced to listen to her daughter's dreadful pronouncements, until a servant enters and whispers a message in her ear. Clytaemnestra has the courtyard illuminated with lamps; she laughs, threatens Elektra and goes to the house in triumph.

Left exhausted by her ecstasy, Elektra remains behind alone, confused, not knowing what to do—until Chrysothemis cries out: 'Orestes! Orestes is dead!' The news is a thunderbolt to the bemused Elektra. She refuses at first to believe what she has heard: 'It is not true!' Then, finally, she accepts the truth, and as if possessed formulates fresh ideas: 'We, we two must do it.' Appalled, Chrysothemis manages not to yield to her sister's demonic entreaties and leaves Elektra alone. Now, cut off from all help, Elektra digs despairingly for the axe she has hidden. A strange man enters. His appearance on the scene disturbs her; she seeks only solitude.

But Orestes, whom she has not recognized, tells her in a remote and solemn voice: 'I must wait here.'

Nationaltheater, Mannheim, 1926
Design by Heinz Grete. An interesting division of the set by a double staircase, although the architecture is a little too decorative.
Producer: Richard Meyer-Walden.
Conductor: Richard Lert.

Metropolitan Opera, New York,
1932
This scene was clearly posed for
the photographer and has little
expressive force.
Producer: Alexander Sanine.
Conductor: Arthur Bodansky.
Sets: Joseph Urban.

San Francisco Opera, 1938
The block-like walls create an atmosphere of threat and immense
power. Less convincing is the
hanging curtain in the foreground. The groups of actors have
adopted poses in the style of
'grand opera'.
Producer: Herbert Graf.
Conductor: Fritz Reiner.
Sets: Harry Hörner.

Staatsoper Berlin, 1940
Design by Emil Preetorius. An
ideally organized set with all the
entrances well balanced. The open
verandah lined with pillars to the
left is particularly beautiful. The
architecture is almost too noble,
given the cruelty of the action.
Producer: Barbara Kemp-von
Schillings. Conductor: Herbert
von Karajan.

Staatsoper, Hamburg, 1950
Design by Alfred Siercke. The
rounded walls emphasize the sense
of oppressive confinement. All the
entrances are arranged in accordance with this concept.
Producer: Wolf Völker.
Conductor: Leopold Ludwig.

With Orestes' entrance, Fate itself has entered the drama; the climax is foreshadowed.
Orestes confirms the news of his own alleged
death: 'Let Orestes be. He enjoyed his life too
much. The gods above cannot tolerate the clear
sound of happiness. So he had to die.'

Elektra's shattering lament leads on to a won-
derfully constructed scene of recognition between brother and sister. 'Who are you then?'
she asks—and from the behaviour of an old servant, who welcomes the homecomer, she finally
realizes whom she has before her. Her cry of:

'Orestes!' unleashes a flood of sound representing immense joy; tears of shock well up in her
eyes. The musical portrayal of such emotion has
arguably never been so convincingly expressed
as in this scene.

Strauss had *felt* what he wanted to say at this
point, a kind of lyrical pause for breath before
the sombre storm breaks loose in the continuing
drama. On 22 June 1908 he wrote to Hofmannsthal: 'On page 77 of *Elektra* I need a great
moment of repose after Elektra's first shout:
"Orest!" I shall fit in a delicately vibrant orches-

Teatro alla Scala, Milan, 1954
The entrances are dramatically
planned in relation to each other,
and the floor-area is well divided
by steps offering good possibilities
for the producer.
Producer: Herbert Graf.
Conductor: Dimitri Mitropoulos.
Sets: Ludwig Sievert.

Salzburg Festival, 1964
Design by Teo Otto, determined
by the very wide stage, with a
fortress-like wall. The performers
have ample opportunity to move
about, but the decorative tree-like
structure to the left is not quite
convincing. On the whole,
though, a free, personal approach.
Producer and conductor: Herbert
von Karajan.

tral interlude while Elektra gazes upon Orestes,
now safely restored to her. I can make her repeat
the stammered words: *"Orest, Orest, Orest!"* several times; of the remainder only the words: *"Es
rührt sich niemand!"* (No one moves!) and *"O
lass Deine Augen mich sehen!"* (Oh, let your eyes
look on me) fit into this mood. Couldn't you
insert here a few beautiful verses until (as
Orestes is about to embrace her gently) I switch
over to the sombre mood, starting with the
words: *"Nein, Du sollst mich nicht berühren..."*
(No, you should not touch me...) etc. ...I

must have material here to work at will towards
a climax. Eight, sixteen, twenty lines, as many
as you can, and all in the same ecstatic mood, rising all the time towards a climax."[9]

By 25 June 1908 Hugo von Hofmannsthal
answered:

'Seite 77.
Elektra: ... Orest!
(flüsternd) Es rührt sich niemand. (zärtlich) O lass
Deine Augen mich sehen. Traumbild, mir geschenk-
tes!

Schöner als alle Träume! Unbegreifliches,
entzückendes Gesicht, o bleib bei mir
lös nicht in Luft Dich auf, vergeh mir nicht—
es sei denn, dass ich jetzt gleich sterben muss
und Du Dich anzeigst und mich holen kommst:
dann sterb ich seliger als ich gelebt!'

(Page 77.
Elektra: ... Orestes!
(whispering) No one moves. *(tenderly)* Oh, let your
eyes light upon me. Dreamlike vision, granted to me!
More beautiful than any dream! a face mysterious
and enchanting, oh stay with me
do not dissolve into the air, do not vanish from me—
but if that must be, then I shall die
and you will come to bear me away:
that would be to die more blessedly than I have lived!)

'I hope this suits you,' the poet added laconically.[10]

It did suit Strauss, and the resulting fusion of
word and sound is one of the finest examples of
creative collaboration.

Orestes and the attendant with him enter the
palace; Elektra 'runs back and forth in front of
the door ... in a terrifying state of tension ... her
head down like an animal in a cage' until the
ear-splitting cry of Clytaemnestra cuts into the
silence. In her demoniacal hatred Elektra then
gives vent to these words to Orestes: 'Strike once

more!' Chrysothemis and the maids come running in; they ask what has happened, and receiv-
ing no answer from Elektra flee from Aegisthus
who is seen coming through the gateway. Pretending subservience, Elektra guides Aegisthus
(who is afraid of the dark) by the light of a sput-
tering torch into the house where his murderers
are waiting. A few moments later Aegisthus can
be seen again at a window, calling for help; he
has been drawn into his dark fate, which is accompanied by the triumphantly contemptuous
cry of Elektra: 'Agamemnon hears you!'

In a state of great agitation Chrysothemis appears again with the maids and says to Elektra:
'Our brother is within!' Cries of: 'Orestes!
Orestes!' echo in joyous excitement round the
walls of the building.

The force of Elektra's clairvoyant powers and
her indomitable will conjured up these events.
Now she has achieved everything. Spiritually
drained and physically exhausted, she manages
with her last breath a macabre dance of triumph,
the shattering apotheosis of her superhuman
hatred. She dies before the eyes of her sister
Chrysothemis on the threshold of the palace.

In actually showing the murder of Aegisthus
Hofmannsthal was adhering to a request made
by Strauss. In a letter dated 22 December 1907
Strauss had written in detail of the sequence of
scenes for *Semiramis* which had blossomed further, but at the end of the letter referred to *Elektra* which was already under way:

As for our recent conversation about *Elektra,* I believe that we can't leave out Aegisthus altogether. He is definitely part of the

Teatro Colón, Buenos Aires, 1966
Costume design for Clytaemnestra
by Roberto Oswald: an elegant,
almost too modish drawing, without real conviction.

Jean Madeira as Clytaemnestra.
She played the part many times
(Vienna, Munich, USA, etc.) to
great effect. The ornamental stick
she holds is characteristically distinctive; the facial make-up is not
obtrusive and everything is left to
the actress's powers of expression.
(Costume designer: unknown.
Period: the 1960s.)

Bayerische Staatsoper, Munich,
1963
The lines of the set point to the
gate. An austere solution of great
expressive force.
Producer: Hans Hartleb.
Conductor: Joseph Keilberth.
Sets: Helmut Jürgens.

Staatsoper, Hamburg, 1973
This design by Majewski impressi-
vely follows the producer's concept, which envisaged a stream of
blood pouring through the gigantic gateway, dominating everything. This was an attempt to free
the set from architectonic forms
and to relate it directly to the
action on stage.
Producer: August Everding.
Conductor: Karl Böhm.

plot and must be killed with the rest, preferably before the eyes of the audience ... It's not a good plan to have all the women come running on stage after the murder of Clytaemnestra, then disappear again, and then, following the murder of Aegisthus, return once more with Chrysothemis. This breaks the line too much. Perhaps something or other will occur to you. Couldn't we let Aegisthus come home immediately after Orestes has entered the house? And perform the murders in quick succession one after the other, possibly in such a way that, the moment Aegisthus has stepped into the house and the door is shut behind him, the distant cry of Clytaemnestra is heard and then, after a short pause, the murder of Aegisthus is done the way it stands now—and after that the final scene with all the women? I think that might work all right.[11]

I recall a performance of *Elektra* at Covent Garden which I arranged jointly with Erich Kleiber when the conductor insisted that the cries of the chorus 'Orest! Orest!' marked at the end of the score should be clearly heard and not left out as is usually the case. He maintained that this would give the blood-soaked stone of the palace a kind of conciliatory, mythic consecration in keeping with Elektra's ecstatic dance. We introduced the cries into the performance and the effect was magnificent: the sombre temple of hatred thereby acquired its final headstone, darkened by the blood that had been spilled.

In conversations over the years, Strauss made almost no mention of *Elektra.* He knew that the work was unique; its grandeur was complete. He had nothing to add. Occasionally he complained about the cuts habitually made in the Clytaemnestra scene and in Elektra's part, on the grounds that although the omissions saved hardly any time in the performance the sections cut were essential for an understanding of the opera in its entirety. This is true. Such cuts having the same effect as though blocks of stone had been torn arbitrarily from a edifice; they are senseless.

The finest tribute to *Elektra,* and one that has since been confirmed by time, came just twelve years after the work's première, when Richard Specht, in 1921, commented as follows with the reference to the many critical opinions expressed: '... Those who lived at that time finally had the most beautiful experience there is: to know that a really great man was among us. A strengthener, and steward of all great music of earlier times; a man who blew open doors into

new realms; one of those rare men who are admired not for what they have done, but for their discovery of new directions of expression, from which all of today's generation (and presumably that of tomorrow as well) can live—and does!'

In shaping this colossal work the producer and the stage-designer were from the start faced with a task which had not to be misunderstood: they had to do justice to the larger-than-life aspect of this plot from Antiquity by constructing a stage setting which would be part of the dramatic action (but would be without distracting details); they had to find the most convincing and logical form, one that would not be subject to a variety of interpretations.

The designers of the early productions of *Elektra* showed that they understood this point by creating imposing sets which were true to the intention of the work and which gave this merciless drama the appropriate background. One or two unsuccessful experiments at supporting the lyrical scenes with botanical embellishments such as placing a tree by the well, soon disappeared. There were interesting variations to the drama's sombre locale, but basically the contours of the work (laid down with chiselled precision) were respected—presumably because the idiom of the work is in itself so convincing that any arbitrary alteration could only weaken the impact.

Some new ideas, developed by individual producers, introduced a number of worthwhile variations to the basic outlines given for the setting. A production of *Elektra* at the ancient Theatre of Herodes Atticus in Athens left one of the most lasting impressions. The designer Helmut Jürgens utilized the second-century A.D. architecture of the theatre, adding only the mighty bronze gate essential for the plot, placing it in an opening already in the theatre. The producer was Heinz Arnold and he, too, drew inspiration from the magic of the setting; the result was an unforgettable artistic experience.

The illustrations in these pages show the work of several famous stage-designers, including Alfred Roller and Emil Preetorius. They are worth studying carefully, because only then do the various ideas (which developed from the work) become apparent in all their diversity—a diversity which at first seems only of minor significance.

In *Elektra,* producer and stage-designer have to co-operate to a degree beyond that of almost any other work since the setting for this one-act drama is unchanging and unchangeable. In this sense it is not really a 'venue', a 'setting' or a

San Francisco Opera, 1973
A scene with Elektra (Amy Shuard) and Aegisthus (Thomas Stewart), both powerful actors.
Producer: Paul Hager.
Conductor: Otmar Suitner.
Sets: Alfred Siercke.

Théâtre National de l'Opéra, Paris, 1974
Birgit Nilsson, who gave an immensely impressive portrayal of Elektra, is an authentic successor to the great interpreters of this part (Marie Gutheil-Schoder, Erna Schlüter, Christel Goltz, Inge Borkh, among others).

background, but a constantly vibrant element of the plot which radiates in tangible fashion the sinister tension of the drama. It introduces us to the *dramatis personae*. Staircases, steps, raised levels, entrance-ways and the great gate, with its central significance, have their own tasks to fulfil in conjunction with the actors. There is nothing coincidental in this mercilessly difficult piece.

In *Salome* a series of details is fused into a whole in *pointilliste* fashion. By contrast all the characters of *Elektra* are sharply delineated, even the maids in the opening scene. One is tempted to describe the characters as solid constructions—and a director has rather to subtract from than to add to their substance; like a sculptor chiselling at grandly conceived, classical forms, so should a director work at a performance of *Elektra*. That means constant control of any gesture which might be open to misinterpretation. In principle, and not just with regard to *Elektra*, Strauss often warned against his

orchestral music being misunderstood and played in an expansive manner. Singers of the roles of Clytaemnestra and Elektra should take special care here, and not dissipate their abilities in hysteria but reinforce the tragic power of the piece by acting with a maximum of self-control.

Opera-houses found less difficulty in casting *Elektra* than they did the vibrant *Salome*. It is clear that the title role demands a dramatic voice, and the two other female parts, Chrysothemis and Clytaemnestra, can be filled by soloists from the normal complement of an operatic company.

Opera programmes give us the names of many famous singers, from Barbara Kemp to Birgit Nilsson, in the part of Elektra; we learn too of the performers of the other main female roles. The men are somewhat less important, even if the Orestes scene does make great demands on the stage presence and personality of the singer.

Théâtre National de l'Opéra, Paris, 1974
Two figures by Majewski in the performance directed by August Everding. A modest, straightforward attempt at free characterization, without adherence to models from Greek antiquity; some affinity to early Russian costume can be discerned.

64

Teatro Colón, Buenos Aires, 1975
The set apparently was conceived
as a stage within a stage. It has
somewhat restricted possibilities.
Note the eccentric frame of the
central doorway, reminiscent of
Christian crosses (in the sixteenth
century B.C.!) A not entirely suc-
cessful attempt to free the set
from the dressed stone style of
Mycenaean architecture.
Producer: Martin Eisler.
Conductor: Leopold Hager.
Sets: Oscar Lagomarsino.

Elektra is a drama about women, and as we mentioned earlier is the first of Strauss's operas inspired by classical Greek mythology. It is tempting to take a comparative look at the last of the 'Greek operas', *Daphne* and *Die Liebe der Danae* ('The Love of Danae'). In *Elektra* Richard Strauss simply had to transmute into music the shattering experience of his first encounter with the essence of Antiquity and the cruel fate to which its people were bound. He had to free himself of the shock of this encounter. The later work *Daphne* is a clear commitment to a spiritually enlightening love. Thirty-two years after *Elektra, Die Liebe der Danae* concluded Strauss's involvement and 'dialogue' with the ancient Greek world. It contains a summary of everything he saw in the classical world: humorous

mockery, loving admiration and the implication that tragedy cannot be avoided by the Master of the Fates himself, the highest of the gods, Jupiter, as he is called in *Danae,* but who here we should call Zeus.

Strauss ended his artistic association with Antiquity in relaxed, considered cheerfulness; this mood could already be discerned within him when he attended a rehearsal of *Elektra* in Dresden. He wrote:

'During one of the first orchestral rehearsals, Schuch [the conductor], who was very sensitive to draughts, noticed in the third balcony of the empty theatre a door which had been left open by a charwoman. Full of annoyance, he shouted: "What are you looking for?" I replied from the front stalls: "A triad".'[12]

Der Rosenkavalier

Imagine a bright day in May, an afternoon for reverie, for falling in love. So it must have been as fine ladies in their elegant carriages promenaded along the avenues of the Prater, the park by the Danube in Vienna, escorted by cavaliers mounted on magnificent steeds. Among the most dazzling women seen in this daily cortège was Princess Werdenberg, wife of a famous field-marshal; with her husband away frequently, she had the time to dally. Indeed, Princess Werdenberg had too much time to spare which she tried to while away in the agreeable style of this gallant epoch. Attentive glances reaped promising responses, and the glowing admiration of the young Count Octavian Rofrano was noticed with a smile . . .

And so it began: an episode with complexities of plot but not a drama; a wafting, magical quality characterized the work from the beginning to the tender, touching encounter at the end.

This relaxed cheerfulness also characterized the new collaboration between Hofmannsthal and Strauss on a comic opera for which the composer had constantly pressed.

Even during the final work on *Elektra* Strauss, ever restless, had been searching for something new, for a cheerful subject which would bring a sense of release. Writing the score and the instrumentation for *Elektra* was for Strauss a purely technical exercise, not a creative one, and after the powerful explosion of *Elektra* he could see no way forward on the course he had taken; even to himself, the music he was working on seemed strangely bold, and he wanted to free himself from it. He wanted to leave behind the tragic and cruel world of Antiquity which had so deeply shaken him and which had led him to a tonal language (for the orchestra) that had not been heard before. Once again he suggested to Hofmannsthal *Semiramis,* based on

This photograph from 1910
shows the leading personalities of
the Dresden Opera. Seated (left to
right): Count Seebach, director-
general; Richard Strauss; Ernst
von Schuch, the conductor.
Standing (left to right): Max
Hasait, technical director; Otto
Altenkirch, scenic artist; Max
Reinhardt, Berlin; Hugo von
Hofmannsthal; Alfred Roller,
Vienna, set designer; Leonhard
Fanto, costume designer; and
Georg Toller, producer.

Königliches Opernhaus, Dresden,
1911
The programme for the première
names the most famous members
of the Dresden ensemble including the producer, Georg Toller.
Max Reinhardt, in effect the producer on this occasion at Strauss's
request, was not named, on the
instructions of Count Seebach.
Roller's design is noted in small
print after the *dramatis personae,* as
was customary at that time.
Conductor: Ernst von Schuch.

the story by Calderón, but the poet evaded the
issue because he himself was working on another
piece based on Casanova and believed that the
latter would be suitable for a musical composition. But then, in the middle of this period of
hesitant waiting, Hofmannsthal wrote on 11
February 1909—a few days after the première of
Elektra—that: '... I have spent three quiet after-
noons here [Weimar] drafting the full and entirely original scenario for an opera...' He made
no mention of the plot and provided only a few
desultory details: '... full of burlesque situations
and characters, with lively action, pellucid, almost like a pantomime. There are opportunities

in it for lyrical passages, for fun and humour,
even for a short ballet... It contains two big ba-
ritone parts and another for a graceful girl dressed up as a man, à la Farrar or Mary Garden.
Period: old Vienna under the Empress Maria
Theresa.'[1]

From the start Strauss's reaction was one of
lively impatience as he waited for the text. Following Strauss's and Hofmannsthal's work on
this opera in their letters is a pleasure which no
music lover should miss.

It is amusing and exciting to read how the
two men, so different in their creative natures,
met in the world of the Baroque, in that great

Königliches Opernhaus, Dresden, 1911

The most outstanding part of Roller's work was his costume design. These designs were published in a separate folio by the publisher Fürstner and every theatre acquiring performing rights had to agree to follow them. They are remarkable for the manner in which they capture the inner natures of the characters. For decades they served as models for every performance.

Königliches Opernhaus, Dresden, 1911

The set for Act II seems strangely simple and 'bourgeois' in the light of later interpretations. Roller subsequently revised his ideas, above all by leaving out the two fireplaces in the corners which served also as scarcely credible entrances for the two intriguers. Producers: Georg Toller and Max Reinhardt. Conductor: Ernst von Schuch.

Der Rosenkavalier
Oper von Dr. Richard Strauß.

Königliches Opernhaus, Dresden,
1911
Count Octavian's entrance in Act
II, with Minnie Nast as Sophie
and Eva von der Osten as Octavian. Note again the economy of
the set, in contrast to the opu-
lence of the music.
Producers: Georg Toller and Max
Reinhardt. Conductor: Ernst von
Schuch. Sets: Alfred Roller.

epoch marked by South German and Austrian influences; how the figures conjured up by the poet gain life through their operatic shape; how the two fought and spurred each other on. Strauss, the clear-thinking man of the theatre, insisted on a fundamental re-shaping of Act II; the more fastidious and sensitive Hofmannsthal was sometimes in danger of overburdening the opera with too much detail. But it was Hof- mannsthal who insisted on the work's brilliant title, *Der Rosenkavalier,* because almost to the last Strauss had held out for the title *Ochs von Lerchenau* ('The Ox of Lerchenau'), and in the end grudgingly agreed to a sub-title which Hof- mannsthal with his linguistic precision had proposed: 'Comedy for music'.

However, these disputes, conducted on both sides with great tenacity, did not begin until work on the new piece was well advanced and indeed almost finished. The prologue and the whole of Act I retain the happy lightness of the initial draft. Hofmannsthal wrote:

The way it arose was as convivial as the work itself. The scenario literally developed in conversation; in conversation, that is, with the friend to whom the text is dedicated, Count Harry Kessler. The figures were sud- denly there and moved before us, even before we had names for them: the clown (buffo), the old man, the young girl, the lady, the cherubino. These were characters whose in- dividual traits were still to be defined in the course of writing. The action sprang from the eternally typical relationship of these figures *almost without us knowing how* ...

When Hofmannsthal merely described the draft to Strauss in Berlin, the composer was fas- cinated: 'Go home quickly and send me the first act as soon as possible.' From then onwards Strauss exerted constant pressure on his libret- tist, with the result that Hofmannsthal was dis- mayed at the pace Strauss demanded and often had to explain that dictation and writing held up faster progress. At the same time he was very sensitive to the weather and needed to feel Na- ture around him if he was to work fruitfully. In this he was like Strauss, who said that he would compose from spring onwards throughout the summer, and use the winter, the dismal part of the year, for the technical labour of writing out the score. On 4 May 1910, admonished by Strauss, Hofmannsthal wrote: '... I would have found the end long ago, but for the appalling weather we have now been having here for weeks; it thoroughly depresses me. The end must be *very* good... In short, it must be done with zest and joy, and so I must sit in the garden and have sun, not icy rain-storms.'[2]

Strauss once said of his own work that 'flow- ers bloom not in winter' but that they need

Königliches Hof- und National-
altheater, Munich, 1911
A few days after the Dresden pre-
mière the Königliches Hof- und
Nationaltheater in Munich put on
Der Rosenkavalier. The sets and
costumes were based on the de-
signs by Alfred Roller.
Producer: Anton Fuchs.
Conductor: Felix Mottl.

warmth and sun; so too with musical ideas. He
composed in the spring and summer; the winter
was for other things.

Hofmannsthal was almost sad when he had to
write 'Curtain' at the end of the libretto. He appreciated the uniqueness of their joint endeavour, which had occasionally led to small
skirmishes but which had been conducted on
both sides with courtesy and forebearance.
(There were none of the serious disputes which
would arise in later years.) Both men found it
difficult to separate themselves from the figures
they had created, which had grown dear to
them, and to hand over the finished work to
routine life in the theatre: a situation which
caused problems, some of them expected but

others surprising. The reservations expressed by the two theatre directors, Count Seebach (Dresden) and Count Hülsen (Berlin), about the great daring of the text were allayed where possible—Hofmannsthal showed great understanding and patience—and the *risqué* bedroom atmosphere of Act I was 'defused' in the way it was portrayed. But Strauss fought side by side with Hofmannsthal to obtain the best cast (in Dresden, Vienna and Munich) and lavish scenery, as well as extensive rehearsals and the best producers. Each asked the other to visit and check on rehearsals in Dresden, Munich and Vienna. On this they were in full agreement, because they both knew the special value of the work, which their creative power had fashioned. A work of complexity had been shaped from free imagination and from many small details. The impact of this work could be sensed even before the first performance, and it therefore seemed natural that the highest demands should be made in terms of its realization on stage. With this in mind, Strauss and Hofmannsthal critically oversaw the preparatory stage work, expressing their frank and often gloomy opinions. Hofmannsthal wrote: '... Oh well, if all the bass buffos are long and lean and only the Quinquins thick and fat, I may as well close down...'[3]

The following comment came from Strauss:
Couldn't you [Hofmannsthal] attend a few Munich rehearsals; then you'll see at once whether Bender is conceivably suitable for Dresden [for the part of Ochs]... I have now written to Schuch, asking that you, Roller and Reinhardt be invited to the setting rehearsals after 9 January. In case you and Reinhardt do not succeed in grooming Perron for the part, I give you full powers of veto to cancel the première with Perron on the 26th. The latter is such a first-class artist that he will understand and share our misgivings. Do

Metropolitan Opera, New York, 1913
Der Rosenkavalier appeared at the Metropolitan Opera in New York for the first time in 1913. The sets were by the Vienna scenic artist Kautsky, an associate of Roller. The decor of Act II is especially noteworthy. Alfred Hertz was the conductor.

treat him tactfully—he's trying terribly hard—but at the same time be implacable, for the fate of our opera is at stake... Therefore: tact and circumspection![4]

In Dresden problems became particularly acute when Strauss demanded that Max Reinhardt collaborate as producer, and, in the teeth of many difficulties, succeeded. Such a request to an opera-house of the standing of Dresden was something hitherto unheard of and it was understandable that the theatre director, Count Seebach, should have sought to protect his own chief producer. Strauss valued Reinhardt above anyone else, particularly since the productions of *Salome* and *Elektra.* He has this to say about the solution that was found:

... When, in Dresden, I listened to the first stage rehearsal with orchestra, I realized during the second act that the producer of the old school who was in charge was completely incapable of producing the opera... Remembering a kind offer made by Max Reinhardt, I asked Generalintendant Graf Seebach whether I could invite Reinhardt to come and help us. Seebach reluctantly permitted this on condition that Reinhardt would not set foot on the stage! Reinhardt came, without making any demands... and thus we all met on the rehearsal stage. Reinhardt as a modest spectator, whilst I in my clumsy way showed the singers as best I could how to play their parts. After a while Reinhardt could be observed whispering to Frau von der Osten in a corner of the hall and then again with Miss Siems, Perron, etc. The next day they came to the rehearsal transformed into fully-fledged actors. Thereupon Seebach graciously permitted Reinhardt to direct operations on the stage instead of watching the rehearsal from the stalls. The result was a new style in opera and a perfect performance in which the trio (Siems, von der Osten, Nast) in particular delighted everyone.[5]

Count Seebach showed himself a master of diplomacy in smoothing over the production difficulties, especially since, by a series of unfortunate coincidences, the resident producer, Georg Toller, had learnt of Reinhardt's presence from the newspapers. But he, too, came to terms with the situation, recognizing Reinhardt's artistic authority, because at the bottom of the theatre programme of the première his name, Georg Toller, appeared as that of producer, and the work of the great Berlin producer was not credited at all. All behaved with great tact, for the good of an exceptional theatrical occasion; this is documented by a photograph which shows Strauss and Hofmannsthal reconciled with everyone else involved in the première. The magic of the silver rose seems to have radiated a spirit of reconciliation even then.

The première in Dresden was on 26 January 1911, and in quick succession Berlin, Munich and Vienna followed with their own first productions: a world success had been born, and it was even more than that—it provided Strauss and Hofmannsthal with a secure platform and gave them both a feeling of security and the courage to undertake further joint projects. *Der Rosenkavalier* had begun its victorious career, which is certain to take it into the next millennium.

Productions throughout the world soon followed rapidly, and Strauss, sure of his achievement, was looking for something new. As early as 8 October 1910 he wrote to Hofmannsthal: '... The time has now almost come to think of *Semiramis*...'[6] But the poet once again had other

plans and ideas which would lead to his next work, *Ariadne auf Naxos.*

The events surrounding the première of *Der Rosenkavalier* give one considerable insight into the great importance of the producer's job. As regards sets and costumes matters had been a little easier because in Alfred Roller, the Viennese artist and designer, Strauss and Hofmanns-

Metropolitan Opera, New York, 1913
This rare photograph shows the leading star of her day, Maria Jeritza, as Octavian in the New York performance—a concession to the fame of this singer, who was not a natural for this trouser-role.

Der Rosenkavalier
Lotte Lehmann — Richard Mayr.

Salzburg Festival, 1929
Two world-famous singers from
the Salzburg performance of 1929:
Lotte Lehmann and Richard
Mayr, here posing for the photo-
grapher.

Metropolitan Opera, New York,
1946
A scene from Act II. The costumes were unchanged from those
in use before the war—Roller's
designs—and the sets were based
on drawings by Kautsky and Roller, revised by Josef Novak.
Octavian: R. Stevens. Sophie:
E. Steber.
Producer: Herbert Graf.
Conductor: Fritz Busch.

Städtische Bühnen, Nuremberg,
1948
Design for Act III by Kurt Hal-
legger. The stage area is interest-
ingly divided up to indicate the
clandestine existence of a *chambre
séparé.*
Producer: Rudolf Hartmann.
Conductor: Alfons Dressel.

thal had found an ideal collaborator whom they
could trust without reservation. Roller's work
remained definitive for decades; it was excellent
in every respect, and Strauss even gave him and
Hofmannsthal the task of drawing up a book of
instructions for the production of *Der Rosenkavalier* which was to be passed on to the many
theatres which planned to perform the work.
Roller's draft was adopted by the Fürstner pub-
lishing house which, at the request of composer
and librettist, for many years required theatres to
adhere to these instructions. This had the advantage of ensuring that even in smaller theatres
quality was maintained in regard to sets and costume, and that performances of the work were
reserved more or less for special festive occasions
(because of the high costs involved in putting
it on). The really small theatres were in
any case not in a position to mount *Der Rosenkavalier* because of the large orchestra needed.

Thus for decades Roller's sets and costumes
dominated performances all over the world.
Experiments with different presentations were
therefore inhibited, and so a certain visual steril-
ity developed. Nevertheless the high standard of

Roller's work remained an almost obligatory
yardstick for the more flexible solutions that
were adopted everywhere after the Second
World War.

The special characteristic of Roller's work,
which is still valid today, is the care with which
he handled detail, not just the painstakingly
created sections of the set, but also the objects
which must 'play their part' at certain points of
emphasis, for example, everything that an actor
touched such as the toilet-set on the dressing-
table, the breakfast china, the silver rose, the
hand mirror and so on. One needs to have experienced, as a producer, how sensitively actors
can often react, in a piece set in the past, to props
and furniture designed in the style of that period
(perhaps even dating from that period), to
understand fully the uncanny emanations given
off by these 'dumb actors' and to marvel at their
effect. Roller understood this magical relationship and it was not just an exaggerated passion
for 'historical realism' which led him to his detailed plans for *Der Rosenkavalier,* in particular
for the costumes. I myself once saw how agitated he became when a singer in the role of Ochs

Two Marschallins from American productions.
Left: Lisa della Casa, New York, 1956
Right: Elisabeth Schwarzkopf, San Francisco, 1955.

San Francisco Opera, 1955
Otto Edelmann, a great Ochs, with Frances Bible in Act III.

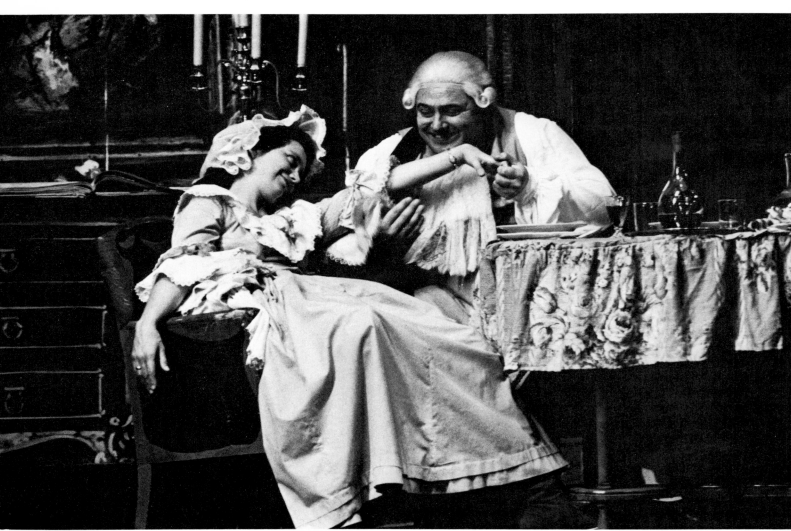

Städtische Bühnen, Frankfurt-am-Main, 1955
Design for Act I by Josef Fenneker. Lively artistic sketch. The areas where the action takes place are convincingly arranged.
Producer: Josef Gielen.
Conductor: Georg Solti.

forgot to wear a bunch of chamberlain's keys with his costume in the second act. To Roller this was unforgivable, because he meant that an important element in the characterization of this seedy representative of the Imperial Court had been omitted.

One may smile at Roller's exactness as pedantry, but it is indeed worth while to consider his and Hofmannsthal's original intentions. These details handed down the poetic ingredients such as the silver rose, and the schematic figures from traditional comedy created an image of the Vienna of Maria Theresa with all its delightful contradictions; so lively that a spectator must feel himself to be part of the scene. The personal experiences of the Marschallin, of Octavian and Sophie mirror, almost inadvertently, an entire epoch, which in this way is brought close to us, inviting us to identity with it.

These sentiments, which ebb away only gradually and which make it difficult for us to return to everyday reality, have often been described—because of their power—as characteristics of what has been called 'culinary theatre'. Its opulent presentation is alleged by some to be the contemptible ideal of petit-bourgeois Philistinism. But of course one can also take the view that a work of art like *Der Rosenkavalier,* which is complete in every sense, deserves love and respect, and that the delight felt by its admirers is an expression of an intensified aesthetic empathy, a yearning for a quality of beauty which has been submerged by the preoccupations of everyday life. There will always be various points of view on this subject. However, the successful fusion of poetry and music in *Der Rosenkavalier* is an artistic triumph, something which should be taken as a starting-point for any discussion of the opera.

Both librettist and composer loved the vivid character of Baron Ochs; in Strauss's case so much so that to the last he preferred Ochs as the title figure. Hofmannsthal followed up every historical clue. He paid great attention to the name and the family of Lerchenau. Following his tracks we learn that north of Vienna there is a small village called Lerchenau, where a somewhat dilapidated manor once existed which could well have been the sort of place where Ochs might have lived. In an article written in a charming *Rosenkavalier* mood Gunther Martin put the matter thus: 'Can anyone be surprised... that one does not need go far outside Vienna to find the village from which Baron Ochs, admittedly in indirect fashion, drew his noble pedigree: Lerchenau, on the stretch north-west of

Korneuburg.' The author then describes how Hofmannsthal sought to give substance to his creations making exact instructions regarding the location for a film of *Der Rosenkavalier* which was made in 1926. Fifteen years after the première of the opera, Hofmannsthal once again enjoyed the happy sense of floating between reality and imagination while writing the screenplay.

Der Rosenkavalier is uniquely bewitching, though its magic and its designers eventually emancipated themselves from Roller's work. Indeed Roller himself indicated the possibility of new developments with his last work, the drafts for a new production in Munich (1937). Later, pompous and imposing Baroque buildings provided the background in Vienna and Salzburg; in Munich this was provided by the graceful Amalienburg in the Nymphenburg Park, which inspired Helmut Jürgens and later Jürgen Rose in their designs for Act II; elsewhere other variations and images developed from similar settings. All these, provided that they were of the same artistic standard, retained the link with the milieu of the period, a link which had been established since the première. Anyone seeking great differences or 'sensational

ideas' must follow through the changes in basic outlines, colours and detailed treatment as they have evolved. There should be no sudden violations of the style—the work itself effectively forbids such developments. There have been occasional attempts at radical change, in the second and above all in the third act, but these attempts have not been fruitful, and indeed are superfluous. In regard to the final trio—whose success Strauss had guaranteed Hofmannsthal——all stagings which deviate from the original intention, no matter how charming they may be, diminish its artistic value.

It is worth recalling here that Strauss believed in the highest professional standards of acting in opera. He knew that he would need the best producer of his day for *Der Rosenkavalier*. This 'comedy for music' required a new, easy-going style of presentation which was in accordance with the way the dialogue had been composed—lively and full of nuance. In short, the new style had to be completely divorced from the rigid pathos of heroic opera. It has taken a long time for producers and singers to fulfil this difficult task. Since 1911 decades of development have taken place which, despite unsatisfying productions in a mixture of styles, have led to the convincing

Deutsche Staatsoper, Berlin, 1960
Design for Act III by Hainer Hill.
The entrances are well positioned, but the architectural elements are rather too heavy.
Producer: Erich Alexander Winds.
Conductor: Franz Konwitschny.

Salzburg Festival, 1960
Construction of the new Salzburg
Festival Hall was a laborious and
lengthy process, but in 1960 it
opened with *Der Rosenkavalier*.
On 26 July Herbert von Karajan
conducted the festival performance, which was directed by
Rudolf Hartmann. Teo Otto designed the sets; the costumes were
by Erni Kniepert. The performance was filmed live (by Rank
Films) and shown all over the
world.

Salzburg Festival, 1960
The outline plan for Act II illustrates the difficulties caused by the
very wide stage. The balconies,
which can be discerned on the
plan, skilfully bounded the set
without restricting the audience's
view of the stage. An elegant and
attractive solution, giving the
producer a chance to develop new
ideas.
Producer: Rudolf Hartmann.
Conductor: Herbert von Karajan.
Sets: Teo Otto.

balance achieved in today's best performances.
The histrionic education of modern singers has
been significantly influenced by the demands
which *Der Rosenkavalier* suddenly made on
opera, out of which musical theatre developed.

To the producer, *Der Rosenkavalier* offers a
rich field. From my own experience I know that
one really has to protect oneself from the sheer
joy of imaginative invention, particularly in relation to the first and third acts, when confronted with so many stimulating ideas. Constant and
strict self-control is essential if one does not wish
to make it more difficult for the audience to
understand the essence of the plot.

Strauss was painstakingly exact about the significance of the setting, even more so than the
imaginative Hofmannsthal, who was more inclined to leave details of the plot to the good-
natured credulity of the public. On 9 August
1909 Strauss again admonished Hofmannsthal:
'... How is the two Italians' change of side
motivated? Is there something at the beginning
of the third act to show how Octavian has won
them over, or that the Baron has not paid them,
etc.?'[7] Hofmannsthal wrote back saying that in
Act III there were enough opportunities for

SALZBURGER
FESTSPIELE
1960

40 JAHRE SALZBURGER FESTSPIELE

26. JULI 1960
FESTVORSTELLUNG ANLÄSSLICH DER ERÖFFNUNG
DES NEUEN HAUSES

DER ROSENKAVALIER

KOMÖDIE FÜR MUSIK IN DREI AUFZÜGEN
VON HUGO VON HOFMANNSTHAL
MUSIK VON
RICHARD STRAUSS
DIRIGENT
HERBERT VON KARAJAN
INSZENIERUNG
RUDOLF HARTMANN
BÜHNENBILD
TEO OTTO
KOSTÜME
ERNI KNIEPERT
ORCHESTER
DIE WIENER PHILHARMONIKER
CHOR DER WIENER STAATSOPER

BEGINN 19.30 UHR

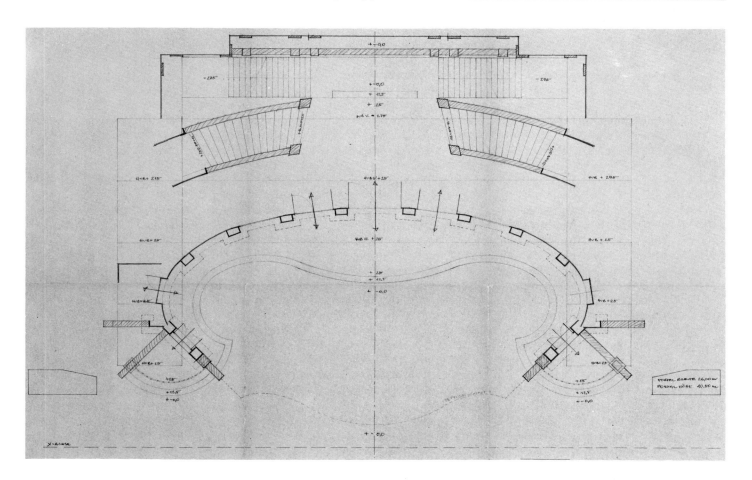

motivating the Italians' change of sides and that the public was very tolerant in such matters.

In such circumstances a producer uses his discretion. In Act II Octavian, forced to take his leave by the enraged Faninal, still has enough time before he actually departs to bribe the Italians over to his side; and at the beginning of Act III Valzacchi receives another full purse. Similarly, too, with the entrance of the Marschallin in the third act. This can be motivated by the bright idea of Ochs's quick-thinking valet Leopold running in order to fetch the Princess as his master's 'saviour'. Silent details like this are an essential part of well thought-out production; they help clarify the plot.

The characters of the main *dramatis personae* have been so exhaustively written about that any repetition would be superfluous. Strauss and Hofmannsthal expressed themselves clearly on the subject. The Marschallin is at the most 32

Salzburg Festival. 1960
The balconies outlined in the plan are visible in this sketch of Act II. The bright, cheerful, room, with its dark floor, effectively enhanced the production.
Producer: Rudolf Hartmann.
Conductor: Herbert von Karajan.
Sets: Teo Otto.

Salzburg Festival, 1960
Act III accorded fully with the director's intentions. The floor-tiles made it possible to site the awkward trap-door unobtrusively. The raised bay area to the left allowed the Marschallin to make an impressive entrance. Teo Otto had freed himself from Roller's model, and found his own solutions for staging the three acts.
Producer: Rudolf Hartmann.
Conductor: Herbert von Karajan.

Salzburg Festival, 1960
In the opening performance in
Salzburg, Lisa della Casa sang the
part of the Marschallin. This scene
shows the entrance of the head
Cook and the Hairdresser.
Producer: Rudolf Hartmann.
Conductor: Herbert von Karajan.
Sets: Teo Otto.
Costumes: Erni Kniepert.

Lisa della Casa as Octavian and
Anneliese Rothenberger as
Sophie, in Act II. A photo of the
Munich set, taken for a record
cover. Lisa della Casa sang the part
of Octavian on a number of occa-
sions, notably at the Metropolitan
Opera, New York.

years old; Ochs is not a peasant yokel, but a somewhat wild noble bachelor of about 35; Sophie a nice bourgeois girl, with a strong temperament; and Octavian is a descendant of Mozart's Cherubino, a young lover with all the talents of another Don Juan.

Everything that pertains to these characters—the milieu, the period, the supporting cast—requires the affectionate touch we have mentioned and impeccable taste.

A producer never ceases to learn from *Der Rosenkavalier*—There is always something new, something that has hitherto remained hidden, that must be discovered and brought to the light. It is a magical, multifaceted masterpiece, whose infinite comic variety confirms its close relationship to *Le nozze di Figaro*.

After the first encounter in the Prater, the Marschallin, experienced in the ways of love, controls and directs the events that follow with grace and skill. When the curtain rises at the start of the first act it reveals the boudoir of a lady used to Rococo luxury. We find the imper-

fectly matched lovers at a tender moment, their previous stormy embraces having been graphically depicted in the overture. This overture is not an 'introduction'; the dashing theme of Octavian, played by the horns, leads directly into the wild love scene, with its ecstatic climaxes, and then into blissful fatigue as the curtain rises. 'As you were, so you are...' whispers the still enraptured Octavian to his beloved, whose face shows an air of remote dreaminess and whose wild passion he experiences again and again as if it were a miracle. The Marschallin, experienced in the ways of love, is enjoying his adulation. She jokes lightly with him and is ready for a fresh embrace; but he does not understand, becomes immersed in his own thoughts and thus breaks the threads which united them in their intimacy. The Marschallin is irritated; she hears something; Octavian has to hide. Through the door a young Negro servant enters, carrying her breakfast; he re-arranges everything and then leaves. This Moorish boy is a fashionable plaything of the kind kept by elegant ladies as ser-

Teatro alla Scala, Milan, 1961
Octavian's entrance with his liveried servants in Act II. The set has become even more luxurious. The costumes and the parade-like arrangement of the liveried servants were retained in performances everywhere.
Octavian: Christa Ludwig.
Sophie: Anneliese Rothenberger.
Producer: Rudolf Hartmann.
Conductor: Karl Böhm.
Sets: Robert Kautsky.

Metropolitan Opera, New York,
1969
The presentation of the rose (Act
II). Too many decorative details
crowd the room.
Producer: Nathaniel Merrill.
Conductor: Karl Böhm.
Sets: Robert O'Hearn.

vants, and for their amusement. Here and there one can see that, taking everything in with a cheeky grin, he is an accessory to the gallant secrets of his mistress. There is a hint of corruption, slightly out of place with the cheerful grace of the overall scene. The Marschallin is clever and has to be very careful. Perhaps her only accomplice in her adventures of love is a taciturn old chambermaid who lets the young lover in at night. But it is not really credible that a talkative child should so obviously be privy to his mistress's nocturnal secrets. This amusing, typically Viennese Sarotti-Mohrl (i.e. Negro servant) would more appropriately be introduced as a Rococo ornament in the following breakfast scene.

The loving couple are without a care in the world and give one another nicknames of endearment—'Bichette', 'Quinquin'. This atmosphere is abruptly disturbed when the Marschallin believes she has heard her husband (the 'quick-march field-marshal') returning home suddenly. Panicking, Octavian has to hide in the niche where the bed stands. The Marschallin

herself fearlessly prepares to face the storm. Then she recognizes the voice in the antechamber as that of someone else, 'Cousin Ochs, old Lerchenau'. What can he want? Oh yes, there was a letter, 'and I have no idea what it contained.'

The secreted lover re-appears from behind the curtains of the bed; he is disguised as 'Mariandl', a country chambermaid, much to the amusement of the Marschallin, who immediately sees the point of this little masquerade. 'He is lightning-quick, this lump...' There is a little parting kiss; Octavian tries to leave skilfully but bumps into Baron Ochs as he enters the room. The Baron has a short exchange with what he takes for a maid, and then greets the Marschallin as she approaches. Remembering the polite forms of greeting which he once learned, Ochs makes a bow in the Spanish-French manner. (This should not be an occasion for exaggerated comic antics, for he learned such chivalrous manners in his youth, as did his great ancestor Falstaff.) He tries to remind the Marschallin of the matter in his letter. During this conversation he finds an amusing way of staying in con-

Opernhaus, Cologne, 1969
In the Cologne production of
1969 both the director and the
designer were searching for new
approaches. The arrangement of
the room in Act I and its decoration has great charm.
Producer: Hans Neugebauer.
Conductor: Janos Kulka.
Sets: Max Bignens.

Opernhaus, Cologne, 1969
In Act III an attempt was made to
expand the set. This gave producer
and singers the chance to enrich
the action; but the value of this
was questionable because it distracted attention from the intimacy of the plot. The effect
became pompous.
Producer: Hans Neugebauer.
Conductor: Janos Kulka.
Sets: Max Bignens.

tact with the chambermaid. The Marschallin is also amused by this cheeky comic relationship between Octavian in his disguise and the 'Don Juan from the country'; she leaves Ochs in the hands of her secretary and retires. The major-domo opens the doors of the antechamber and the daily crowd of petitioners seeking her patronage streams in. There follows a scene of great charm which aptly portrays the milieu of the opera, a scene inspired by paintings and engravings of the period. In a letter dated 4 May 1909 Strauss wrote: 'The middle part (antechamber) [is] not easy to put into shape, but I'll manage it all right. Anyway I've got the whole summer in front of me...'[8]

And manage he did. The various episodes with the characters in this scene are masterfully interwoven: the hairdresser, the *bel canto* singers, the aristocratic orphans, the animal seller, the milliner, followed by the important conversation between Ochs and the Notary about the marriage contract. From this scene the acting of Act I develops so the producer must make it entirely comprehensible! Ochs gets angry with the Notary, forgets where he is, and abruptly interrupts the recital given by the tenor and the flautist; confusion reigns everywhere and Ochs has to leave on the orders of the Marschallin. A pair of intriguers, Valzacchi and Annina, approach Baron Ochs, who is searching in vain for the pretty maid, and offer him their confidential services. Ochs is astonished: 'Hm, the things you find in this Vienna!', but deliberately ignores the outstretched hands of the two Italians. Then he presents his personal servant, Leopold, his natural son, to the Marschallin. With the son is the silver rose for the bearer, whose duties the Marschallin has previously suggested should be carried out by Octavian. Ochs leaves with his retinue; the Marschallin remains, deep in thought, a little wistful, but not descending into tragic mood; she has suddenly become aware that time is passing unperceived and that the years are creeping up on her.

Not even the return of Octavian can lift her out of this mood. (The motive for his return is nicely conceived: he comes back to fetch his sword which he was unable to take with him when disguised as a maid. I saw this very logical nuance for the first time in a production by Joseph Gielen in Berlin and gladly adopted it later as a useful embellishment of the plot.) Octavian does not understand the Marschallin; perhaps he is too young to do so. He feels cast aside and hurt, with the result that she asks him to join her in the Prater that afternoon and to ride next to her carriage... just as he had done when

their magically amorous encounter first began. She does not guess that it is she herself who is about to send him into a new adventure with the silver rose.

Octavian leaves, still aggrieved; the Marschallin gives the silver rose, which has been left behind, to her little black servant to take care of. 'My Lord the Count knows in any case.' On her own again, she falls back into her earlier sad mood, but does not weep, merely dwelling on her thoughts:

Light must one be;
light of heart and light of hand;
hold and take, hold and let go...

The enchanting figure of Princess Maria Theresa disappears from view during Act II. The stirring musical introduction takes us to Herr von Faninal's new city palace, full of excitement and expectancy. This rich war-time profiteer ('he has the supplies for the army which now stands in the Netherlands') has had a house built by Vienna's most expensive architect and has equipped it with everything that goes with such extravagance: a large number of servants, magnificent coaches ('with sky-blue curtains, and drawn by four dapple-greys') and a major-domo whose distinguished bearing makes Faninal feel irritable. Sophie, an only child, together with her duenna from Leitmeritz is waiting for the Rose Cavalier who has announced his coming. Faninal has to leave rapidly to fetch the bridegroom from his quarters. With loud cries of 'Rofrano' the runners accompanying Count Octavian announce his arrival. He enters, surrounded by his magnificently attired liveried servants; he is holding the silver rose in his hand, and Sophie is not the only one who is excited; he is, too. He is performing the ceremonial duty with which he has been entrusted, and Sophie von Faninal, whom he has never met before, has turned out to be a girl of disconcerting beauty. Their encounter has all the radiance of youth, for he looks absolutely captivating: 'entirely in silver is he adorned, from head to foot, like a holy angel.' During the presentation of the rose the two have time to fall head over heels in love and the easy-going conversation they have afterwards only helps to deepen the growing sense of attachment between them.

Faninal comes in with the pompous bridegroom, who marvels at the magnificence of the reception room and is overjoyed at the youthful bride, whom he now sees for the first time. Sophie makes no attempt to hide her disappointment, indeed her horror, at Baron Ochs, her intended husband. ('So that's my future husband! And, heavens above, pock-marked as well!') The duenna does all she can to console Sophie: 'Well, if he doesn't please you from the front, you haughty young maid, then look at him from the back... and you will see that he's an Imperial Chamberlain whom your patron saint has granted you as a husband...' (She points out to Sophie the chamberlain's keys which Ochs carries on his tunic.)

Ochs tries to make polite conversation with his bride, but his talk veers towards the bawdy, with the result that Sophie begins to cry, and the enraged Octavian—whose protective instincts are aroused—can hardly contain his fury. Faninal invites the bridegroom into the next room to discuss the legal aspects of the proposed union. Ochs agrees, but not without first having committed his bride to the care of Count Octavian: '... cousin Taverl will keep you company!'

The two young people are alone. They whisper hastily to one another, constantly on guard against the duenna, who is present as chaperone but is distracted by her various domestic tasks. Octavian to Sophie: 'Will you marry that fellow there, *ma cousine?*' 'Not for all the world!...' replies the agitated Sophie, seeking his help. Their clandestine conversation is interrupted by the drunken servants from Lerchenau chasing the housemaids. After the din has died down, and the duenna, too, has disappeared, Sophie and Octavian continue their conversation, which leads to an embrace and a kiss. The intriguers, Valzacchi and Annina, always on the look-out for a potentially profitable opportunity, surprise the young lovers and call Ochs. In the dispute which follows Octavian holds true to his role as Sophie's protector; there is a short duel in which Octavian wounds Ochs in the arm. Thereupon uproar breaks out: the servants run excitedly about the house; Ochs von Lerchenau roars; Faninal rages and finally shows Count Octavian the door. He leaves, but not before arranging a rendezvous with Sophie and acquiring the services of the two intriguers by greasing their palms. In the meantime Ochs has calmed himself with wine and is in the best of moods when Annina, now in the service of Octavian, brings him a love letter from the pretty chambermaid of Act I. He yields happily to the pleasure he anticipates: '... with me, with me no night will be for you too long....'

Hofmannsthal wanted a turbulent ending to this act, but Strauss persuaded him to accept a 'quiet close', and as with the whole structure of this difficult act he was right to do so.

Théâtre National de l'Opéra, Paris, 1976
A sketch by Ezio Frigerio in the style of the old masters showing the Marschallin in intimate *déshabillé* in Act I.
Producer: Rudolf Steinboeck.
Conductor: Horst Stein.

Now we come to Act III, which according to Hofmannsthal was to be the best. A single room in an inn is the setting. Here the intrigue worked out between Valzacchi and Octavian—who is dressed as a maid—at Ochs's expense will be carried out with precision. An extended pantomime scene explains the point and reveals the tricks which have been prepared in order to instil anxiety in the lecherous Baron Ochs. For example, Annina is to pretend to be the wife he allegedly deserted, with numerous children; there are to be ghostly apparitions in all corners of the room, and so forth. (The instructions themselves offer so many possibilities that one must beware of adding anything excessive. The overall effect should remain graceful.)

Everything goes flawlessly until Ochs, who has grown suspicious, unexpectedly calls the police, putting all those involved in the charade in an embarrassing position. Confronted by the austere police chief, the landlord stammers excuses; Ochs is preening himself for victory, when he is inadvertently taken for the main culprit, and Octavian—as a girl who has been seduced—tries to salvage the situation to his own advantage. Things get more and more complicated. The score reads: 'The personal servant is very confused about the situation. But then he seems to have an idea which can save the

Théâtre National de l'Opéra, Paris, 1976
A free, open, spacious setting with good backdrops. Act I produced a noble, distinguished and slightly cool effect.

A similar atmosphere in Act II, with the characters freely grouped. On the whole a development away from schematic presentation.
Producer: Rudolf Steinboeck.
Conductor: Horst Stein.
Sets and costumes: Ezio Frigerio.

day and rushes suddenly out of the central door.' He leaves to call the Marschallin to the aid of his hard-pressed master. In the meantime Ochs has claimed that the girl discovered with him is his bride, Fräulein Faninal, but this impertinent lie causes him considerable embarrassment when her father, called by Octavian, suddenly arrives. Under persistent questioning by the police Commissar, Ochs finally 'recognizes' his father-in-law and offers all kinds of excuses. The enraged Faninal calls his daughter Sophie, who has been waiting below in her sedan-chair; thus the chaos is complete. Faninal begins to feel unwell; accompanied by Sophie he is taken into the next room and things calm down. Baron Ochs, re-

gaining his self-esteem, then says to the Commissar: 'You're clear about all this now. I'll pay, I'll go!' and tries to leave the room. Apprehended by the Commissar, Ochs then has to watch as the alleged chambermaid whispers something to the policeman and as the clothes of Mariandl are thrown one by one out of the niche where the bed stands. This greatly amuses the Commissar. The Baron rages and is about to become violent when the Marschallin makes a surprise entry and forestalls a row. With magnificent authority she clarifies the confusion; the Commissar salutes and leaves.

Now we see Ochs standing between the Marschallin and Sophie on one side, and on the

Staatstheater, Darmstadt, 1979
The set here (for Act II) has been freed of traditional elements. The classical or Renaissance architecture may be accounted for as representing the spacious entrance hall of a palace whose inner rooms could well be in contrasting baroque style. A valid way of reconciling an apparent contradiction.
Producer: Kurt Horres.
Conductor: Hans Drewanz.
Sets: Jürgen Dreier.
Costumes: Inge Glenz.

other Octavian, still half-hidden, and trying to fathom out why the Marschallin should suddenly have appeared. Sophie informs Ochs that her father has said no to the match; Ochs objects but the Marschallin indicates that he should go. Because he remains stubborn, the Marschallin calls 'His Grace, my Lord Count Rofrano' to her aid. Ochs understands but the Marschallin dismisses the matter lightly: 'A Viennese masquerade and nothing more.'

Ochs begins to suspect the connection and is emboldened. He tries a little blackmail but is firmly shown the door by the Marschallin: 'Does he not understand when a matter is at an end? The betrothal and all that goes with it is now nullified.' Baron Ochs and Sophie are each deeply affected by this in their own way.

At this point the whole throng erupts on to the scene in a great uproar as the landlord brazenly tries to present his bill. Ochs escapes with Leopold, followed by the outraged crowd, to the sound of loud, exuberant waltzes. The Marschallin is left behind with the two young lovers.

The final scene begins; once again a 'quiet close', of whose effect Strauss had been so certain. The Marschallin draws everything to a serene conclusion with a magnificent gesture of renunciation by mastering her own passions: 'I prided myself that I held him dear . . .' By foregoing the affections of Octavian the Marschallin helps lead the young Count into his new adventure with Sophie, who has the advantage of youth. The tiny Moor is the last on stage. He retrieves a forgotten handkerchief which flutters in his hand—and rushes off with a happy grin.

In an afterword by Hofmannsthal written in 1911, the poet took a valedictory look at the figures he had brought to life:

The Marschallin does not exist for herself, nor does Ochs. They stand opposite one another and indeed belong to one another; the boy Octavian is between them and unites them; Sophie is against the Marschallin—the girl versus the woman; and again Octavian steps between them, separating them and holding them together. Sophie is, in her inner thoughts, bourgeois like her father; and this group therefore stands against the great nobilty who can take many liberties. Ochs, be he as he may, is still an aristocrat of a kind; Faninal and he complement one another; one needs the other, not just in this world but also, as it were, in the metaphysical sense. Octavian attracts Sophie to him—but does he really, and for always? This much is perhaps in doubt. Group stands against group; allies are separated and the separated linked together. They all belong to one another, and the best lies between them: it is momentary yet eternal, and here there is room for music. The music is endlessly loving and unites everything: the Marschallin's lament is as sweet a sound as Sophie's child-like joy. The music has only one aim: to pour forth the harmony of all that lives, to the joy of every soul.

ΑΠΟΦΑΙΝΕΤΑΙ ΠΑΜΨΗΦΕΙ

Ἡ πόλις τῆς Νάξου διὰ τοῦ Κοινοτικοῦ αὐτῆς Συμ
βουλίου τιμὴν ἀποδίδουσα εἰς τὸν Μέγαν τῆς ἐπο-
χῆς μας μουσικοσυνθέτην ἐντιμότατον κ. ΡΙΧΑΡΔΟΝ
ΣΤΡΑΟΥΣ, ἀνακηρύττει Αὐτὸν Ἐπίτιμον Πολίτην Νάξου
καὶ ἐκφράζει Αὐτῷ τὴν ἄπειρον εὐγνωμοσύνην καὶ εὐ
λάβειαν τῆς πόλεως Νάξου διὰ τὸ ἐπιτελεσθὲν ἔργον
Αὐτοῦ δι' οὗ ἔδωκεν ἔκφρασιν ἀνωτάτης τέχνης εἰς
τὸν μῦθον τῆς Νάξου καὶ κατέστησεν παγκοσμίως
γνωστὴν αὐτήν, καὶ ἐντέλλεται τὸν κ. Πρόεδρον τοῦ
Κοινοτικοῦ Συμβουλίου τὴν προσήκουσαν διαβίβασιν
τοῦ παρόντος.————————

— Τοῦ Κοινοτικοῦ Συμβουλίου Νάξου

Ὁ Πρόεδρος   Τὰ Μέλη

Χ.Δ. Ἁγιοπετρίτης   Γεώργ. Λύκαρης

                              Μ. Δρύλλης

                              Ἐμμ. Γ. Κοραξίτης

                              Ι.Χ. Φραγκουδάκης

                              Μ. Μαρμαρᾶς

                              Λ. Θεόφιλος

                              Ἐμμ. Πολυκρέτης

                              Κ. Λάσκαρης

                        Ἀκριβὲς ἀντίγραφον

                        Ἐν Νάξῳ αὐθημερόν.

                        Ὁ Πρόεδρος τοῦ Κοινοτικοῦ Συμβουλίου

Richard Strauss's prize award in a glass case at his home, giving him honorary citizenship of the city of Naxos.

Ariadne auf Naxos

Among the many honours and awards that Richard Strauss kept behind glass in the library of his home at Garmisch there was one item he never failed to show his guests: a declaration in Greek proclaiming him an honorary citizen of the town of Naxos, on the island of that name. He was especially fond of this honour and of its associations with the Naxos of ancient Greek legend.

The declaration states that he received the honour on account of the opera *Ariadne auf Naxos* ('Ariadne on Naxos'). Many stock theatrical figures appear in this light, gracious work which deals in a playful manner with change and transformation. There are buffo-like comedy characters and more serious roles; yet, in contrast to *Der Rosenkavalier,* it did not emerge out of a mood of cheerfulness and harmony. This finely wrought work, which still evokes undiminished delight, produced serious tension, even ill feeling, between librettist and composer. It required two versions before the 'hybrid', as Strauss once called it, assumed its final form.

The letters exchanged by Hofmannsthal and Strauss best illumine the development of the composition.

Following the success of *Der Rosenkavalier,* a hesitant wait-and-see atmosphere developed between composer and librettist. Strauss, ever impatient, was whiling away his time after Hofmannsthal's rejection of his plans for *Semiramis:* '*Semiramis* is miles away; no intellectual or material inducements could extract from me a play on this subject.'[1] Strauss was waiting for new ideas; one was *Das steinerne Herz* ('The Stone Heart') based on Hauff's original. It was discussed, but then vanished. However, in a letter from Hofmannsthal dated 20 March 1911 we find the following passage, which, among other things, dealt with a new major project: 'If we were to work together once more on something (and by this I mean something important, not the thirty-minute opera for small chamber orchestra

which is as good as complete in my head; it is
called *Ariadne auf Naxos* and is made up of a
combination of heroic mythological figures in
eighteenth-century costume with hooped skirts
and ostrich feathers and, interwoven in it,
characters from the *commedia dell'arte,* har-
lequins and scaramouches, representing the
buffo element which is thoroughly interwoven
with the heroic) ...'[2]

We have to consider this outline of the intended short opera carefully, because artistic fusion of all theatrical elements was a concept
which meant a great deal to Hofmannsthal and
was something he struggled passionately and

single-mindedly to achieve. Yet he mentioned it
only in passing, almost shamefacedly. Strauss,
although well disposed to the plan, was more interested in the framework for *Die Frau ohne
Schatten* ('The Woman without a Shadow'),
mentioned in the same letter.

A few lines further on Hofmannsthal returned to the idea of *Ariadne:*

About *Ariadne* too, we must talk; it can,
I believe, turn into something most charming, a new genre which to all appearances
reaches back to a much earlier one, just as all
development goes in cycles. I am also inclined
to think that this interim work is necessary,

Königliches Hoftheater, Stuttgart, 1912
Stuttgart celebrated the opening of its new Königliches Hoftheater in 1912 with a Strauss Week. (The theatre was built by the Munich architect Max Littmann.) The special event of the week was the première of the new work *Ariadne auf Naxos,* which joined the ranks of *Feuersnot, Salome, Elektra* and *Der Rosenkavalier.*

at least for me, to make myself still more familiar with music, especially with your music, and to achieve something that brings us closer together even than in *Rosenkavalier*—which as a fusion of word and music satisfies me greatly, but not wholly.[3]

The impression conveyed by these lines is worthy of particular note. At this juncture Hofmannsthal was caught in the vagaries of the age-old contest between words and music; indeed, he had suffered a little from the victory of the music in *Der Rosenkavalier.* Some respected men of letters even felt sorry for him, believing that his fine poetry had been ill served by the music. With *Ariadne,* though, Hofmannsthal laid down the form and content definitively from the start, even to the extent of specifying a chamber orchestra, so as not to put the poetry at a disadvantage. Strauss pretended to overlook this point and then asked: 'Dear Poet, I want to enquire how *Frau ohne Schatten* is doing: can't I get a finished draft or maybe even a first act to look at some time soon? I would also be interested to know what's happening to the Molière.'[4]

Hofmannsthal reacted tetchily to Strauss's insistence: 'My dear Doctor Strauss, I like you very much indeed, I enjoy working for you.'[5] Then came the great 'but' with which Hofmannsthal warded off any sense of haste over *Die Frau ohne Schatten.* On one occasion he even wrote curtly: 'Had you made me choose between producing

this work on the spot or doing without your music, I should have chosen the latter.'[6]

The concepts for Molière's *Le Bourgeois Gentilhomme* and *Ariadne* were then detailed in a similary determined fashion: 'The divertissement *Ariadne auf Naxos* itself is to be performed after dinner in the presence of Jourdain, the Count and the dubious Marquise... The playbill looks like this:

Le Bourgeois Gentilhomme
A comedy with dances by Molière, arranged by Hugo von Hofmannsthal from the old translation by Bierling (1751)
at the end of Act II
Divertissement
Ariadne auf Naxos
(Music by Richard Strauss)[7]

This was followed by the list of characters and by precise requirements regarding the music——in the case of *Ariadne* one can feel how the poet wanted to be the main guiding force. He continued to seek this role in the work on the opera that followed. On one or two occasions Strauss made some dry criticisms, and although not uninterested in work on *Ariadne,* seemed little affected by it. Hofmannsthal, ever sensitive, fought for his basic concept. From the beginning he was aware that in view of the high demands made by an evening which combined

Königliches Hoftheater, Stuttgart, 1912
The sets and costumes by Ernst
Stern were among the great delights of the première. The finely
worked details corresponded to
the elegance of the basic concept
and were in keeping with Hofmannsthal's intentions.

play and opera, only one man could be considered as producer: Max Reinhardt.

For his part Strauss replied with exact instructions on the musical items and the castings of
the singers. Initially he considered a contralto
voice for Ariadne but remained sceptical on this
point:

'*Ariadne* may turn out very pretty. However,
as the dramatic framework is rather thin
everything will depend on the poetic execution.
But with you one doesn't have to worry about
flowing verse. So get your Pegasus saddled!'[8]
His work gave inspiration to Hofmannsthal,
who replied at once:

You call the scenario a little thin—that is
quite true. Perhaps a still better way of putting it would be: a little rectilinear, possibly
a little too rectilinear... When I think of
heroic opera, whose spirit we mean to invoke,
when I think of Gluck, of *Titus* or *Idomeneo*,
this kind of thin rectilinear quality does not
seem to me a fault. Moreover, the intermingling with the other, the buffo element, possesses great attractions and eliminates monotony.[9]

Hofmannsthal placed his fundamental concept for this difficult work in the forefront once
again and also made proposals as to the casting.
Strauss remained cool: 'Personally, I am not par-

ticularly interested by the whole thing myself:
that was why I asked you to spur your Pegasus
a bit, so that the ring of the verses should stimulate me a little.'[10]

Hofmannsthal's answer was not long in coming: 'We have always understood each other
well, but on this occasion I feel we may have to
agree not to understand one another.'[11]

In the same letter, after giving details of the
work, Hofmannsthal wrote: 'That is how I feel
about *Ariadne* and about the trimmings, Zerbinetta, and so forth, we are in any case entirely
d'accord. But if my libretto, when you have it,
does not attract you in this way, then by all
means leave it alone; there will be no hard feelings. What matters is the central idea of the
piece and though two men like us who know
their job should not despise the flourishes, they
can never be a substitute for the main thing.'[12]

Hofmannsthal, nursing injured feelings, was
suggesting that they drop the entire project. But
that was not what Strauss wanted: 'We don't
misunderstand each other at all.'[13] They continued to make practical proposals. But then
correspondence ceased for a time. Hofmannsthal
became unsettled. After that the sparks again
began to fly across their joint horizon. Hofmannsthal was deeply disappointed by Strauss's
somewhat aloof reaction to the finished libretto:

Königliches Hoftheater, Stuttgart, 1912
The final scene with its decorative Baroque canopy was especially beautiful: a harmonious collaboration between producer and designer.
Producer: Max Reinhardt.
Conductor: Richard Strauss.
Sets: Ernst Stern.

'I must confess I was somewhat piqued by your scant and cool reception of the finished manuscript of *Ariadne,* compared with the warm welcome you gave to every single act of *Der Rosenkavalier,* which stands out in my memory as one of the most significant pleasures connected with that work.'[14]

Strauss again took a more conciliatory line, but also conceded that he had been disappointed by the libretto: 'Perhaps because I had expected too much . . . Be patient therefore: maybe my incomprehension will spur you on after all—and don't take it as anything else. After all we want to bring out the very best in each other.'[15]

In this exchange of letters, besides writing at length of his plans for *Ariadne,* Hofmannsthal also dealt generally with the principal issues in the relationship between word and music. These letters are very well worth reading.

The atmosphere between the two men had now become less tense, and the issues involved in working on *Ariadne* gradually moved to the forefront. But Hofmannsthal now became somewhat inflexible, thereby almost bringing

further complications. He insisted on having Max Reinhardt as producer, and also wished to have the première in Reinhardt's theatre in Berlin, partly so that his excellent company would be available for the first part of the evening, Molière's comedy.

Strauss was not at all certain: 'On Friday I'll discuss with Reinhardt whether he is in a position to stage *Ariadne* at all; I still don't see where he is to get his orchestra and singers from. The best hope might be Munich in the summer.'[16]

Hofmannsthal insisted stubbornly that Reinhardt must direct, and rejected all other suggestions: 'A world première of this work at some court theatre or other would mean a complete flop.'[17]

Disagreement persisted. How seriously Hofmannsthal took the matter is shown by a long and moving letter: 'I am writing this letter at leisure, quite alone here, after due deliberation and in high seriousness, and ask you to read it in the same spirit, to re-read it and to remember how much is at stake between the two of us who have been brought together by something high-

95

er, perhaps, than mere accident; between the two of us who are meant to derive joy from each other and who must do all in our power not to be deflected from this purpose—a danger which seems to threaten us at this critical juncture... I must tell you that you would be doing a grave injustice to the work and to me if, without absolute and compelling necessity... you were to take away the original première, which is decisive for the impact of this work, from the one theatre for which, and for the special qualities of which, I have devised and executed it in every detail... It is one of my most personal works and one I cherish most highly... Here I must dig my heels in, or show myself as an amateurish bungler and worse.'[18]

A little incautiously, Strauss had made proposals which would, inevitably, have excluded Reinhardt's participation. The cities of Berlin, Dresden and Munich were mentioned. Hofmannsthal maintained the hurt and reproachful tone: 'That you should find it possible to disregard all that the realization of this work of my imagination means to me... *does* touch me... and hurts me more than just momentarily. Here I find myself misunderstood and injured by you at the most vulnerable point in our relationship as artists.'[19]

Hofmannsthal then went on to recall that he had put aside his own work on *Jedermann* ('Everyman') to help Strauss, and later had great difficulty in overcoming 'this violent interruption'.[20] The letter contained an almost despairing cry, characteristic of Hofmannsthal's oversensitivity: 'I am not saying this as a reproach to you, but because it is true. I beg you, do not inflict on me this injury! Do not injure us both, do not injure our relationship!... Don't injure our work...'[21] The letter concluded with Hofmannsthal earnestly pointing out that Reinhardt had abandoned plans for a Molière comedy with ballet, proposed by another party, in favour of *Ariadne*: 'One cannot and must not treat a man like Reinhardt in such a way; it is madness for the few of us, of our kind, of our rank, scattered in this desert crowded with mediocrity, to act in such a manner; for then we lose our last hold, and before that is lost I would rather stop writing for the theatre altogether—I tell you this quite calmly.'[22]

Strauss, for his part did not allow himself to lose his composure. At the beginning of 1912 (2 January) he again rejected Reinhardt's theatre in Berlin, but at the close of his letter he wished Hofmannsthal '... a good 1912 in health and happiness and steady progress, and in it a fine *Frau ohne Schatten*'.[23]

His sights were set beyond *Ariadne* towards the next *major* work—and towards developing their joint work. None the less, he turned his attention energetically and skilfully to the production problems of *Ariadne*. Since the major theatres in Berlin, Dresden and Munich remained out of the question (Vienna was not even mentioned), he arranged a performance at Stuttgart through Max von Schillings; and the small theatre there ultimately seemed to appeal to Hofmannsthal too. Reinhardt agreed to direct and to place his actors at their disposal for the Molière comedy, so the way was clear for the première. In a letter dated 10 February 1912 Hofmannsthal, now reassured, signed himself: 'With best regards from your librettist, who considers you by no means a fool and is very well disposed towards you.'[24]

The storm-clouds which had gathered over the island of Naxos and her fair inhabitant had finally dispersed. On 25 October 1912 the work received its première at the small Königliches Hoftheater in Stuttgart.

In his *Recollections and Reflections* Richard Strauss recalled the external circumstances surrounding *Ariadne auf Naxos*, but made no mention of the dispute with Hofmannsthal, which at times had been quite fierce. For Strauss this dispute had been an internal matter, one which was not—so far as he was concerned—for the public at large. His esteem and affection for Hofmannsthal's genius remained unaltered to the end of his days.

This is what he said about *Ariadne auf Naxos:*

Hofmannsthal conceived *Ariadne* as an act of homage to Max Reinhardt, in the form of an epilogue to a comedy by Molière. *Ariadne,* split into three parts and provided (like a well known mythological snake) with nine heads, was eventually resolved into two new comedies. The first idea was fascinating: beginning in the most sober of comic prose and proceeding via ballet and *commedia dell'arte* into the heights of the purest symphonic music, it ultimately failed owing to a certain lack of culture on the part of the audience. The play-going public did not get its money's worth, the opera public did not know what to make of the Molière. The producer had to assemble two separate dramatic and operatic casts, and instead of two box-office successes he had only one doubtful one.

But let us start with the history of the opera: I enjoyed composing the incidental music to the play which, like almost everything I dashed off, as it were 'with my left hand', turned out so well that it continued its

existence successfully as a small suite for orchestra. The little opera, too, went very well up to the appearance of Bacchus, when I began to fear that the small chamber orchestra would be inadequate for my dionysiac urges. I informed Hofmannsthal of my fears and asked him whether I could not change over at this point to the 'full orchestra', if necessary behind the stage. Admittedly a stupid idea! Hofmannsthal implored me to give it up and under this benevolent imperative the second half has turned out to be characteristic enough.[25]

If one thinks of the glorious sound of the orchestra from the point of Bacchus' entrance onwards, then one cannot be grateful enough to Hofmannsthal for his intervention. Strauss—with his humorous self-criticism—was well aware of Hofmannsthal's vigorous 'assistance'. Continuing, he described the production difficulties in Stuttgart, Berlin and elsewhere and the fundamental revision of the whole work:

The charming idea—from the most sober of prose comedies to the experience of purest music—had proved a failure in practice; to put it bluntly, because the play-going public has no wish to listen to opera and *vice versa*. The proper cultural soil for this pretty hybrid was lacking. Thus Hofmannsthal and I were forced, four years later, to undertake the oper-ation of separating Molière and Hofmannsthal-Strauss, although the work had been successfully performed on many stages (amongst others in the Munich Residenztheater and the Berlin Schauspielhaus).[26]

This decision led to the revised composition of the prologue; thereby *Ariadne auf Naxos* achieved the final form with which we are familiar today. It was given its first performance on 4 October 1916 in Vienna, with Lotte Lehmann as the 'composer'; the conductor was Franz Schalk.

We have followed the comments of composer and librettist on the development and creation of this unique work because its crystal-clear form—seemingly fashioned in one continuous process—gives no indication of the obstacles and difficulties that arose while it was being shaped. Hofmannsthal was well aware of the work's exceptional quality and for that reason passionately supported his original conception, from which developed a many-faceted, exquisitely polished jewel. The brief prologue (as Strauss described it, a stylistic precursor to *Intermezzo*) and the *opera seria* (happily associated with *commedia dell'arte*) fused together without apparent effort into a homogeneous artistic entity. The music for *Le Bourgeois Gentilhomme*, left over from the original idea, was expanded into a ballet score.

Bayerische Staatsoper, Munich, 1937
Commedia dell'arte scene. Zerbinetta (the unforgettable Adele Kern, who died in 1980) with her four lovers: Joseph Knapp, Walter Carnuth, Georg Wieter and Emil Graf.
Producer: Rudolf Hartmann.
Conductor: Clemens Krauss.

Teatro alla Scala, Milan, 1950
A variation by Ludwig Sievert on
his 1937 design for Ariadne's island. The structure above the cave
is somewhat simplified. The front
of the stage is divided off for the
commedia dell'arte scenes.
Producer: Giorgio Strehler.
Conductor: Issay Dobrowen.

Prologue

A lively and exciting musical introduction leads
straight into hectic activity at the house of the
'richest man in Vienna'.

'A low, sparsely furnished and dimly-lit room
in the house of a grand gentleman. To the left
and right, two doors on either side; in the
middle, a round table. In the background, preparations for a private theatre are being made.
Decorators and workers have erected a stage set,
the back of which can be seen. An open corridor
runs between this part of the stage and the space
in front.'

The Major Domo appears; the Music Master,
mentor of the young Composer, anxiously pro-
tests about plans to present a cheap farce in the
Italian buffo manner. 'The Composer will never
allow it!' he exclaims (referring to the creator
of the serious opera, *Ariadne auf Naxos.*) The ar-
rogant steward, who is only impressed by his
master's money, insultingly rejects any protest

about the programme (which is also to include
a firework display), pointing out that high fees
are being paid. The Music Master crushed, remains behind. 'How am I tell my pupil about
this?'

An Officer enters Zerbinetta's dressing-
room. He is her admirer; she is the celebrated
star of the *buffo* troupe, and the declared enemy
of the Prima Donna from the opera ensemble
—their performing skills and styles are irrecon-
cilably different.

The young Composer hurries in. He asks a
servant to bring some of the musicians to him,
but receives a hurtful and scornful reply; angered, he comments: 'Idiot! Impudent, cheeky ass!
This fool has left me alone at the door—at the
door, he leaves me standing and has gone.'

In his agitation a delightful new melody oc-
curs to him, which he is keen to note down
straight away. The angry Tenor, who clips the
Wigmaker round the ear, interrupts him; he requests in vain a 'piece of paper' from the man-

handled Wigmaker and then—aside—meditates on his new musical idea.

On the other side of the stage, as yet unseen by the Composer, Zerbinetta appears at the door of her dressing-room with the Officer. She is very pretty and flirts with her admirer. Opposite, the Music Master appears from the Prima Donna's room. The Composer is keen to go to her but is held back by the Music Master. Suddenly he sees Zerbinetta, walking with the Officer to the Dancing Master [entering backwards]. He asks: 'Who is this girl?... Who is this enchanting girl?' The Music Master seizes the opportunity to tell the Composer of the 'jolly piece' which Zerbinetta and her four partners will be putting on after the opera.

The Composer is appalled and outraged: 'After my opera? A jolly piece? Dances and ditties? Vulgar gestures, *double entendres* after *Ariadne?*... The secret of life will come close to them, will take them by the hand—and they order a foolish comedy to wash the resonance of eternity from their unspeakably frivolous skulls? Oh, what a fool am I!'

The Music Master tries in vain to calm his excited pupil; only the recurrence of the melody which he chanced upon earlier (and now sings to his teacher) helps to cheer him up.

Zerbinetta's four partners appear; with her they improvise a make-up scene and engage in the battle of words which breaks out between Zerbinetta and the Prima Donna across the room. The Servant announces that the ladies and gentlemen have ended their banquet and tells everyone to hurry; thereupon the Major Domo enters with an important announcement: 'I have a sudden new instruction for you all from my gracious master!'

In the meantime the opera ensemble, too, is almost complete; the Tenor and the three Nymphs have joined the Prima Donna. The two very different theatre troupes stand opposite one another, each trying to outdo the other. Their two spokesmen are the Dancing Master and Music Master. General consternation follows the new instruction: 'The masquerade will be presented neither as prologue nor as epilogue,

but will be presented simultaneously with *Ariadne.'*

Astonishment, horror and protest greet the announcement—but all to no avail. The Major Domo reminds them earnestly of the fees they have already received, and the comedy players and singers resign themselves to the situation, leaving the Dancing Master and Music Master to find a way out, if possible. The Composer wants to flee, but his teacher reminds him of the urgent need of money. He allows himself to be persuaded by the skilful Dancing-Master as to the necessary cuts that are to be made in his opera. The Prima Donna and Tenor jealously supervise every change, and Zerbinetta is briefed about the content of the opera, which she then transposes into her style of comedy. She instructs her partners thus on the new procedure:

Take note, we shall now be playing in the piece *Ariadne auf Naxos.* The story is as follows: a princess has been jilted by her bride groom and her second admirer has not yet arrived. The stage is like a desert island. We are a cheerful company which by chance finds itself on the island. The wings are cliffs and

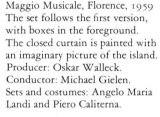

Maggio Musicale, Florence, 1959
The set follows the first version, with boxes in the foreground. The closed curtain is painted with an imaginary picture of the island. Producer: Oskar Walleck. Conductor: Michael Gielen. Sets and costumes: Angelo Maria Landi and Piero Caliterna.

we are to place ourselves between them. You will follow my lead and as soon as an opportunity presents itself we will enter and mingle in the action of the plot.

This explanation is quite sufficient for the players, who are used to improvisation. They disappear into their dressing-rooms; Zerbinetta remains behind with the young Composer who is alone and down-hearted, musing on the noble concepts of his opera. The shrewd actress employs her coquettish charm and a touching dialogue ensues. It is taken seriously by the Composer, but is of course cleverly stage-managed by Zerbinetta.

The dialogue is interrupted abruptly by the Music Master, who announces the start of the strange performance. At the sight of the buffo figures the Composer is once again thrown into the depths of despair and runs headlong from the room, fleeing from the monstrous event he has been persuaded to condone.

The Opera

'The stage represents a desert island—Ariadne is on the ground before the cave—Echo at the rear by the wall of the grotto'; this is the full extent of the instructions about the setting for the opera. From the start the stage-designer was given plenty of scope for invention.

After a sombre yet lyrical orchestral introduction the curtain rises. The three Nymphs observe Ariadne resting; in simple tones they bewail the fate of the heavy-hearted sleeper. She awakes to renewed pain and fresh memories of her lost love, Theseus. As she sinks back, the buffo figures look out from the proscenium, observing her beauty and her sorrow.

The players thereby slip into the action of the plot in a discreet and harmonious fashion. They leave immediately when Ariadne begins her great lament to Theseus' memory, closing with the wish that she may die. The players make use

Metropolitan Opera, New York, 1962
Introduction. Prologue. A spacious room in a grandiose palace, which is in contrast to the informal groupings of the characters. Producer: Carl Ebert. Conductor: Karl Böhm. Sets: Oliver Messel.

of the natural pause after this monologue to return in order to cheer her up. Following Zerbinetta's instruction: 'Oh, at least try a little song!', Harlequin, accompanying himself on the lute, sings a few consoling verses—but to no avail. Zerbinetta notices his strong interest in Ariadne: 'You are completely beside yourself.' Harlequin concedes: 'Never has a human soul touched me so deeply.'

At once Zerbinetta teases him: 'You're like that with every woman!', whereupon he retorts: 'And what about you with every man?' With this short, stinging dialogue the players skilfully introduce one of their characteristic teases – jealous love—which will re-appear later in the plot.

Alone again, Ariadne begins another great lament, wishing for the arrival of Hermes, the Messenger of Death and closing with an ecstatically passionate appeal: 'I will lose myself entirely in you, it is with you that Ariadne must be.'

After this farewell the players stage a major interlude. Dancing around her, they attempt to console Ariadne: 'Beautiful eyes must be clear of tears if dancing and singing are to count for a thing.'

Zerbinetta tells them that she is pleased with them but then recalls that she is supposed to be cheering Ariadne up. Because these efforts seem to be a failure she sends her partners away and—woman to woman—begins a lengthy address to Ariadne.

This is the now famous Zerbinetta aria, 'Grossmächtige Prinzessin', which calls for the finest display of coloratura virtuosity. Zerbinetta tells of her own richly varied experience with men and points consolingly to the next man who is bound to come along. Ariadne does not react; she has withdrawn into the cave.

Harlequin springs out from the wings, mocks the vain attempts of Zerbinetta and then tries to kiss her.

Metropolitan Opera, New York, 1962
The meeting between Ariadne and Bacchus (Leonie Rysanek and James King). Oliver Messel's set adheres to the first version with boxes on the stage. Because of this the stage seems very restricted.
Producer: Carl Ebert. Conductor: Karl Böhm.

Salzburg Festival, 1964
The island has become a modest dais-like structure between the cliff-like wings of the stage. The design makes a stronger impact than did the actual set.
Producer: Günther Rennert.
Conductor: Karl Böhm.
Sets: Ita Maximowna.

Salzburg Festival, 1964
When the set was built, the lightness evidenced in the sketch was lost. Here we see the Nymphs with Ariadne. On the whole this is an elegant solution, but it offers no new developments.
Producer: Günther Rennert.
Conductor: Karl Böhm.
Sets: Ita Maximowna.

Munich Festival, 1969
The arrival of Bacchus. A beautiful, free approach to the scene, done in a very artistic way. The decorative features follow the lines of Baroque proscenium stages. Producer: Günther Rennert. Conductor: Wolfgang Sawallisch. Sets: Rudolf Heinrich.

Munich Festival, 1969
The final scene from the same performance with the canopy above the two lovers. The fantastic starry sky and the glow of the Aegean are emphasized. The Baroque chandeliers are discreetly placed.

The other three buffo characters come running in, pretending to be in love with Zerbinetta, and a well-rehearsed scene from the players' repertoire develops: Zerbinetta and her four lovers. Jokes and dances give them a chance to show all their skills. They put on masks and throw themselves energetically into the scene, but Harlequin is more cunning than they: he abducts Zerbinetta and they ultimately find themselves embracing and kissing each other.

The island then reverts entirely to grand opera. The excited Nymphs announce the arrival of a young god and relate the tale of his first adventure with Circe, from whom he escaped without being transformed: 'All her art is in vain because no animal descends to earth!... Untransformed, and unbound, a young god stands before you!' Circe's magic, which she uses to transform young men on her island into animals, has failed in the face of Bacchus' divinity.

The Nymphs call Ariadne, who comes forth from the cave. She hears the still distant voice and remains preoccupied with her thoughts of death: 'Oh, Messenger of Death! How sweet is your voice! It is balsam to the blood and slumber to the soul!'

When Bacchus can be seen, she is startled: 'Theseus!' She believes she has espied her lost love, but quickly regains her composure and welcomes him solemnly as the Messenger of Death. Bacchus, still bound up in thoughts of his adventures with Circe, imagines Ariadne to be an equally dangerous magician. Ariadne does not understand what he is talking about. She believes she is to undertake 'the crossing', the journey aboard the dark ship of the god into kingdom of the dead. Bacchus embraces and kisses her; the surroundings change; Ariadne is transformed, believing she has died and is in Hades; but Bacchus convinces her with his triumphant jubilation in which she acquiesces: 'And the eternal stars will sooner perish, than you should die apart from me!'

Zerbinetta returns once more, points to the couple with her fan and sings mockingly: 'When the new god comes along, we silently surrender.'

Mounting this inspired baroque fusion of all elements of the theatre – which is what Hofmannsthal aimed at—is one of the most attractive challenges for an opera producer. It is also one of the most difficult, because besides music, there is speech, dance and pantomime; all these heterogeneous elements, including the heroic style of grand opera, have to be united in the graceful and delicate form which librettist and composer intended. The sharply etched figures of the Prologue, with vain singers 'without a mask', players, Music Master and so forth, up to and including the Major Domo with his pompous speech—all these elements offer us as much in a half-hour play as can often be found in one of in several acts. The constant alternation between dialogue, recitative and aria calls for careful attention to acoustic balance. The audience must understand every word in the Prologue: this is an essential condition, for otherwise no one will be able to perceive the elements in it which lay the groundwork for the complicated interaction of comedy and serious opera in the second part of the work. Following the Prologue, the audience must be eagerly waiting for the *simultaneous* performance of two completely different pieces which has been demanded by the 'rich master of the house'—an absurd idea which leads to a perfect work of art.

For the orchestra Strauss demanded players of the highest quality, and the same applied to the singers and actors. A single miscasting, whether of the Composer or the Major Domo, can endanger the success of the whole work—more so than in other works, where weaknesses of casting can be covered up. Some characters only appear briefly (the Servant, the Officer, the Wigmaker etc.), but still must be sketched with bold strokes. Following the lively, sparkling parade of the Prologue, the opera itself appears slightly more easy-going because it takes place in a familiar framework. The naturalness of the three Nymphs should not just be expressed by their costumes, but more by their positions and their movements around Ariadne. The essential qualities of the main characters are unambiguous: sadness, loneliness and a yearning for death in the case of Ariadne, together with her exalted transformation by new love. Bacchus should above all appear young, inexperienced, and god-like in the exuberance with which he throws himself into the new adventure.

The buffo figures, together with Zerbinetta, are embellishments for the blossoming love of Bacchus and Ariadne; they provide a commentary and an element of calm, which contrasts with the passion of the classical figures; they do no more than that. It is the producer's task to bring artistic unity to all these factors, in a manner which appears graceful and natural to the audience and which leaves no unanswered questions; he must also get across a sense of elegance and rapture.

The stage-designer has to combine the almost dry reality of the Prologue with the baroque representation of the island. He must make one believe that one is watching a theatrical performance in the palace of a rich patron, an entertainment which manages to attain the heights of true art.

The instructions as to the location are broad enough to allow an almost boundless use of imagination. The extent to which relics of the Molière scenes remain tangible (chandeliers over the island, an awning, fixed lights and other elements) will vary from one production to another. Some designers have undoubtedly responded most elegantly to the sophistication of combining all theatrical elements. *Ariadne auf Naxos* renders homage to baroque theatre by its mastery of rhetoric, dance, pantomime and song, and not least by the scope it offers for virtuosity in free invention.

The score bears the inscription:
Dedicated to Max Reinhardt
in admiration and gratitude.

Richard Strauss   Hugo von Hofmannsthal

Diaghilew et Nijinsky   Jean Cocteau
                                              x 1913

108

Josephslegende

An exuberant and witty sketch by the young Jean Cocteau of Diaghilev and Nijinsky, done in Paris during preparations for *Josephslegende*. The overbearing personality of the impresario almost absorbs that of his star dancer.

Paris in the summer of 1912: international society is still little troubled by the political discord gathering on the horizon. People are strolling along the fine boulevards or gossiping at the street tables of the Café de la Paix. Any talk of politics is conducted with elegant reserve; men still respect and value one another's company, as yet unaware that a little later they will be shooting each another in the uniforms of opposing sides—indeed they will suddenly have become 'the enemy' because world politics has so demanded it... But for the moment none of this is evident. Parisian life is like a late Impressionist painting, a dazzling array of sun and light, and one of the topics of conversation is the Russian ballet. The Diaghilev company, with the most famous dancer of the day, Nijinsky, is making a guest appearance at the Opéra.

One can easily imagine the poet Hofmannsthal and the aesthete Count Kessler moving in these sophisticated artistic circles. Both had long been enthusiastic devotees of ballet and mime. They would never miss an event such as the Russian visitors' tour, which also included Germany.

On 23 June 1912 Hofmannsthal wrote to Strauss from his home in Rodaun:

> ... Together with Kessler, who possesses a most fertile, and quite specifically a designer's imagination, I have produced a short ballet for the Russians, *Joseph in Egypt,* the episode with Potiphar's wife; the boyish part of Joseph of course for Nijinsky, the most extraordinary personality on the stage today... The sketch has, if I am not mistaken, two good points: the idea of dressing a biblical subject in the costume of Paolo Veronese and of treating it in his spirit; and dramatically, the sharp antithesis between the two main characters, which in the end leads them to opposite poles: one upwards to a bright heaven, the other to sudden death and damnation... [1]

Strauss and Hofmannsthal made these plans even though they were still preparing the first performance of *Ariadne auf Naxos* (25 October 1912), so deeply were they committed to their partnership. Strauss briefly informed Hofmannsthal, to the latter's satisfaction, that he accepted the idea of *Joseph,* and on 2 July wrote in more detail:

> Once again, *Joseph* is excellent: I'll bite! Have already started sketching it out. Count Kessler's remarks, I am bound to admit, do not convince me entirely, but never mind, I'll get over the difficulty somehow, especially if the character of Potiphar's wife is accurately outlined in the libretto (possibly in the list of characters). We can't have *Joseph in Ägypten* as a title, because that's the name of Méhul's well-known opera which is still in the repertoire. It must be *Joseph bei Potiphar* ...[2]

In the second part of this letter Strauss discussed scenic difficulties in *Ariadne* which were still bothering him. The new major plan, *Die Frau ohne Schatten,* was also mentioned. Strauss saw *Joseph* as an interim work in the same manner as he had placed *Ariadne* between *Der Rosenkavalier* and *Die Frau ohne Schatten.* The composer was by now almost fifty; and after his successes he felt his creative muse to be at full strength. He and Hofmannsthal were aspiring to the pinnacle of their artistic association and their lesser projects had to fit into this process. Complying with Hofmannsthal's request, Strauss exercised great self-restraint in not asking impatient questions about the libretto realizing that it was making slow progress.

However, it is impossible to separate this preparatory phase for *Die Frau ohne Schatten* from *Ariadne* or especially from *Josephslegende.* Again and again we find ideas which overlap. These three works basically occupy the same period of creativity and their development occured more

or less simultaneously. For this reason few details (except for passing reference) are given in the correspondence about progress on *Josephslegende*. In particular, Strauss did however make it clear that he was having difficulties with the composition. On 11 September 1912 he wrote: '...*Joseph* isn't progressing as quickly as I expected. The chaste Joseph isn't at all up my street, and if a thing bores me I find it difficult to set to music. This God-seeker Joseph—he's going to be a hell of an effort! Well, maybe there's a pious tune for good boy Joseph lying about in some atavistic recess of my appendix...'[3]

Strauss's free and easy style of expression upset the linguistically sensitive Hofmannsthal on the grounds of both form and content. He replied at once:

I am amazed to hear that you are stuck over the character of Joseph; to me he is the best and most successfully conceived character, the only thing in the whole ballet which is genuinely unusual and engaging. I must say, however, that the way you describe it, as the 'chaste Joseph' for whom a pious tune must be found, this character bores me too and I should be equally unable to find music for it...[4]

He then provided a fine and noble explanation of *Joseph* as he and Kessler saw him, and appealed to Strauss to look for the appropriate music not in his appendix but in the most exalted regions of his brain: '...I cannot believe that you should be incapable of finding some bridge between this boy and the recollection of your own adolescence...'[5]

Théâtre National de l'Opéra, Paris, 1914
The set for the première followed the author's instructions exactly: 'in the style of Paolo Veronese'. Léon Bakst's costumes with their splendid colours and imaginative design won him world renown. Choreography and production: Michel Fokine. Conductor: Richard Strauss. Sets: José Maria Sert.

THÉÂTRE NATIONAL DE L'OPÉRA

Les bureaux ouvriront à 8 h. 1/2 — On commencera à 9 heures

Aujourd'hui **JEUDI 14 MAI 1914** — 1re Représentation (1er Abonnement)

SAISON DE BALLETS RUSSES

De Serge de DIAGHILEW

Direction Générale : M. Serge de DIAGHILEW et le Baron Dimitri de GUNZBOURG

Directeur Chorégraphique : M. Michel FOKINE

LES PAPILLONS

Ballet en un 1 acte, de Michel FOKINE — Musique de Robert SCHUMANN

Orchestré par N. TCHEREPNINE

Scènes et Groupes de Michel FOKINE — Décor composé et réglé par M. DOBOUJINSKY

Mᵐᵉ THAMAR KARSAVINA   M. MICHEL FOKINE

Mᵉˡˡᵉ Schollar — Mᵐᵉˢ Kopycinska, Pflanz, Wasilewska, Gouliouk

L'Orchestre sera dirigé par **M. PIERRE MONTEUX**

LA LÉGENDE DE JOSEPH

Ballet en 1 acte du Comte Harry de KESSLER et de M. Hugo de HOFFMANSTHAL — Musique de Richard STRAUSS

Décor de José-Maria SERT — Costumes de Léon BAKST — Chorégraphie de Michel FOKINE

Mᵐᵉ Marie KOUSNEZOFF   M. L. MIASSINE   Mᵐᵉ Vera FOKINA

M. Boulgakow   Mˡˡᵉ Fokina II   M. Serge Grigorieff

Mᵐᵉˢ Tchernicheva, Pflanz, Majkerska, Kopycinska, Wasilewska

L'Orchestre sera dirigé par **M. RICHARD STRAUSS**

SHÉHÉRAZADE

Drame chorégraphique en 1 acte, de MM. Michel FOKINE et L. BAKST — Musique de RIMSKY-KORSAKOW

Danses et Scènes de Michel FOKINE — Décor et Costumes dessinés par L. BAKST

Décor exécuté par MM. BAKST, ANISFELD, ALLEGRI — Costumes de Mᵐᵉ MUELLE, de Paris

M. MICHEL FOKINE   Mᵐᵉ KARSAVINA   M. BOULGAKOW

Mᵐᵉˢ Tchernicheva, Schollar, Frohman, Pflanz, Wasilewska, Majkerska, Kopycinska

MM. Cacchetti, Frohmann

L'Orchestre sera dirigé par **M. PIERRE MONTEUX**

Régisseur en Chef : M. Serge GRIGORIEFF

Théâtre National de l'Opéra, Paris, 1914
The première of *Josephslegende* is announced between two other ballets conducted by Pierre Monteux. *Josephslegende* was conducted by Strauss himself.
Choreography and production: Michel Fokine. Sets: José Maria Sert.

In the meantime the attention of composer and librettist had been taken up by the première of *Ariadne* in Stuttgart; they exchanged details of their impressions, and the second version was already beginning to emerge. Strauss was waiting for *Die Frau ohne Schatten; Joseph* seemed to have faded into the background, at least for a time. Not until 15 June 1913 was there any further reference to the planned ballet: 'I will try in the meantime to get down to *Joseph,* which our dear old Count Kessler is doing his best to make palatable to me. It's not because of any lack of goodwill, that I haven't got any further, but simply that artistic creation, as of course you know better than anybody, can't be commanded…'[6]

The composing continued, however, and occasionally he was able to report good progress. In December 1912 Strauss played what he had written to Hofmannsthal, only to receive a 'horrified' reply from the poet over the style of the *Josephslegende* themes:

I am so miserably incompetent at expressing myself accurately and precisely in musical terms, that I can only appeal again and again, and on behalf of the three of us—the perturbed Kessler, the perturbed Nijinsky, as well as myself—to your goodwill, to your open mind, to your willingness to understand...I fear it is the idea of ballet, of the need for accentuated rhythms, which has misled and confused you. Therefore I must make myself the spokesman for Nijinky who implores you to write the most unrestrained, the least dance-like music in the world, to put down pure Strauss for this leaping towards God which is a struggle for God. To be taken by you beyond all bounds of convention is exactly what he longs for...[7]

Strauss was clearly moved by this urgent appeal to find something new, for a few days later (on 22 December) a letter of Hofmannsthal revealed a sense of relief at Strauss's reaction:

I am very glad you took my letters in such good part...and that you have already carried your changed purpose into effect, i.e. into music...I hope we are agreed about the stylistic intention of the ballet, which is simply meant to give you again every conceivable freedom in polyphony as well as modernism: that is, to express your own personality in a manner as bold and as bizarre as you may wish...[8]

Hofmannsthal and Kessler followed the preparations for the première in Paris and at the beginning of May 1914 Strauss, too, arrived in the French capital. *Josephslegende* appeared on stage on 14 May 1914.

Serge Diaghilev, whom Hofmannsthal had from the start referred to as a Russian of 'the most likeable sort', cast his best dancers. Shortly before the première serious personal differences led to a breach between Diaghilev and Nijinsky, whom the former summarily dismissed. The embarrassing business was dealt with very discreetly by everyone who knew about it, but a new dancer had to be found for the part of Joseph. Fokine was both director and choreographer and the part of Joseph was danced by the young Massine. The ballerina Kuznetzova appeared as Potiphar's wife (later in London the part was danced also by Tamara Karsavina), the set—based on the style of Paolo Veronese—was designed by the Spaniard, José Maria Sert, and

This etching by Ernst Oppler shows a rehearsal in Paris. Strauss is at the piano; in the group to the right are: Michel Fokine (in a shirt), Serge Diaghilev (seated), Count Harry Kessler and Hugo von Hofmannsthal. The part of Joseph was danced by Leonid Massine. Germans, Russians and Austrians all worked on the French première.

the costumes were prepared by Léon Bakst. Contemporary reports show that the première at the Opéra was a magnificent success, above all for Richard Strauss who had to take frequent curtain-calls. After the Paris performance, Diaghilev was able to put on *Joseph* only in London before the First World War broke out. That performance was at the Drury Lane Theatre.

It was not until after the war that *Joseph* came to Germany, Austria or other countries. In Strauss's *Recollections and Reflections,* we find the following short passage, written in 1941:

My intention in *Josephslegende* was to revive the Dance. The Dance, the Mother of the Arts, standing as it were, like a mediator between them. The Dance as an expression of the dramatic, but not only of the dramatic. The modern variant of the Dance, in which it is nothing but rhythmic or paraphrased action, only too frequently leads us away from the essence of the genuine, purely inspirational, form of the Dance dedicated to movement and absolute beauty, i. e. the Ballet. It was this that I intended to rejuvenate. I think

it was the Russian dancers who first put the idea into my head. My *Joseph* contains both elements: dance as drama and dance as—dance. We must not lose the sense of the purely graceful just as, analogously, in the realm of music the element of absolute beauty must never be neglected in favour of the characteristic, programmatic and elemental. This, if you will, was my intention in writing *Josephslegende.*[9]

A further comment from the same source, written in 1942, summarizes the origins of the work:

In the last years before the First World War the Russian ballet under its inspired leader Diaghilev, and with the incomparable Nijinsky, caused a stir in Germany, as elsewhere. A guest performance in Berlin delighted me so much that I gladly took up a suggestion made by Hofmannsthal and Count Harry Kessler that I should write something for this unique troupe, when I was shown the pantomime *Josephslegende,* the title-part of which had been designed for

Nijinsky. The work was first performed at the Paris Opéra on 12 May 1914 [actually, 14 May], without him, his place being taken by Massine, a weaker and not quite adequate dancer. This successful performance was followed by six further performances at Covent Garden, although anti-German feeling ran high there that June and Diaghilev, who was always in financial difficulties, did not pay me my conductor's fee (six thousand gold francs) nor has he done so to this day. But it was beautiful for all that!... When war broke out two months later we were in S. Martino di Castrozza. We succeeded with difficulty in making our way home through Austrian troop transports over the Brenner Pass... On 1 August, the British confiscated my capital deposited in London with Edgar Speyer—the savings of thirty years... *Josephslegende* was revived (in 1922) in Vienna, produced by Alfred Roller and the excellent ballet-master Kröller...[10]

Heinrich Kröller, a famous choreographer of the twenties, also mounted a distinguished production at the Nationaltheater in Munich: the stage-designer was Leo Pasetti.

Thenceforward this fine ballet has re-appeared in the repertoires of all major theatres. The part of Potiphar's wife, a key figure, was played alternately by singers or actresses and ballerinas who were capable of living up to the demands made by the role. We find such names as the Russian prima ballerinas already mentioned as well as Marie Gutheil-Schoder, Tilla Durieux, Alice Verden and Zdenka Mottl-Fassbender. The casting of these parts is determined by the intentions of the director, who may also be the choreographer. But a co-operative effort between a director and a choreographer has often been successful.

In all the performances the ballet is influenced by the set and above all by the costumes. Leading designers have dedicated themselves to *Josephslegende*, using Paolo Veronese as an inspiration

Staatsoper, Berlin, 1921
Two stylish designs by Emil Pirchan, from the folio of illustrations edited and produced by Franz Ludwig Hörth (published by Fritz Gurlitt, Berlin, 1922).
Left: Vision of the final scene.
Right: probably the dance of Sulamith, or of Potiphar's Wife in the seduction scene.
Choreographer: Heinrich Kröller.
Conductor: Otto Urack.

but at other times attempting free interpretations.

The tasks facing the producer, or more precisely the choreographer, are closely linked to those of the set-designer. They are manifold but interconnected, and all develop from the basic concept of the work. Productions by new choreographers such as Pia and Pino Mlakar in Munich, although very different in approach and style, have made a powerful impact.

Let us now look at the content of this biblical ballet. The best approach would be to follow the introductory explanation of the co-author Count Kessler and the foreword by Hofmannsthal:

The stories of ancient legend are inexhaustible in two ways. Within themselves they contain both concrete characters and abstract notions about humanity distilled in such a way that they resist the march of millennia—so that to each generation their impact is fresh and unblemished by time. Outwardly, they independently set the imagination of the world in motion, as in the case of the Egyptian Joseph, whom so many musicians, painters and poets—even Goethe—could not pass by without being moved...

Hofmannsthal backed up his choice of material by citing impressive authorities, and justified the link with the style of Paolo Veronese, which he had conceived with Strauss, Léon Bakst, and 'Serge Diaghilev's wonderful ballet corps' in mind.

Count Kessler provided an introductory summary of the ballet's content, from which extracts will be quoted. The count's detailed

115

Bayerische Staatsoper, Munich,
1941
Joseph freed by the Angel. Pino
Mlakar danced Joseph with a
compelling gravity. Pia Mlakar's
interpretation of Potiphar's Wife
was very erotic in its effect. The
Berlin designer Rochus Gliese
adhered to the style of Paolo
Veronese.
Sets and costumes: Rochus Gliese.
Choreography and production:
Pia and Pino Mlakar.

Salzburg Festival, 1964
The same scene. The two Yugo-
slav choreographers, Pia and Pino
Mlakar—who previously had
danced the main roles themselves—created a convincing production with strong visual
images. The company was that of
the Croatian National Ballet.
Joseph: Aleksey Judenič. Sets and
costumes: Dusvan Ristic. Choreography and production: Pia and
Pino Mlakar. Conductor: Mladem
Basič.

choreographic instructions, in a series of four-
teen scenes, are interesting as a detailed description of events on stage although they are not
binding, because every choreographer will work
out his own ideas and follow them through. But
the emphatic way in which Kessler describes elements of the colourful set (giving rein to his pic-
torial imagination so praised by Hofmannsthal)
is still remarkable.

Here is a short example:

At the foremost table on a dais sit Potiphar
and his wife, the latter in a very low-necked
dress of gold brocade with strings of pearls
hanging down over it. In her hair, too, are

strings of pearls. At her feet, a young slave-girl on the lowest step of the dais.

Waiting at the tables are eight Negro slaves in semi-oriental costumes of pink and gold adorned with red and white feathers. Behind the dais, in the corner to the left beneath the gallery, stand the members of Potiphar's bodyguard—giant mulattoes in black Toledo armour inlaid with gold and decorated with black feathered crests. They bear golden halberds and golden-handled whips.

With his somewhat luxuriant taste Kessler painted a picture of oriental splendour and magnificence for the series of scenes which, viewed in the context of the ballet as a whole, emphasized the contrast with the final spiritualized apotheosis—the transfiguration of Joseph.

'The action of *Josephslegende*.

The content of *Joseph* portrays the contradiction and struggle between two worlds. The contrast extends from the costumes to inner spiritual mood through gestures and music which reveal the characters' souls. One world, that of Potiphar, has risen high and gathered within it all riches, power, beauty and the art of living;

Bayerische Staatsoper, Munich, 1980
A free approach unrelated to Veronese, with the purely balletic qualities emphasized and brought into the foreground.
Sets: Klaus Hellenstein.
Costumes: Silvia Strahammer.
Choreographer and producer: John Neumeier. Conductor: Heinrich Bender.

but because of their sheer abundance these elements have so depreciated, have created a mood of satiation, that a world such as this no longer contains any charm, challenge or tension. It is a splendid, luxurious, stifling world full of strange scents and creatures from a tropical garden, but a world without secrets or mystery, balanced in itself, classical, hard, oppressive, a world in which even the air seems loaded with gold dust. What must impress itself on the audience is this world's richness in gold, its size, its great and gracious gestures.

The other world is that of Joseph, who comes from the desert, a shepherd boy, the son of a prince. He is gentle, wild and caustic... And because he is still virtually a child, an aristocratic child, he adheres to the customs of his people... The morality which lives within him is that of the shepherd from the bright, free desert and is nothing less than the natural stance of a spiritual and corporeal being who has been drenched in sunlight, kept intensely vigilant by the sands of the desert and made strong and sinewy through extensive travels across the desert's endless plain... The central motif of this figure is a sense of soaring, flying, floating—now in dance, now in dreams, now in an intimate fusion of fantasy and movement. Joseph is a dancer and a dreamer...'

This exposition is followed by an explanation of the various stages of inner development in Joseph's character, from childlike lad to strong hero and herald of a new, still distant world. The major dance of the shepherd boy portrays this development: his naive, cheerful existence, his dreams of heroism, his yearning for total clarity which he cannot yet attain.

Potiphar's wife, 'inside as dead as a dark, cold sea never warmed by a ray of sunlight', is suddenly moved by the strange and unfamiliar appearance of the shepherd boy; she wants to possess him and has him taken to her chambers. Then, at night, she creeps secretly into Joseph's new quarters. The shepherd boy recoils from her in horror. The plot follows the ancient legend exactly. Potiphar's wife reviles Joseph with hatred, makes false accusations against him and, with all the other witnesses, watches Joseph withstand the agony of torture.

'A great sense of gloom descends upon her. The more Joseph flourishes, the darker her world becomes. When Joseph's world appears almost tangibly before her in a vision, in the form of the Archangel, she once more makes a hopeless, child-like gesture at following the apparition into that world. After that, nothing remains for her but death.'

After the list of *dramatis personae* Count Kessler then provided details about some of the 'dance configurations'. He closed his comments with the transfiguring appearance of the Archangel, who leads Joseph—now free of his chains—up to heaven, while Potiphar's wife kills herself in despair. The two worlds which were momentarily in contact have separated for ever.

The première of this biblical dance pantomime, held in the brilliant setting of the Opéra, was the last international cultural event of the era between the wars of 1870 and 1914.

Die Frau ohne Schatten
('The Woman without a Shadow')

This design for *Die Frau ohne Schatten* by Panos Aravantinos (Berlin, early 1920s) is beautiful and complete in itself. It shows the scene at the Emperor's hunting lodge, and is in the best traditions of popular decorative art.

First World War August 1914 — November 1918

'*Die Frau ohne Schatten,* a child of sorrow, was completed in the midst of trouble and worries during the war...'—so runs Strauss's own comment. [1]

He called the work 'a child of sorrow' because there were inordinate difficulties over its first performance, and because it failed to win the same degree of success as *Der Rosenkavalier.* Both Strauss and Hofmannsthal felt this to be their most important work, the climax of their artistic collaboration, and had anticipated a much stronger and more lasting response. Their disappointment following the première in Vienna was bitter and not without its consequences.

Strauss noted:

... In Vienna itself, owing to the strenuous vocal parts and to difficulties over the sets, the opera had to be withdrawn more often than it was performed. At the second theatre (Dresden otherwise the location of so many Strauss premières) it came to grief because of the imperfections of the *mise en scène*... which forced me to ask Count Seebach after the dress rehearsal to postpone the first performance for several days... It was a serious blunder, to entrust this opera, difficult as it was to cast and produce, to medium and even small theatres immediately after the war. When, on another occasion, I saw the Stuttgart post-war production (on the cheap!) I realized that the opera would never have more success. But it has succeeded nevertheless and has made a deep impression, especially in the Vienna and Salzburg production (Krauss—Wallerstein) and finally in the Munich one (Krauss—Sievert—Hartmann); music-lovers in particular consider it to be my most important work. [2]

Strauss did not live to see world-wide recognition given to his 'child of sorrow'. In the years following the Second World War it was pro-duced at international opera-houses, above all on festive occasions, and increasingly attracted the favour of the public. The rebuilt National-altheater in Munich (1963) and the New Metropolitan Opera in New York (September 1966) were both opened by performances of *Die Frau ohne Schatten.* The work also appeared in the festival programme to celebrate the restoration of the Vienna Opera, and in quick succession it was likewise performed for the first time in Brussels, London, Paris and elsewhere.

Librettist and composer had unswerving faith in the opera's value—and they were right. It is unfortunate that neither of them was able to witness the growing success of *Die Frau ohne Schatten,* which—despite the works that follow-ed *(Die ägyptische Helena, Arabella)*—without doubt takes pride of place among their joint creations.

Hofmannsthal noted that it was on 26 February 1911 that the idea for this opera first arose. Originally conceived as a popular entertainment, soon, following a conversation with Strauss, it took on the form of grand opera. Both composer and librettist had noticed that the basic idea bore a relationship to that of *The Magic Flute.* 'In July 1914, only a few days before mobilization, I had finished the third act. By 1915 the opera was completed, but it then lay in Strauss's desk-drawer for four years. We could not bring ourselves to have it performed while the war was on.' Hofmannsthal did not write his prose version of the fairy-tale until the libretto for the composition had been finished.

Ernst Roth, for many years head of the London music publishers Boosey and Hawkes, was very close to Strauss in the composer's later years. On the outbreak of war in 1914 he wrote:

Politics, war and nationalism were totally alien to Richard Strauss. He escaped from a world he did not understand into the world of poetic imagination opened up for him by Hofmannsthal... While war raged at the

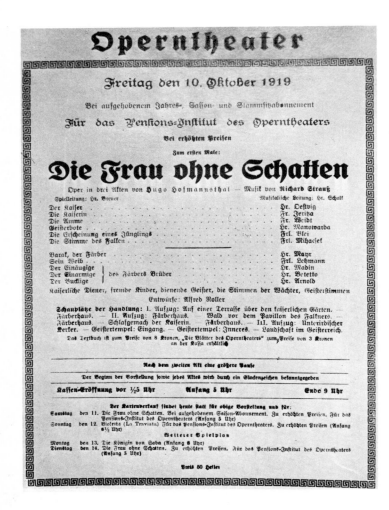

four corners of the earth, Strauss buried himself in the atmosphere of wonder, horror, and
conciliation of *Die Frau ohne Schatten,* which
became his greatest and in many respects his
most beautiful work. The score was complete
by 4 June 1917 but only after the return of
peace did it receive its first performance, on
10 October 1919 in Vienna.

ACT I

'On a flat roof above the imperial gardens. To
one side is the entrance to the chambers, dimly
lit.' The Nurse cowers in the darkness; there is
a sudden flood of light, and the Spirit Messenger
from Keikobad's kingdom appears, bathed in
magical light.

This scene, immediately after the curtain
rises, is the first magical event which producer,
stage-designer, and technical director must solve
convincingly. Keikobad is to be understood as
an invisible, commanding divinity, who remains mysterious and intangible, as does the

world to which he belongs. Past, present and
hereafter are united in him. The Spirit Messenger, the twelfth within the space of a year, demands to know from the Nurse the condition
of the Empress who has been entrusted to her
care: 'Does she cast a shadow? Then, woe to you!
Woe to us all!' The Nurse is triumphant:
'None! By the all-powerful Name! None!
None! Her body refracts light as if she were of
glass.' (The shadow is of course the symbol of
female fertility.)

The Spirit Messenger reminds the Nurse that
she allowed the Empress to be stolen from her,
but the Nurse defends herself by pointing out
that her charge has the ability to change herself
at will into an animal, and that she yearns to be
among people, a desire she inherited from her
mortal mother. The Nurse speaks derogatively
of the Emperor, whom she hates: 'He is a hunter
and love-sick, otherwise he is nothing!'

The Spirit Messenger recalls the moons that
have passed by and the command issued by
Keikobad: 'He has her for only three more days.
When they have passed, she returns to her fa-

Staatsoper, Vienna, 1919
Alfred Roller's design for the pre-mière shows the Dyer's hut. The colours of the scene, imbued with Middle Eastern elements, are clearly arranged and all the props have been well thought out.
Producer: Hans Breuer.
Conductor: Franz Schalk.

Staatsoper, Vienna, 1919
The Empress's bedchamber in Act II: a magnificent design and admirable for the presentation of the dream scene, with its threaten-ing glimpse of the spirit world. As always in Roller's work, the colours are subdued and harmo-nious.

Staatsoper, Dresden, 1919
Only twelve days after the Viennese première, the Dresden Staatsoper, which normally put on Strauss's premières, performed the work for the first time. As usual the cast was excellent, but the sets, based on Alfred Roller's work in Vienna, displeased Strauss because of their modest scale, due to post-war conditions.
Producer: Alexander d'Arnals.
Conductor: Fritz Reiner.

Sächsische Landestheater
Opernhaus

Mittwoch, am 22. Oktober 1919
Anfang 6 Uhr

Zum ersten Mal:

Die Frau ohne Schatten

Oper in drei Akten von Hugo Hofmannsthal

Musik von Richard Strauß

Musikalische Leitung: **Fritz Reiner**   Spielleitung: **Aleg. d'Arnals**

Personen:

Der Kaiser	Fritz Vogelstrom
Die Kaiserin	Elisabeth Rethberg
Die Amme	O. Metzger-Lattermann
Der Geisterbote	Robert Burg
Ein Hüter der Schwelle des Tempels	Grete Schubert
Erscheinung eines Jünglings	Friedrich Zobiel
Die Stimme des Falken	Hedwig Erl
Eine Stimme von oben	Emilia Poffzert
Barak, der Färber	Friedrich Plaschke
Sein Weib	Eva Plaschke-v. d. Osten
Der Einäugige	Erik Wildhagen
Der Einarmige } des Färbers Brüder	Ludwig Ermold
Der Bucklige	Hanns Lange
Die Stimme des Wächters der Stadt	Robert Burg

Kaiserliche Diener, Fremde, Kinder, dienende Geister, die Stimmen der Wächter, Geisterstimmen

Erster Aufzug: Auf einer Terrasse über den kaiserlichen Gärten. — Färberhaus
Zweiter Aufzug: Färberhaus. — Wald vor dem Pavillon des Falkners — Färberhaus. — Schlafgemach der Kaiserin — Färberhaus
Dritter Aufzug: Unterirdischer Kerker. — Geistertempel: Eingang. — Geistertempel: Inneres. — Landschaft im Geisterreich

Einstudierung der Chöre: **Karl Pembaur**

Die Dekorationen sind nach den Entwürfen des Professors A. Roller von der Firma Baruch & Co. in Berlin angefertigt

Nach dem zweiten Akt eine längere Pause

Textbücher sind für 2.- an der Kasse und bei den Türschließern zu haben

Der freie Eintritt ist aufgehoben

Krank: Margit von Luffan, Adolf Lutzmann. Heiser: Rudolf Schmalnauer

Eintrittspreise

Mittelloge des I. Ranges	30 .- ./	IV. Rang Mittelgalerie und Proszeniumslogen	12 x 10 ./
I. Rang Logen	40	IV. Rang Seitengalerie, Seitenlogen	4 .-
II. Rang Fremdenlogen	25	V. Rang Mittelgalerie	3 .-
II. Rang Mittellogen	25	V. Rang Sitz- und Stehgalerie, Proszeniumsloge	2 .- 50
II. Rang Seitenlogen	20	Parkettlogen	25 .-
III. Rang Proszeniumslogen	17.50	Parkett, 1. bis 4. Reihe	20 .-
III. Rang Mittellogen	17.50	Parkett, 5. bis 14. Reihe	15 .-
III. Rang Seitenlogen	15	Parkett, 15. bis 19. Reihe	10 .-
IV. Rang Balkon	15	IV. Rang Mittel-Stehplätze	6 .-

ausschließlich Wohlfahrtssteuer

ther's arms.' The Nurse (stifling her jubilation): 'And I with her! Oh, blessed day! But he?' 'He will be returned to stone!... Protect her well! Three days! Think on this!'

Having delivered this message, so fateful for the Emperor, the threatening, sombre Spirit Messenger disappears again as swiftly as he came.

It is clear that a scene with this kind of content cannot be treated as a brief, unimportant introduction. The appearance of the Spirit Messenger out of nowhere must have a powerful and frightening impact. The gradual process whereby he becomes visible requires sophisticated technical methods (projection, gauzes, tracking, trap-doors, etc.), indeed the use of whatever gives the scene conviction. It is also essential that the singer who plays the Spirit Messenger is positioned in such a way that his words can be clearly understood. Wherever possible the use of a microphone and loudspeaker should, however, be avoided. Technical aids should never be obtrusive. The theatrical spirit of the fairytale is baroque and must be presented accordingly.

The Emperor appears, leaving his wife's chambers in the palace. He tells the Nurse that he is going hunting and then becomes lost in recollection of the time he hunted the white gazelle which cast no shadow. Dazzled by the wings of the red Falcon the gazelle had fallen—'I bore down on her with spear drawn—whereupon as the animal's body fell away, a frightened woman emerged in my arms.' This was how he won the Empress as his wife. The cunning Nurse learns that he will probably be away for three days. He commends the lady of the house to the care and heightened watchfulness of her servant and leaves quickly. The verse that Hofmannsthal wrote for the passionate Emperor inspired Strauss to compose the most beautiful cantabile vocal line for him.

The Nurse is now alone again, awaiting her mistress, the second female figure of the opera; the third is the Dyer's Wife, who appears in the second scene. The three female roles bear a resemblance to those of *Elektra,* where the radically different characters of Chrysothemis and Clytaemnestra appear alongside the title figure of Elektra. Indeed, from *Salome* onwards women dominate Strauss's operas, with the men almost always occupying a lesser position. The fascination which the female character held for Strauss repeatedly provided him with inspiration. Up to and including his last work, *Capriccio,* Strauss never tired of portraying woman in her infinite variety, from the demonic to the vulnerable and submissive.

Of the three female characters in *Die Frau ohne Schatten* (Empress, Dyer's Wife, Nurse) the Nurse is a dangerous female Mephistopheles who exudes evil to the point of self-destruction. She is bound to the Empress by a relationship at once loving and hating; she scorns humanity because of its primitive, mean existence; the world of the Emperor is something remote and incomprehensible to her, and only the power of Keikobad inspires her with abject fear. Her approach embodies the three planes on which the plot revolves: the lower human world with its simplicity and poverty; the lofty, glass-like sphere of the Emperor; and the dread spirit kingdom, an impenetrable realm beyond the grave.

The Empress appears on the terrace: 'Is my beloved away? Why wake me so early?' She laments the loss of the talisman which gave her the gift of metamorphosis; she yearns for the body of the white gazelle or the wings of a bird: 'Would that I were the fleeing game which his falcons savage...'

The red Falcon of former times appears. The Empress recognizes him and sees tears in his eyes: 'Falcon! Falcon! why do you weep?' The Falcon answers: 'Why should I not weep? The Woman casts no shadow and the Emperor must be turned to stone!'

This short scene is full of difficulties: The Empress must not cast a shadow—a demand very difficult to fulfil but essential to the plot. Producers and stage-designers cannot avoid the problem by taking refuge in excuses such as 'it's only a symbolic image'. The audience must go by what it sees and does not see. Technical solutions on stage are possible (a translucent glass floor, softly illuminated from below, an iron grid, etc.), particularly when it is remembered that the terrace does not require an extensive area but can be treated as a narrow fore-stage area. In the more realistic scenes in the Dyer's house, the problem of shadows becomes less acute. The producer can position the Empress in front of solid objects, such as pillars or rolls of material, so that her shadow is, as it were, absorbed by those cast by the objects; the actress playing the part of the Empress cannot of course be left in darkness all the time.

The milky, glass-like quality of the atmosphere on the terrace in the morning light demands the finest of lighting transitions. The entrance of the red Falcon also makes technical demands; his presence cannot just be understood. How otherwise is the audience to make sense of the singing voice of the Falcon? The words uttered by the Falcon must be clearly audible. That is why the Falcon repeats himself, and why his words are also echoed by the Nurse and the Empress. It is inadvisable to use a loudspeaker here for the same reasons as in the first scene. Placing the singer for the red Falcon in the orchestra pit is the best solution, so long as she can be kept hidden from the audience.

Shocked by the Falcon's ominous prophecy, the Empress declares her desire to acquire a shadow. She begs the Nurse to help her. The latter, with a display of malicious readiness, points the way to the lower world of humans, where the shadow the Empress seeks is to be found.

'They descend into the abyss of the human world; the orchestra takes up the theme of their flight to earth. The intermediate curtain closes quickly.' These stage directions led Hofmannsthal to make the following amusing comment to Strauss (in a letter of 18 September 1919):

Only one thing: I am told that at the end of the first scene on the terrace you wanted to make the Nurse and the Empress *vanish through the trap-door* instead of running off into the bed-chamber. This really will not do, for five reasons:

1. It is expressly stated here that the orchestra takes up their 'flight to the earth', i.e. a flight through the air, gradually ap-

proaching the human sphere—not plunging through the dark centre of the earth.[3]

The other four reasons given are similarly hard-hitting and to the point, Hofmannsthal already sensed there would be objections and attempted to pre-empt them: 'I am quite prepared for a certain incomprehension of the subject, for stupid interpretations and guesses where everything is simply picture and fairy-tale. All this will pass, and what really counts will remain.'[4]

The intermediate curtain closes quickly. This raises a question: should the curtain close or not? Modern stage equipment allows transitions from one scene to another without the distracting rise and fall of the curtain. In the Vienna–Munich version by Emil Preetorius there was a 'weightless', truly 'fairy-tale' transition behind a gauze curtain, to which subtle lighting brought added conviction.

We enter the room in the Dyer's house, realistically depicted as poor and miserable—yet given an air of oriental colour by the bright pieces of cloth and leather, and other materials of his trade. Barak's three brothers, the One-Eyed, the Hunchback and the One-Armed, are scuffling on the floor. The Dyer's Wife throws a bucket of water over them as if they were fighting dogs. The Dyer enters and orders his battling brothers—who hate their sister-in-law—outside to work. His Wife starts nagging and demands that they go for good. But Barak ignores her ill-humour: 'Here are the bowls from which they drink. Where should they live if not in their father's house?' He looks at her, repeats his desire for children—a wish he has expressed many times in the past—but she remains adamant and is deaf to his entreaties. Barak stays calm and replies 'with unforced solemnity and heartfelt piety': 'Out of a young mouth come forth harsh words and defiance, but they are blessed with the gift of revocation. I am not angry but will live in confident expectation of giving thankful praise to the ones to come.'

Strauss composed an expansive, powerful cantilena for these beautiful lines—followed by an orchestral passage deeply expressive of Barak's feelings; his Wife is forced to stop and think, but she makes malicious comments and parries his entreaties. Laden with his wares, Barak then leaves the house.

At the same time the light changes. 'A sense of soaring, dawning, a flash of light fills the air. The Nurse, in a garment of black and white patches, and the Empress are suddenly there without having entered through the door.'

The way in which the producer and designer plan their entrance is very important. The sudden appearance of the Nurse and the Empress can be made credible in several ways. It is the arrival of the two spirit-like beings which triggers the development of the drama.

The Dyer's Wife is startled, and made suspicious by the Nurse's flattering attention. The Empress is irresistibly drawn by the sight of the shadow which the woman casts. (At this moment a shadow from the Wife is as essential as the absence of one from the Empress.) The Wife finally bursts into tears, feeling humiliated by the *hauteur* of the Nurse, who regains her attention and excites her curiosity by mention of a 'secret'; the Nurse speaks temptingly of doing a deal over the shadow, and convinces the hesitant woman by conjuring a jewelled bracelet out of the air. With the words: 'Allow me to adorn you!' she transforms the room.

Salzburg Festival, 1932
Once more Alfred Roller's sets and costumes were used, this time at the Salzburg Festival of 1932, where, again, the best singers were cast. The producer, Lothar Wallerstein, and the conductor, Clemens Krauss, belonged to Strauss's circle of close friends.

Staatsoper, Dresden, 1939
In 1939 Dresden presented a new production. The sets were by Adolf Mahnke; the producer was Max Hofmüller; the conductor was Karl Böhm.

Staatsoper, Dresden, 1939
This illustration from the same production shows the hut of the Dyer, Barak: an individual approach, which makes a powerful effect and offers great scope to the singers.

'In place of the Dyer's hut there now stands a glorious pavilion...the boudoir of a princess...'

The Dyer's Wife, drawn on by the Nurse, finds herself surrounded by slave-girls, is adorned with jewels, sees an Apparition of a Youth, and succumbs to the Nurse's magic when she catches sight of herself in the mirror.

This scene demands a convincing transformation of the setting, which is doubly difficult because of the very short passage of music available and because the pavilion must as quickly be transformed back into the Dyer's house. The words of the Empress here are important: 'For this image in the mirror will you not give me your empty shadow?' Thereby she plays an active part in the attempt to deceive the Wife and rob her of her shadow. The actual appearance of the Youth is not explicitly demanded, but he should be seen because at this point disembodied voices would only be confusing.

The Wife is delighted by what she sees: immediately the conjured illusion dissolves. Back in her real world, she decides to part with her shadow and agrees to the Nurse's terms. Suddenly she hears Barak returning and is afraid because she has not prepared the evening meal. The Nurse again comes to her aid. She conjures up a fish which lands in the oil being heated on the fire ('Fischlein aus Fischers Zuber'), divides the bed in two with a wave of her hand, announces that the Empress and herself will be staying for three days as her servants, and then disappears with her 'daughter'.

The Wife, now alone, is frightened by voices of children which she hears in the air, 'We are in the dark and in fear! Mother, mother, let us in! Or call our dear father, that he may open the door to us!'

The unborn are calling their hard-hearted mother from everywhere, around her, not from the fire, as the woman at first suspects, and their voices are *not* those of the fish! This overlap between the magic scene and the children's voices has led to many misinterpretations, and critics of the opera have frequently made mocking remarks, such as: 'The Dyer, I suppose, will be eating his own children for supper.'

As with *Der Rosenkavalier,* the work on *Die Frau ohne Schatten* led to a lively and fruitful correspondence between Strauss and Hofmannsthal. In a letter of 5 July 1914 Strauss wrote thus about the 'Fischlein' scene:

Today I merely want to settle a few minor doubts concerning the text of my first act: On page 16 the Wife says: 'Now, he will demand his supper which is not ready.'

Nevertheless on page 18 the Wife says: 'There is food to eat' and Barak does in fact sit down on the ground to eat; a moment earlier, however, he says: 'A wonderful aroma of fish and oil'. Won't this suggest that he is about to eat the freshly fried little fish—which would be rather distasteful and revolting? Do please consider this food problem—whether one ought not to delete the passage: 'A wonderful aroma of fish and oil' to avoid any misunderstanding.[5]

Hofmannsthal replied on 8 July: 'The objection to the eating of the fish seems to me, frankly, over-subtle. The little fish are not, after all, the children: they are merely vehicles of magic...'[6]

Strauss did not give up. On 10 July he wrote: '...You have not dispelled my misgivings about Barak eating his own children. If one didn't hear the children singing you'd be right! But as it is, one is bound to identify the unborn children with the little fish in the frying-pan!...'[7]

He then made a detailed suggestion as to how the problem might be solved, and on 12 July Hofmannsthal replied thus with the final version:

... Now for the 'supper scene'... Very well, let him not touch the fish, but I need the point of repose where he sits on the floor and eats, instead of always working! Let him then be resigned... take a piece of bread out of his pocket and eat it... Therefore on page 18 at the bottom: the woman rises wearily, goes to her bed and says *nothing*.

Thereupon he exclaims 'A wonderful aroma of fish and oil', etc. (this passage expressing naive pleasure I would hate to take away from him), and she says harshly and angrily: 'There is no food here... Your bed is over there. I'm going to mine'... and so on as it stands... In this way the passage gains both from your point of view and mine.[8]

Both Strauss and Hofmannsthal were concerned to clarify the action. Despite this, however, the scene can still easily be misinterpreted unless the producer helps it along. The Wife must perceive the children's voices not just coming from the fire but from everywhere around her, and when she collapses in despair she must do so *well away from the fire*. Above all the producer must correct one error in the vocal score. Hofmannsthal wrote this line for the Wife: 'Hier ist *kein* Essen!' (here is *no* food) but in print we find 'Hier ist *dein* Essen!' (here is *your* food), a sentence which naturally leads to misunderstandings since it may erroneously seem to refer to the fish.

Bayerische Staatsoper, Munich,
1954
Emil Preetorius based his design
for Act I, Scene I freely on Persian
miniature paintings.
Producer: Rudolf Hartmann.
Conductor: Rudolf Kempe.

Act I closes with Barak going to his rest and with the hauntingly poetic Night Watchmen's song.

The scene after Barak's return has been treated so explicitly here because the exchange of views between composer and librettist makes it plain that the producer must go to great pains to clarify the action in this difficult scene in an opera which is inherently problematic. The Dyer's house should be absolutely realistically portrayed throughout, but the three brothers should be characterized as grotesques.

ACT II

Strauss was delighted by the five-scene form of the second act. These scenes entail production difficulties similar to those of Act I.

Act II opens in the Dyer's house: the maids (the Nurse and the disguised Empress) accompany Barak, who is leaving, to the door. The Nurse is talking to the Wife, almost as if she were a match-maker, about a handsome youth. The Wife is at first confused and does not want to understand what the Nurse is saying. But then she concedes: 'I was on a bridge among many people when someone came towards me, almost a boy, but he took no notice of me—he had a superior look. From time to time I thought of him secretly, just day-dreaming!'

The Nurse conjures up the apparition of the Youth, who appears strangely lifeless. But they are interrupted by Barak's return. The Empress has sensed him approaching: 'Ah, that they should meet, the thief and he to whom the house belongs, one with a heart and the other without!'

With these words the Empress for the first time reveals her sympathy for Barak and her doubts about the Nurse's machinations. She begins to examine and reconsider her motives; a process of purification and trial has started. The Nurse makes the apparition of the Youth disappear again, whereupon Barak enters with his brothers and a host of beggar-children. He is carrying a gigantic bowl of food; the brothers have wine-skins and smaller bowls. Barak is happy, but his Wife turns her back on him. He invites the children and everyone who has gathered at the door of his hut to a meal; the room is filled with the sounds of happiness and good cheer. Barak sends the Empress with sweetmeats to his Wife, who rounds on her angrily, brushing aside the food offered.

The Wife is also beginning to change. Without being aware of it she is becoming jealous of the Empress, the 'servant'. Her words are drowned by the singing of the brothers and the children.

The scene changes to the imperial falconry, a lonely spot in the woods. The Falcon has been found again and has led the Emperor here. He finds the house empty, his wife absent. His suspicions are awakened. Hiding himself, he observes the secret arrival of the Nurse and the Empress, who slip silently into the house. The Emperor is filled with anger and pain; in his jealousy he thinks of killing his wife. He too has entered a phase of trial and suffering.

The scene again changes rapidly back to the Dyer's house. Barak is working; the Nurse and his Wife are waiting impatiently for him to leave. The Dyer is tired and thirsty, the Nurse secretly pours a potion into his cup. Drugged, Barak sinks into a deep sleep. Once more the Nurse conjures up the Youth, and the Wife, at first resisting the lure of the apparition, ultimately approaches it: 'I dreamed that I flew to you with unending kisses, like a dove which feeds its young, and that my dream killed you!' When she is quite close to the apparition she recognizes it for what it is and recoils in horror. She calls for help to Barak, who, waking from his drugged sleep, looks about him in bewilderment: 'Robbers here? Give me the hammer! Brothers, help me quickly!' In jumping up he shatters a vat. The Nurse makes the apparition of the Youth disappear again, and watches the Dyer and his Wife with spiteful glee. The Empress weeps; increasingly filled with pity and affection for Barak, she concerns herself with him. The Wife, now feeling herself completely free, takes up her shawl to go into the town. The Nurse accompanies her; the Empress is waved away and remains beside Barak, kneeling at his feet. It is a moment when both are very close, a further moment of trial and self-examination.

The scene changes to the Empress's bedchamber at the falconry. The Empress is talking in her sleep, while the Nurse lies at her feet. The Empress's words show clearly that her feelings are torn between the two men, the Emperor and the Dyer: 'Look—Nurse—the man's eyes, how tormented they are! [This is the vision of the Emperor turned to stone] ...Barak—what am I doing to you?'

She sinks back and seems to sleep more deeply. The wall of the chamber disappears to reveal

San Francisco Opera, 1959
A scene in the Dyer's hut in Act II. A free interpretation, richly detailed. The impact is imaginative, despite the somewhat restricted area.
Producer: Paul Hager. Conductor: Leopold Ludwig. Sets: Jean-Pierre Ponnelle.

Bayerische Staatsoper, Munich, 1963
A new production for the opening of the re-built Nationaltheater in Munich on 21 November 1963. Design for the first scene: the appearance of the Spirit Messenger. The effect of the fountain on the terrace is a little awkward.
Producer: Rudolf Hartmann.
Conductor: Joseph Keilberth.
Sets: Helmut Jürgens.

a giant cave with a small fissure leading out into the open. Dim lamps here and there in the dark cave reveal ancient tombs hewn into basalt rock. To the right can be seen a bronze door leading into the heart of the mountain. The cry of the Falcon is heard and then the Emperor enters through the fissure in the rock as if following the Falcon; his hands are stretched out in front of him.

The Empress moves in her sleep and sighs once, gently. The Emperor takes a lamp from a tomb, and in his hand it suddenly brightens. He notices the bronze door, behind which can be heard a sound like that of rushing water, and moves towards it. The Falcon flies round him uttering mournful cries of warning. The Emperor hammers on the door, which opens, allowing him to enter again.

The Falcon cries out: 'The woman casts no shadow, the Emperor must be turned to stone!' The dread kingdom of Keikobad disappears; the bed-chamber is as it was before.

The Emperor's entrance into the darkness of the unknown, which the Empress witnesses in her sleep, is once again a scene which demands great technical skill. It should illustrate the

Bayerische Staatsoper, Munich, 1963
The Empress (Ingrid Bjoner) and Barak (Dietrich Fischer-Dieskau) in Act II. The set for the Dyer's hut by Helmut Jürgens is very much in keeping with the style of the work without being overburdened by detail.
Producer: Rudolf Hartmann.
Conductor: Joseph Keilberth.

process of purification undergone by both Emperor and Empress as they move towards understanding and the experience of the deepest human emotions.

At the height of her torment the Empress sees the Emperor turned to stone and feels compassion for Barak: 'Both here and there, everything is my fault—I gave no help to him [the Emperor], I brought ruin to the other [Barak].' The only way out, it seems, is through her own death: 'Woe is me! Rather would I be turned to stone!'

Rapid change of scene to the Dyer's house... The room is in twilight, growing darker and darker. The brothers, fearing disaster, come to Barak seeking help: '... The sun goes down in the middle of the day...' The Nurse too, is afraid: 'Higher powers are at work here, madam; something threatens us...' She knows that she has evoked Keikobad's wrath by her sacrilegious machinations, but cannot stop their develop-

ment. A demonic force drives her further towards her downfall. Meanwhile the Empress has matured through her experience, and she admits: '... I am thankful that I have found this man (Barak) among men, for he shows me what a human being is, and for his sake I will stay among humans, breathe their breath and bear their troubles.'

The Wife is still angry and stubborn. She confronts Barak—who persists in his gloomy fear—with false confessions of her unfaithfulness and tells him that she has agreed to give up her shadow: 'I shall put away from my body the unborn children, and my womb will not be fertile for you nor for any other...' In a state of great agitation Barak calls for light, and his brothers hold their lamps over his Wife. They see that she no longer casts a shadow. Barak tries to throttle her, but is held back by his brothers.

The Nurse has now achieved the object of her demonic ambitions and signifies to the Empress

Metropolitan Opera, New York, 1966
The Dyer's Wife (Christa Ludwig), the Nurse (Irene Dalis), Barak (Walter Berry) and the Empress (Leonie Rysanek) in Act II.
Producer: Nathaniel Merrill.
Conductor: Karl Böhm.
Sets: Robert O'Hearn.

Metropolitan Opera, New York, 1966
The Empress (Leonie Rysanek) before entering the spirit world in Act II. An impressive piece of scenic design by Robert O'Hearn.
Producer: Nathaniel Merrill.
Conductor: Karl Böhm.

that she should now assume the shadow. But the Empress refuses to accept the theft: 'I do not want the shadow: there is blood on it; I will not touch it. I raise my hands into the air, to keep them free of human blood. I invoke the names of the stars to save this person come what may!' Her compassion, a newly acquired human quality, leads her to decide to sacrifice herself.

The Nurse conjures a shining sword into the hand of the enraged Barak: 'He who cries for blood yet has no sword, shall be armed by us! Let the dark blood flow fast; we have the shadow, and for us that is good!'

Now the Wife, undergoing a profound inner transformation ('radiant, with an expression she has never worn before')—offers herself to the sword, with words of committed love: 'Barak, I did not do it! I have not done it yet! . . . If I must die before your eyes, if I must die for what was never done, mighty Barak, whom I never saw before, severe judge, lord and husband—Barak, then kill me quickly!'

As Barak raises his hand to strike, the shining sword suddenly disappears, as if wrenched from his hand—a dull rumbling makes the whole building shake, the earth opens and the river floods into the room, bursting through the side wall. While the brothers try to escape we see Barak and his Wife, who lies at his feet devoid of any will, each sinking separately into the flood waters. The Nurse has meanwhile pulled the Empress with her on to a raised ledge in the wall of the vaulted room. She covers her mistress with her cloak. Out of the all-embracing darkness her voice echoes: 'Powers beyond us are at work! Come here to me!'

This is where Act II closes: following the test of Barak and his Wife, and after the Empress's first victory over herself and her desire for the shadow, Keikobad has caused a natural catastrophe. This event leads into the domain beyond the human world, and thus into Act III. By including details of the very demanding scenic changes I have sought to make clear the growing demands placed on the producer and stage-designer. As in any fable these changes are an integral part of the plot, and their symbolism is more than a mere direction for the staging. The stage directions for the close—resembling a miniature *Götterdämmerung*—illustrate the extent of the demands made on the lighting and technical staff.

In his *Recollections* Strauss commented as follows on the development of Act III: '. . . These wartime worries may be responsible for a certain nervous irritation in the score, especially halfway through the third act, which was to "explode" into melodrama.'[9]

The 'wartime worries' which Strauss mentioned were his concern for his only son, who had enlisted in Mainz for service in the foot artillery; he was discharged later on health grounds. Nor could Strauss bear the idea that Hofmannsthal was serving as an officer in Poland and France. The composer withdrew entirely into his work, living in an ivory tower and giving vent

Teatro Colón, Buenos Aires, 1970
The Dyer's hut presented in a free, non-representational form. The motif of the woven carpets has become a principal feature. The focal points of the set are well accentuated.
Producer: Ernst Poettgen.
Conductor: Ferdinand Leitner.
Sets: Roberto Oswald.

Théâtre National de l'Opéra, Paris, 1972
Jörg Zimmermann's set stressed colour and the element of the fantastic. The singers were: James King (Emperor), Leonie Rysanek (Empress), Walter Berry (Barak) and Christa Ludwig (Dyer's Wife). This scene shows the Dyer's Wife and the Nurse in Act II, Scene 3.
Producer: Nikolaus Lehnhoff.
Conductor: Karl Böhm.

Théâtre National de l'Opéra, Paris, 1972
The first scene on the terrace of the Emperor's palace. An impressive design by Jörg Zimmermann.

only occasionally to his disgust at the events of the day.

In a letter of 14 October 1914 to Hofmannsthal, he wrote: 'Dear friend. The second act is nearly ready: it's going to be really splendid; it almost composes itself, so good and well-suited to the music is your poetry...'[10]

His harmonious collaboration with Hofmannsthal was disturbed by external events. Strauss waited impatiently for Act III, but it was not until the beginning of 1915 that Hofmannsthal was able to continue his work. He advised Strauss to consider Act III carefully: 'For we would run a grave risk if we were to be at cross purposes anywhere in this work, as happened for instance, as you know, more than once over *Ariadne*...'[11]

Wisdom prevailed. Strauss also agreed with Hofmannsthal that it would not be a good idea at present to perform *Josephslegende* in Germany; this ballet had after all been written for the Russians and first put on in Paris. There were accusations of a lack of patriotism, a lack of honour and so forth. Strauss was irritated by this, and concentrated more than ever on *Die Frau ohne Schatten,* not least because Hofmannsthal gave him hope. On 26 March 1915 the latter wrote: 'The act will delight you; it is wholly music, meets the music all the way, and at the same time is rich and varied and brief (only eighteen pages). You will and must summon up all your strength to make this act hold all that is most rich and sublime in what we two together have to give...'[12]

Strauss was overjoyed, and immediately suggested dates: '... I am definitely thinking of starting the composition of Act III at the beginning of May...'[13]

In the same letter of 30 March 1915 Strauss encouraged Hofmannsthal, who was worried about the war: 'But as for politics: I think we'll view them from a little way off and leave them to the care of those concerned with them. Only hard work can console us...'[14] For Strauss, work in hand was the only thing that mattered.

He was untouched by the uncomfortable and distracting changes in daily life and expressed his ill-ease at the prospect of the return of Germany's youth from the war: '... when in fact one must be thankful if the poor blighters are at least cleansed of their lice and bed-bugs and cured of their infections and once more weaned from murder!'[15]

On 5 April 1915 Strauss put a significant question to Hofmannsthal: '... Before you send me Act III I must convey to you a few misgivings which may perhaps still give you some im-

portant ideas for the third act. What happens to the shadow which the Dyer's Wife has lost in Act II and which the Empress refuses to accept?... The shadow hangs in the air. Moreover, the Empress's words, 'I do not want the shadow; there is blood on it' are lost to the audience because they are sung in an ensemble...'[16]

Hofmannsthal answered immediately and gave a concise and convincing explanation of the third act:

You are quite right; at the end of Act II the shadow hangs in the air: one woman has lost it, the other has not rightfully acquired it. This pending transaction, its final settlement by a judgement of Solomon by higher forces, whose spokesmen are the 'unborn children'—this is indeed the focal point of

Théâtre National de l'Opéra, Paris, 1972
The final scene with the players grouped in somewhat conventional manner. No emphasis on the distinction between the worlds of the Emperor and Barak. The singers are: James King (Emperor), Leonie Rysanek (Empress), Walter Berry (Barak) and Christa Ludwig (Dyer's Wife).
Producer: Nikolaus Lehnhoff.
Conductor: Karl Böhm.
Sets: Jörg Zimmermann.

Salzburg Festival, 1974–5
Scene from Act II. A vividly
imagined fairy-tale world, making
full use of the broad stage.
Producer: Günther Rennert.
Conductor: Karl Böhm.
Sets: Günther Schneider-Siemssen.

Salzburg Festival, 1974–5
The final scene, showing the
Dyer's Wife and the shadow she
has regained—her bridge to a new
life.

the third act. The big scene of the Empress in the temple is the spiritual core of the entire opera which helps us to see Acts I and II in their true light...[17]

Strauss worked on the score at a furious pace, asking, in places, for more verses, suggesting changes which would help make the action as clear as possible, making additions, and writing letter after letter. When Hofmannsthal returned from Poland on 21 June 1915 he found four long letters from Strauss waiting for him. They all contained expressions of the composer's con-

cern and impatience. On 8 June 1915 he had written: 'Since I am now stuck in my composing, while you, most unnecessarily, are consorting with lice and bed-bugs instead of writing poetry, I have now begun orchestrating the score of Act I. But I'd much prefer, while the sun shines, to finish composing Act III, which I could manage in one go...'[18]

Months of continuous work followed, although here and there it was interrupted by other things. Both authors were much occupied with the new version of *Ariadne* being produced

Opernhaus, Dortmund, 1975
Two figures by Lore Haas. The costume designs, with their striking ornamentation of oriental motifs, are exceptionally imaginative.

in Vienna. Hofmannsthal had to go to Belgium and France, and then again to Poland. It was not until summer of 1916 that *Die Frau ohne Schatten* again came to the forefront of their attention. By then, though, the steady flow of thought had been interrupted and Act III was beginning to cause them concern. Hofmannsthal felt that the music (except for the first scene) was too heavy and oppressive, and Strauss himself, quite contrary to his normal mood, was uncertain of himself; although he took heart from Hofmannsthal's encouragement, his mind was straying to other ideas. A comedy was taking shape on the horizon: *Intermezzo*. Hofmannsthal, too, was overburdened with his own work, and both men were also collaborating on *Le Bourgeois Gentilhomme* for Max Reinhardt, something which took up much time and energy but which brought little success.

Work on *Die Frau ohne Schatten* came to a standstill. On 12 July 1918 Strauss wrote to spur Hofmannsthal on:

Don't be angry that I have 'prodded' you. It was not meant as a reminder—but you can't blame me for dying to get something from you again soon. I am fifty-four years of age—how long my productive vigour will continue to yield something good, who can tell? And we could both give the world a

good many fine things yet. What was it you said at the time? Every few years a delightful little *Singspiel*, in between a comedy with music (like the *Bourgeois*), then a satirical operetta, and then—as it goes in *The Magic Flute*—another little Papageno, then another Papagena, until the spring runs dry...[19]

In the meantime Strauss had been appointed joint-director of the Vienna Opera with Franz Schalk, and it was not until the end of 1918 that he and Hofmannsthal could begin to see their way through to the first performance of *Die Frau ohne Schatten*. By 1919 preparations were under way for this 'child of sorrow' to be introduced to the public. The première was given on 10 October, and on 18 April 1920 the Staatsoper in Berlin followed with its own first performance.

ACT III

The contrast between the realism of the Dyer's hut and the unearthly world of the Emperor, which we saw in Acts I and II, has ended. Keikobad's mysterious spirit kingdom opens up before us. The Wife and Barak meet again in the subterranean chambers of this strange world, each unaware of the other and enduring the pangs of remorse and dawning self-knowledge. In their own separate ways they still have to face the final, great test. They recognize their undying love for one another, and experience self-reproach yet also hope. Hofmannsthal's beautiful lines: 'Mir anvertraut, dass ich sie hege, dass ich sie trage auf diesen Händen...' (Entrusted to me that I should care for her, that I should cherish her with these hands...) and the thoughts of the Wife as a distant answer: 'Serving, loving, to bow before you: to see you! to breathe, to live! to give you, good husband, children...!' led Strauss to write an inspired duet. A Voice from on High tells them: 'The way is clear' and a beam of light falls on them. They go towards their last trial, and to freedom. The words sung by the contralto voice must be heard; for this reason it is important that the singer be placed as far forward as possible (behind a rock or similar object).

The vault sinks out of sight. Clouds appear, and divide, revealing a rocky terrace, like the one that was visible as the Empress slept. Stone steps lead away from the water upwards to a mighty, temple-like entrance into the heart of the mountain. Opposite, dark water flows, cutting into the base of the rock... A boat without a helmsman floats along in the water. Lying in the boat, slumbering, is the Empress, the Nurse kneels beside her...

Some fundamental points about Act III should not be overlooked. In the first place, the

Opernhaus, Dortmund, 1975
The set-designer Hans Schavernoch hit upon impressive solutions for the terrace in Act I and for the Dyer's hut which, overshadowed by the stone mass of the town, creates a convincing impression of poverty and cramped living conditions.
Producer: Paul Hager.
Conductor: Marek Janowski.

first three sets of the act should be dissimilar and contrasted in colouring. Scenes 2 and 3 are relatively long, with only two people, at times only one, on stage at a time. The audience will soon tire of these scenes if only grey or bluish grey predominate. Such colours become monotonous. At this point the stage-designer must avoid monotony without damaging the basic unity of the spirit kingdom.

The whole of Act III also requires careful attention if it is not to fall disappointingly flat after the concentrated flow of events in the second act. The temple scene and the complicated finale, with its realization of the spirit figures, are particularly important. The audience must also be able to follow the ebb and flow of the water in the temple if its dangerous attraction for the Empress is to be understood.

In contrast to Hofmannsthal, who planned a very short third act, Strauss called for more text, new verses, to extend his musical ideas. For instance, he wanted to give the Nurse a major aria, and to expand the duet between the Emperor and the Empress. In practice it was found that the resulting length was too great, and that the Nurse's scene was too exhausting for many singers. Cuts became inevitable. Conductors and producers had to try to find the right balance without tearing apart the fabric of the plot. Several productions were exemplary in this respect, but unfortunately not all. Strauss said to me that he was happy with the version and sets for Act III used in the productions at Vienna and Munich.

Despite Strauss's oft-repeated aversion to voices off-stage which the audience could not clearly identify, such effects accumulate in Act III: Barak and his wife; the voice of the spirit servants; the unborn children, and so forth. However, Strauss's efforts to make everything comprehensible were not in vain. The spirit servants did not appear on stage and the number of their calls from the darkness was reduced, thus making it easier for the audience to follow the plot. What, though, does it really need to know? That Barak and his Wife must search for one another; that each is lost and calling the other; that the Empress must pass the last test in front of her father, the god Keikobad; and that the Nurse is to be cast out from the kingdom of the spirits. The calls of the Dyer and his Wife can be shortened without adverse effect, as can the voices of the spirit servants, above all when they are not visible. The Nurse's scene has already been mentioned.

In contrast to the first version, where subterranean voices and a Voice from on High were to be heard in the scene of the Empress at the Golden Fountain, the final form included the figure of the Guardian of the Threshold. This was clearly an improvement: the words became more intelligible and the temptation more convincing. In practice, with Strauss's agreement, the male Guardian became a female one, a light soprano voice which could cope more effectively with the fast tempo required.

But to go back to the two women in the boat. The Empress recalls the mysterious gateway. She recognizes the course she has been ordered to take and bids farewell for ever to the Nurse, who desperately attempts to hold her back. The door opens for the Empress, who enters Keikobad's kingdom, but the Spirit Messenger bars the way for the Nurse, who is carried back to the human world by the boat. There she must remain in despair, cast out, damned. The Spirit Messenger tells her: 'Let grief consume you! You have been dealt with according to the law!' The curse is accompanied by a short but severe storm, with brilliant lightning and thunder. The scene then changes to the temple.

During the intervening passage of music it is best entirely to cut the calls of the Dyer and his Wife and the voices of the spirits. The orchestra alone speaks: until the violin solo accompanying the entrance of the Empress. The stage shows a large temple-like room, lost in mysterious half-darkness. Moving to the centre of the room is the Empress, subdued, awed by her surroundings. She says: 'Father? Is it you?...' She wishes to subjugate herself to Keikobad's command. As she is crossing the room, a Golden Fountain springs up, which she rejects: 'Within me is love; that is far more...' Even the temptation of the shadow of the Dyer's Wife offered by the Guardian of the Threshold fails to distract her. 'But what will become of her?' The Empress's compassion for the Wife prevents her from accepting water from the fountain, particularly when she hears the voices of the Dyer and his Wife. She recalls with a sense of guilt her attempted deception of Barak and moves away from the fountain: '... I will not drink.' The fountain vanishes. The Empress is still seeking her unseen father, and wants to present herself to him: '... Wherever you may hide in the darkness, in my heart is light to reveal you by. I desire my just deserts! Show yourself, father! My judge, come forth!' Light fills the depths of the temple and we behold, seated on his throne, the Emperor turned to stone: 'he is rigid and of stone, only his eyes seem to live'.

The Empress screams out and recoils in horror. Strauss chose to employ melodrama for the major scene that follows (the Empress's last phase of trial) to ensure that every word would be understood. To what extent cuts should made is something which must be left to the producer's judgement, but nothing that aids the work's comprehensibility should be sacrificed.

Subterranean voices roar in the ears of the Empress, who has collapsed. The Emperor's eyes are filled with a silent plea: 'The woman casts no shadow, the Emperor must turn to stone.' The statue of the Emperor darkens, the Golden Fountain re-appears, the Guardian of the Threshold beckons again: 'Say: "I will" and the shadow is yours. This man will rise and will come to life and will go with you. As a sign of this, bow down and drink!' After a terrible inner battle with herself, the Empress manages to utter a tortured, groaning cry: 'I—will—not.'

The water sinks away suddenly, everything grows completely dark. After a short period of darkness, light fills the room from above. The Empress, as if unknowingly, has raised herself to her feet, and away from her now stretches a sharply-defined shadow right across the room. The Emperor rises from his throne and begins to descend the stairs.

During the following duet the light in the room becomes ever brighter; the room is, as it were, uplifted by enlightenment. The Emperor, freed from his torment, understands the task before him and instructs the hesitant, confused Empress: 'You have overcome yourself. Now heavenly messengers have freed father and children, the unborn. They have found us, and now speed towards us.' The couple, liberated, embrace; the voices of the unborn resound cheerfully from the light, which is increasing in brightness. Even this scene, which contains no action, just shining apotheosis, can conceivably be shortened if done with care. The stylized gestures of Persian or Indian miniatures are almost perfect at this point.

The lively, bright transformation music leads into the next scene: 'A beautiful landscape, climbing steeply, is the main feature. In the centre: a golden waterfall cascading through a fissure. The Emperor and Empress are to be seen above the waterfall, climbing down from the heights.' This scene with actions taking place at different levels is not easy to realize in the short transition period available. The lightning should not initially be too bright, lest it detract from the final climax.

Barak and his wife finally find one another; they meet in the middle of her shadow—now in the foreground—which has re-appeared and forms a bridge between them. The two couples, re-united, remain on their different levels.

This scene makes great technical demands. After the two couples have been re-united, the plot as such is concluded. A broad, spacious musical apotheosis, accompanied by the constantly increasing intensity of light already mentioned, brings the final scene to a close: the love of married partners has vanquished the darkness of suffering *(Fidelio)*; all tests and trials have been overcome *(The Magic Flute)*; the main characters have found one another, on the highest ethical plane conceivable in a relationship between a man and a woman *(Frau ohne Schatten)*.

* * *

After *Die Frau ohne Schatten* was finished there was a lull in the collaboration between Hofmannsthal and Strauss as they waited for the première of the great work. They went their own ways. Several times Hofmannsthal turned down suggestions for a cheerful opera of 'bourgeois' character; Strauss proceeded with his plan for *Intermezzo,* for which he ultimately was to write the libretto as well.

After *Elektra, Der Rosenkavalier, Ariadne auf Naxos, Josephslegende* and *Die Frau ohne Schatten,* the collaboration between composer and librettist ceased. It was resumed almost nine years later, for *Die ägyptische Helena.*

Measured against Strauss's long life and against the entirety of his stage works, *Die Frau ohne Schatten* represents the conclusion of the first half of his overall work.

The Confirmation candidate in
the ceremonial coach. The
Munich artist Franziska Bilek,
who was famous for her humorous drawings, was invited to design the decorated Viennese *Fiaker*
(coach) carrying the hero of the
ballet *Schlagobers*.

Schlagobers

Richard Strauss's sixtieth birthday fell on 11 June 1924. The event was anticipated the month before with a major celebration in Vienna, where Strauss had a share in the directorship of the State Opera. There were official functions and honours, musical events, and performances at the opera-house of all his stage works with the exception of *Guntram*. In addition, on 9 May 1924, the composer himself conducted the première of his ballet *Schlagobers*.

Heinrich Kralik, a Viennese music critic, well describes the milieu portrayed in this cheerful little piece:

... The idea for the whole work, the plot and the dance scenes came entirely from Strauss. He found the inspiration for the piece right from the start of his activities in Vienna... Strauss set to music the culinary specialities of the city, the aroma of tea and coffee, the crispness of Viennese *Semmel* (rolls) and *Kipferl* (croissants)... The ballet plot is handled in an easy-going manner, but none of the tight artistic concentration of true Strauss music is sacrificed; and this piece contains rhythmic, melodic and harmonic delicacies in delightful abundance. The sweet

Staatsoper, Vienna, 1924
This group, photographed in the style of the period, shows the Confirmation candidate in the première, together with the ladies of *Schlagobers*. The costumes were by Ada Nigrin. Choreographer: Heinrich Kröller. Conductor: Richard Strauss.

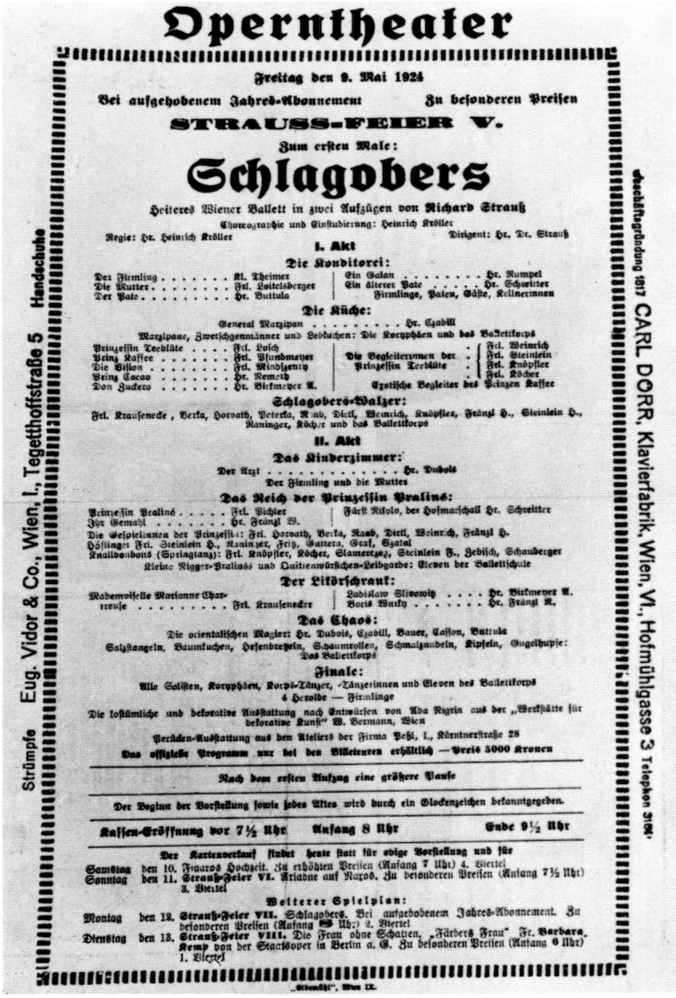

Operntheater

Freitag den 9. Mai 1924

Bei aufgehobenem Jahres-Abonnement — Zu besonderen Preisen

STRAUSS-FEIER V.

Zum ersten Male:

Schlagobers

Heiteres Wiener Ballett in zwei Aufzügen von Richard Strauß

Choreographie und Einstudierung: Heinrich Kröller

Regie: Hr. Heinrich Kröller — Dirigent: Hr. Dr. Strauß

I. Akt

Die Konditorei:

Der Firmling . . . . Kl. Theimer | Ein Galan . . . . Hr. Rumpel
Die Mutter . . . . Frl. Loitelsberger | Ein älterer Pate . . . . . Hr. Schreitter
Der Pate . . . . Hr. Buttula | Firmlinge, Paten, Gäste, Kellnerinnen

Die Küche:

General Marzipan . . . . Hr. Czabill
Marzipane, Zwetschgenmänner und Lebkuchen: Die Koryphäen und das Ballettkorps

Prinzessin Teeblüte . . . . Frl. Loich
Prinz Kaffee . . . . Frl. Pfundmeyer
Die Vision . . . . Frl. Mindszenty
Prinz Cacao . . . . Hr. Nemeth
Don Zucero . . . . Hr. Birkmeyer A.

Die Begleiterinnen der Prinzessin Teeblüte: Frl. Weinrich, Frl. Steinlein, Frl. Knöpfler, Frl. Köcher
Exotische Begleiter des Prinzen Kaffee

Schlagobers-Walzer:

Frl. Krausenecke, Berka, Horvath, Peterka, Raab, Dirtl, Weinrich, Knöpfler, Fränzl H., Steinlein H., Raninger, Köcher und das Ballettkorps

II. Akt

Das Kinderzimmer:

Der Arzt . . . . Hr. Dubois
Der Firmling und die Mutter

Das Reich der Prinzessin Pralinée:

Prinzessin Pralinée . . . . . Frl. Pichler | Fürst Nikolo, der Hofmarschall Hr. Schreitter
Ihr Gemahl . . . . Hr. Fränzl W.

Die Gespielinnen der Prinzessin: Frl. Horvath, Berka, Raab, Dirtl, Weinrich, Fränzl H.
Höflinge: Frl. Steinlein H., Raninger, Fritz, Buttera, Graf, Szatal
Knallbonbons (Springtanz): Frl. Knöpfler, Köcher, Slamerczeg, Steinlein F., Zebisch, Schauberger
Kleine Nigger-Pralinés und Quittenwürstchen-Leibgarde: Eleven der Ballettschule

Der Likörschrank:

Mademoiselle Marianne Chartreuse . . . . Frl. Krausenecker | Ladislaw Slivowitz . . . . Hr. Birkmeyer A.
Boris Wutky . . . . Hr. Fränzl R.

Das Chaos:

Die orientalischen Magier: Hr. Dubois, Czabill, Bauer, Casson, Buttula
Salzstangerln, Baumkuchen, Hefenbretzeln, Schaumrollen, Schmalznudeln, Kipfeln, Gugelhupfe: Das Ballettkorps

Finale:

Alle Solisten, Koryphäen, Korps-Tänzer, -Tänzerinnen und Eleven des Ballettkorps
4 Herolde — Firmlinge

Die kostümliche und dekorative Ausstattung nach Entwürfen von Ada Nigrin aus der „Werkstätte für dekorative Kunst" W. Bermann, Wien

Perücken-Ausstattung aus den Ateliers der Firma Peßl, I., Kärntnerstraße 28

Das offizielle Programm nur bei den Billeteuren erhältlich — Preis 5000 Kronen

Nach dem ersten Aufzug eine größere Pause

Der Beginn der Vorstellung sowie jedes Aktes wird durch ein Glockenzeichen bekanntgegeben.

Kassen-Eröffnung vor 7½ Uhr — Anfang 8 Uhr — Ende 9½ Uhr

Der Kartenverkauf findet heute statt für obige Vorstellung und für
Samstag den 10. Figaros Hochzeit. Zu erhöhten Preisen (Anfang 7 Uhr) 4. Viertel
Sonntag den 11. Strauß-Feier VI. Ariadne auf Naxos. Zu besonderen Preisen (Anfang 7½ Uhr) 3. Viertel

Weiterer Spielplan:

Montag den 12. Strauß-Feier VII. Schlagobers. Bei aufgehobenem Jahres-Abonnement. Zu besonderen Preisen (Anfang [illegible] Uhr) 2. Viertel
Dienstag den 13. Strauß-Feier VIII. Die Frau ohne Schatten. „Färbers Frau" Fr. Barbara Kemp von der Staatsoper in Berlin a. G. Zu besonderen Preisen (Anfang 6 Uhr) 1. Viertel

„Elbemühl", Wien IX.

Staatsoper, Vienna, 1924
The première of *Schlagobers* took place in Vienna on the fifth evening of the celebration of Strauss's sixtieth birthday. Ada Nigrin's decor and costumes were superb.

content of the work is something you can be proud to smack your lips at, rather than relish at the back of the palate...

However, the composer's humorous homage to Vienna was not a success. It was misunderstood; as Kralik noted: 'The reaction to this sweet offering was a sour one...' And that was virtually the end of the matter. Apart from one production in Breslau (where the Viennese term *Schlagobers* was altered to *Schlagsahne**) there have been no other productions.

The Viennese première was presented with loving care and the witty costumes and sets (by A. Nigrin) have lost none of their gracious charm. The ballet, like the old *divertissements,* contained everything that could be successfully danced: classical and popular dances, and to crown all, of course, a waltz. This obviously called for a large ballet company, and an imaginative choreographer and director; in Vienna this role fell to Heinrich Kröller.

Strauss devised the scenario entirely by himself. He also wrote a synopsis of the ballet:

> Anyone who wanders down the *Hauptallee* of the Vienna Prater, shaded by lush chestnut-trees, on a sunny Whit Sunday, will meet a number of carriages decked out with white elder-blossoms and roses and drawn by a pair of smart 'Iuckers' [light Hungarian carriage-horses], and even they are garlanded. There will also be bevies of girls in white and young lads in black jackets accompanied by their uncles and aunts as godparents. They will be going at an easy pace towards the famous summer-house of the great Empress Maria Theresa.

* *Schlagobers/Schlagsahne:* the meaning is the same,—whipped cream for coffee, cakes, etc.—but to German ears the amusing aspect arises from the differencies of regional terminology. The effect is similar to calling Yorkshire pudding 'batter cake'—*Translator's note.*

Staatsoper, Vienna, 1924
Gusti Pichler (prima ballerina)
and her partner (Don Sugaro),
Willy Fränzl (soloist and, later,
ballet-master). Choreographer:
Heinrich Kröller. Conductor:
Richard Strauss.

These are Confirmation candidates who have taken Communion in the morning, and after a festive lunch are enjoying the pleasure of a drive in one of the old, much-loved, rubber-wheeled Viennese 'fiacres' (carriages), usually for the first time in their young lives. And where else could this pleasant excursion end but in that Eldorado of youth: one of the no less famous patisseries, eating a cake—whether it be a *Sachertorte, Linzertorte, Bischingertorte* or *Doboschtorte*—with whipped cream *(Schlagobers)*.

The venue for the ballet is, then, a Viennese patisserie where the Confirmation candidates are devouring chocolate with whipped cream and many other sweet delicacies. They show their thanks with a country-style round dance; only one small lad makes himself ill after eating too much *Schlagobers* and is taken home by a concerned godfather. After the doctor has declared his illness to be harmless, the boy conjures up in his imagination lively games in the patisserie. The figures that appear are good company with well-known names and characters:

Princess Pralinée
Prince Nicolo, her Lord Chamberlain
Princess Tea-blossom
Prince Coffee
Prince Cocoa
Don Sugaro
Mademoiselle Marianne Chartreuse
Ladislav Slivovitz }
Boris Vutki   }   Liqueurs

The court of Princess Pralinée: crackers, small pralines, quince 'sausages', four heralds with trumpets; then the army of marzipans, ginger-breads and plum-men; the choir of the giant *Gugelhupf* cakes, *Baumkuchen* (tree-shaped cakes), Christmas loaves, yeast bretzels, dripping noodles, cream horns, crullers, oriental magicians and *Schlagobers*.

Prinzess Pralinée
12337.

12337

Staatsoper, Vienna, 1924
Design by Ada Nigrin for
Princess Pralinée. Like all the
other costumes, it has charm and
is well suited to this ballet.

Staatsoper, Vienna, 1924
One of the dream scenes, designed
by Ada Nigrin. The graceful quality apparent here was a dominant
feature of the première, given on
9 May 1924.

Staatsoper, Vienna, 1924
Design by Ada Nigrin for Prince
Cocoa.
Conductor: Richard Strauss.
Choreographer: Heinrich Kröller.

Stadttheater, Breslau, 1924
Two sets from the German pre-
mière in Breslau, which to a great
extent followed suggestions by
Ada Nigrin.
Choreographer and producer: Max
Semmler. Conductor: Richard
Strauss.

ACT I

In Act I the marzipans, plum-men and ginger-breads emerge from their boxes in the patisserie together with the warlike soft-ices. After that Princess Tea-blossom and her four companions appear to perform an exotic dance. 'Prince Coffee and his entourage enter in the style of a Brazilian folk-dance and dance a romantic *notturno* which ends in a dream-like sequence in an exotic pavilion.'

Then, one after the other, Prince Cocoa, and—in polka rhythm—Don Sugaro enter. All three join in a cheerful round dance, in which Princess Tea-blossom later takes part. In the background a giant bowl appears with *Schlagobers* spilling out of it—i.e. the girls of the ballet corps in white costumes—and the act concludes with a 'great waltz climax'.

ACT II

The Confirmation candidate who has been taken ill is lying in bed with the doctor examining him. He is given something to reduce his fever, immediately falls asleep and has vivid dreams.

The stage is transformed several times: first of all for the entrance of Princess Pralinée with her courtiers. There is a dance solo, then an Upper-Palatine two-step (a folk-dance) by the praline children, a leaping dance by the crackers. After another change of scene we see glass cases containing liqueur bottles. Mademoiselle Chartreuse dances a minuet and is courted by Ladislav Slivovitz and Boris Vutki (*pas de deux* and exit all three). Now the stage is transformed into a Viennese suburb. A *passacaglia* accompanies the entrance of the household pastries and cakes, such as the *Gugelhupfs,* Christmas loaves and dripping noodles. Led by oriental magicians they advance in warlike fashion on the sweetmeats of the patisserie. Marianne Chartreuse, Ladislav Slivovitz and Boris Vutki march with the revolutionaries, as do the marzipans, ginger-breads and plum-men, all of them bearing arms.

A lightning polka is heard; the set changes completely; and the excited crowd passes through the streets of Vienna to the patisserie in the Kärntnerstrasse, where the defending forces use tea, coffee and cocoa as weapons to overwhelm the attackers. Only when Hofbräu beer, in giant beer mugs, is brought into action is the revolt brought under control. Attention turns to another spectacle: accompanied by her 'quince sausage' lifeguards in Frankfurter uniforms and her full court Princess Pralinée appears and placates the people by distributing endless quantities of chocolates and honours.

Under her direction the crowd, now in a mood of enthusiastic excitement, pays homage to the princess in a great dance finale.

Schlagobers makes heavy technical demands for its magical effects, and calls for a large corps de ballet, so it has proved virtually impossible to stage the work in smaller theatres. Moreover it requires an immense number of costumes, placing a burden on any budget; and its typical Viennese setting and plot has further diminished the work's chances of production. In addition, the period of dire need after the war had not yet passed, and people were shocked rather than amused by the celebration of Viennese delights which they had to forego. The 'uprising', too, reminded people of the hunger revolts in the city streets and was considered tactless and embarassing. *Schlagobers* thus held a bitter after-taste for the public.

Strauss remained calm and detached about the cool response of the Viennese. Only once did he complain in a letter that people had held this harmless ballet against him. In my opinion he was right in his reaction, because a quick glance at great classical composers like Beethoven, Bach or Mozart shows that they all undertook such humorous trivia when taken by the mood of the moment.

That is, of course, a different matter from the practice of certain companies to base new ballets on music from Beethoven's string quartets, or on Strauss's Four Last Songs, which have been danced as well as sung. Still, even that makes some sort of change from the all-to-familiar repertory of *Giselle, Swan Lake, The Sleeping Beauty* and other popular favourites.

Verklungene Feste
('Faded Festivities')

Strauss maintained his interest in ballet. He often inserted ballet passages in his later operas. In 1941, at the request of Clemens Krauss and Pino Mlakar, he extended his *Tanzsuite* (Dance Suite), based on piano pieces by François Couperin, by several numbers. The suite was given an attractive plot to frame the various pieces; with choreography by Pia and Pino Mlakar it provided an opportunity to present classical dances from the Baroque period up to the Napoleonic era. The stage-designer Rochus Gliese created a set depicting a beautiful melancholy park, and a series of unforgettable costumes. These were made of rare antique materials, acquired with difficulty from Venice; after the war they were cut up or destroyed.

Verklungene Feste, which received its première in Munich in 1941, was not an original Strauss work but an arrangement. Pia and Pino Mlakar danced a serious sarabande of unforgettable beauty; its final tableau, when the woman kissed the hand and the ring of the Cardinal, was more than just a pose. It was a wistful farewell to a faded epoch.

Bayerische Staatsoper, Munich, 1941
The Cardinal is shown dancing, with an aristocratic lady, the serious sarabande—here performed by Walter Matthes and Helen Kraus. Sets and costumes: Rochus Gliese. Choreographers: Pia and Pino Mlakar. Conductor: Clemens Krauss.

Bayerische Staatsoper, Munich, 1941
A couple from the group performing the elegant contre-danse.

Intermezzo

The old Vierjahreszeiten Hotel in Munich had a restaurant which Richard Strauss frequented whenever he was in town because of its excellent food. My wife and I were often invited to join him. On one of these evenings Strauss was in a particularly good mood and some remark or other led him to mention his opera *Intermezzo*. I have written about this occasion elsewhere:

> I almost believe he did so deliberately because his delight was immense when his wife—as if reacting to a cue—immediately interjected with some derogatory comments. She declared categorically that she had been jealous all her life, because 'men are all no good!' and that even today, at her advanced age, she would scratch the eyes out of any woman who came too close to Richard. But one didn't need to write a play, let alone an opera, about that. She had always been greatly vexed by it as had Anna, her servant of many years. Strauss amused himself royally over her outraged zeal and then smoothed things over with the comment: 'But I did write a beautiful duet of reconciliation at the end!' His wife paused, smiled—she could be absolutely charming—and then said endearingly, like a little girl: 'Yes, that's true, you did!' And with a glance the good atmosphere was restored.

This little episode was like a passage from the opera itself—for instance, the temperamental opening tableau: 'Anna, Anna! Where is the stupid girl?'—or the passage later on in the first scene, before the husband's departure, when a lively domestic altercation develops.

Strauss wrote a detailed foreword to this dialogue explaining how it had to be handled:

> Perhaps it was inevitable that the peculiar subject matter taken from real life and embracing the whole gamut from the sober prose of everyday life through the various shades of dialogue to sentimental song, should induce me, who had in my previous works taken so much care to render the dialogue natural, to adopt the style realised in *Intermezzo*.[1]

Citing several examples he explains his intentions clearly and gives advice based on the scores of his other works. He concludes with an appeal to theatre managers, producers and conductors to do justice to the individual style of *Intermezzo*:

> I would ask the producers when distributing the parts to disregard all demands of the prima donna assoluta or the first baritone. Just as the actors in this opera *Intermezzo* are not operatic heroes but should represent genuine human beings, the casting of the singers for *Intermezzo* should be governed by any existing talent for a light conversational tone, and by musical and physical aptitude for the characters to be portrayed.[2]

Thus Strauss outlined the demands made by a work which at that time was seen as unusual, even capricious. For years productions of *Intermezzo* (often at theatres which were really too large) suffered from 'heavy' casting, so that the conversation in the work took on a charged Wagnerian atmosphere, which was the opposite of what Strauss had laid down. So too with the staging of the work. Justice had do be done—so it was held—to the massive 'Straussian' orchestra involved; little thought was given to what Strauss himself wanted.

Another factor unfavourable to *Intermezzo*'s reception was its emphasis on personal matters. The basic idea for the piece had stemmed from a true event in Strauss's own married life. This aroused harsh criticism: tasteless self-representation, vain self-reflection, over-blown triviality were some of the reproaches directed at Strauss at the time.

On the other hand, the music of the opera,—above all that of the interludes, the *intermezzi*—was owing to its originality and startling freshness, given the recognition and admiration that it deserved.

◁ This lively drawing by the Dresden artist Adolf Mahnke shows the 'accident' which leads to the amusing *Intermezzo*: the collision between Christine Storch on the sledge and the Baron on skis.

A third element in *Intermezzo* has yet to be fully appreciated: the rapid succession of scenes. Strauss chose to have only one break, after the eighth scene; apart from this, the audience must digest the thirteen scenes, some of them quite short, during the various musical interludes. In 1924 this approach to opera had been tried here and there before but had never been followed through with such consistency. It is possible, if you like, to call *Intermezzo* a 'musical' on the operatic stage. It became a fruitful inspiration which influenced such later works as Hindemith's *Neues vom Tage* and many others.

Strauss had wanted to write a comic opera with modern dialogue ever since work on *Die Frau ohne Schatten* was nearing completion. But Hofmannsthal, whom Strauss tried to win over to the idea, refused to participate because he was tied up with his own projects. He did, however, suggest the Austrian comedy playwright, Hermann Bahr; Strauss told him about the material he was considering and Bahr then drafted one or two scenes. However, Bahr strongly recommended that Strauss should write the libretto himself, on the grounds that its author would have to be able to draw on his own experiences. After some hesitation, Strauss did begin to draft the first scene—writing on 'hospital paper' during a period spent at a clinic. At this point none of the characters received names, being referred to simply by the initials 'A' and 'B'. Strauss enjoyed the task because he was not forced to write poetry, for which he had had no inclination following his attempt with *Guntram.* The work simply involved writing down 'his own experiences' in everyday dialogue.

Things progressed rapidly. Strauss noted: 'The first performance in Dresden coincided with my dismissal from Vienna'.[3]

Once the autobiographical elements in *Intermezzo* had been recognized, its première (4 November 1924) was transferred from the Dresden opera-house to a smaller theatre. This created a sensation on account of the sets being virtually a photographic reproduction of the actual rooms in Strauss's Garmisch villa (a practice also followed in other productions), so that the connections between the opera's principal characters and their originals, the composer and his wife Pauline, were evident to all.

Later, Strauss admitted that it had been a mistake to stress the aspects of the work which related directly to his own life. Heinrich Kralik adds that *Intermezzo* was particularly close to its author's heart. Strauss himself wrote: 'Harmless and insignificant as the incidents which prompted this piece may be, when all is said and done,

Sächsische Staatstheater
Schauspielhaus

Dienstag, am 4. November 1924

☛ Außer Anrecht ☚

Anfang 7 Uhr

6. Veranstaltung zur Feier von Richard Strauß' 60. Geburtstag:

Uraufführung:

Intermezzo

Eine bürgerliche Komödie mit sinfonischen Zwischenspielen in zwei Aufzügen von Richard Strauß

Musikalische Leitung: **Fritz Busch**   In Szene gesetzt von **Alois Mora**

Personen:

Christine	Lotte Lehmann
Der kleine Franzl (8-jährig), ihr Sohn	Fritz Sonntag
Hofkapellmeister Robert Storch, ihr Mann	Josef Correck
Anna, ihre Kammerjungfer	Liesel v. Schuch
Baron Lummer	Theo Strack
Der Notar	Robert Büssel
Seine Frau	Elfriede Haberkorn
Ein Kapellmeister / Ein Kommerzienrat / Ein Justizrat / Ein Kammersänger } Roberts Skat-Partner	Hanns Lange / Ludwig Ermold / Adolf Schoepflin / Willy Bader
Ein junges Mädchen	Irmgard Quitzow
Stubenmädchen / Köchin } bei Storch	Erna Frese / Anna Bolze

Die Handlung spielt teils am Grundlsee, teils in Wien

Bühnenbild: **Adolf Mahnke** und **Georg Brandt**

Kostüme aus dem Atelier **Birsch & Co.** in Dresden

Nach dem ersten Akt eine längere Pause

Piano C. Bechstein aus dem Magazin **F. Ries, Dresden, Seestraße 21**

Sämtliche Plätze müssen vor Beginn der Vorstellung eingenommen werden

Textbücher sind für 1.— Goldmark an der Kasse und bei den Türschließern zu haben

Gekaufte Karten werden nur bei Änderung der Vorstellung zurückgenommen

Einlaß und Kassenöffnung ¼7 Uhr – Anfang 7 Uhr – Ende gegen 10 Uhr

Spielplan:

Opernhaus:	Schauspielhaus:
Mittwoch, am 5. November: Außer Anrecht: Zum ersten Mal: **Die Orestie.** Anfang ½ 8 Uhr. (D. V. Nr. 9458—9553.)	**Mittwoch, am 5. November:** Außer Anrecht: **Intermezzo.** Anfang 7 Uhr
Donnerstag, am 6. November: Anrechtsreihe B: **Xerxes.** Anfang ½ 8 Uhr. (D. V. Nr. 3501—3566.)	**Donnerstag, am 6. November:** Außer Anrecht: **Die heilige Johanna.** Anfang 7 Uhr. (D. V. Nr. 9554 — 9650.)

Buchdruckerei der Wilhelm und Bertha v. Baensch Stiftung, Dresden.   Unerlaubter Nachdruck verboten.

Schauspielhaus, Dresden, 1924
As the programme indicates the première, on 4 November 1924, was held at the Schauspielhaus des Dresdener Staatstheaters, a clever choice for this work which depends so much on conversation. The set was designed by Adolf Mahnke; the producer was Alois Mora; the conductor was Fritz Busch. Lotte Lehmann sang the first Christine.

Schauspielhaus, Dresden, 1924
Frau Storch's room was an exact
reconstruction of a room in
Strauss's villa at Garmisch, so too
was the dining-room in the final
scene. The designs for the première were by Adolf Mahnke.
Producer: Alois Mora.
Conductor: Fritz Busch.

Staatstheater, Darmstadt, 1929
The design for the dressing-room
by Lothar Schenk von Trapp followed modern trends but contributed little to the work itself.
Producer: Renato Mordo.
Conductor: Carl Bamberger.

they nevertheless led to difficult and disturbing psychological conflicts.'[4]

Strauss was proud of a remark by Max Reinhardt that *Intermezzo* was good enough to be produced as a straight play, without music. But his reaction to Hofmannsthal's not very favourable critique was one of superior reserve:

> Of course it has little 'action'; on the contrary, the action is from the outset trivialized (as you quite rightly observe regarding the character of the Baron) and treated ironically. But then, what are these so-called dramatic plots? They've remained the same for two thousand years: murder and destruction, intrigue of mean minds against the hero, betrothal after overcoming obstacles, or separation—surely all this is uninteresting and has been seen heaven knows how many times before... That is why I consider an attractive and consistent character portrait as in *Intermezzo* more interesting than any so-called plot...[5]

Hofmannsthal never altered his opinion, but neither did Strauss. Both soon began to work together again: *Die ägyptische Helena* was beginning to take shape.

A new Strauss work always meant an enrichment of the repertoire which no opera-house could ignore. Because of its modest demands on the orchestra, *Intermezzo* could also be performed at smaller theatres and for some years after 1924 producers seized the opportunity to put on this work, which seemed to be so easy to cast.

But then less was heard of *Intermezzo,* and it was not until 1950 that interest in the opera was renewed. Recent productions have benefited from earlier experiences with casting and of the problems associated with the autobiographical nature of the work.

Technically speaking, *Intermezzo* will always make high demands on a theatre. None the less, technical improvements have meant that where previously the frequent scene changes had to be effected with hand-moved trolleys or carriages, nowadays turn-tables, elevateable platforms and moveable 'side-stages' can be used—one positive consequence of the building of many new theatres after war-time destruction. Successful, too, have been the attempts of stage-designers to abandon photographic realism and so to transpose the characters into settings that are universally relevant.

For the producer it is sheer delight to work with the actors in creating the characters, who communicate with one another in musical recitatives and arioso-like passages. The producer can catch every nuance and shape the performance, as it were, in 'constant close-up'. This style of production is in great contrast to the *al fresco* style adopted in the early years, when the contours of grand opera were followed (deriving largely from weighty casting). Producers are now able to achieve the effect of light irony which Strauss intended.

Let us now look at the plot of *Intermezzo*. Strauss described the location as follows: 'The action takes place partly at the "Grundlsee" inn and partly in Vienna.' No mention was made of the house in Garmisch or of nearby Munich. The locale is unconnected with any setting in Strauss's personal life.

ACT I

Scene I. The dressing-room, prior to the departure of the husband, Hofkapellmeister Storch. Open travelling-bags, complete disorder. It is 7 a.m.

The Hofkapellmeister's wife, Christine, is in a state of nervous excitement which she tries to hide by frantically rushing about. Her husband, Robert Storch, endeavours to calm her, but fails because of her temperament. His parting remarks are therefore frosty and hurtful: 'All right then, go to the devil! Goodbye!' She has upset him because she refuses to write to him. Her answer as he leaves angrily is characteristic: 'May God go with you. And don't miss the train!'

Christine is pleased that she has managed to hide her real feelings, but immediately after her husband leaves the room asks her maid, Anna, whether her husband is waving goodbye as he departs; then she pours her heart out to her confidante. Every now and then she snaps at Anna, particularly when the latter defends her master, whom she greatly admires. Christine then receives a visit from one of her friends who invites her out for a walk. The invitation is cheerfully accepted.

The scene changes quickly to a toboggan-run. The transition through this scene is problematic because the toboggan-run needs the appropriate structures and a certain amount of

Cuvilliéstheater, Munich, 1960
Hanny Steffek and Hermann Prey in a successful production at the Cuvilliéstheater. The illustration shows the 'Schuhplattler' scene at the inn.
Producer: Rudolf Hartmann.
Conductor: Joseph Keilberth.
Sets: Jean-Pierre Ponnelle.

space, while the dressing-room set has to remain complete so that it can be used again later. The best solution is to combine suspended flats (backdrops) with specially constructed trolleys; a turntable could also be used. The main point is that the technical operations should not prove disruptive.

In the first scene the producer has many opportunities to delineate Christine's character with colourful and amusing details. He can show her both as the shrew and as the concerned, faithful wife; as an enchantingly charming woman and as an intolerably hurtful creature. All these elements are contained in the two conversations which she has with her husband and with her maid, Anna, conversations in which the dialogue often jumps from one subject to another.

By subtle characterization, the producer can help the Hofkapellmeister's wife become an endearing figure whose lapses of temperament occasion only an amused smile. Her hurtful remarks which bubble up from time to time have little weight to them and are quickly forgotten.

Scene II: at the toboggan-run.

One toboggan after another appears on the run and then disappears into the wings. Baron Lummer comes in on skis. He is an agreeable Austrian playboy type, on the look-out for pretty girls, and so fails to hear Christine's warning cry: 'Make way!' She runs into him with her sledge and they both tumble to the ground. She explodes in a rage: 'You fool! Can't you see people are tobogganing here?' She will not accept his semi-apology, discovers that she 'has hurt herself terribly' and threatens to inform her husband. The Baron introduces himself and immediately Christine's mood changes. It turns out that she knows his parents. She chats in lively fashion and begins to flirt a little (the Baron is young and handsome), having completely forgotten her 'terrible' pain. She invites him to visit her and leaves in the best of tempers.

The orchestral interlude, a cheerful waltz, prepares us for the third scene: a ball given by the landlord at the Grundlsee inn. The atmosphere is festive and cheerful. Guests are amusing themselves by watching skilful *Schuhplattler*

Cuvilliéstheater, Munich, 1960
Frau Storch (Hanny Steffek) in conversation with Baron Lummer (Ferry Gruber). A few details are enough to catch the right atmosphere.
Producer: Rudolf Hartmann.
Conductor: Joseph Keilberth.
Sets: Jean-Pierre Ponnelle.

Cuvilliéstheater, Munich, 1960
Frau Storch inspects the room she
has rented from the Notary's wife
for the Baron. An attractive set in
rustic style. The details of set and
costumes were designed by Jean-
Pierre Ponnelle with characteristic
elegance.
Producer: Rudolf Hartmann.
Conductor: Joseph Keilberth.

Volksoper, Vienna, 1969
The reconciliation scene in the
final tableau with Hanny Steffek
and Karlheinz Peters.
Producer: Rudolf Hartmann.
Conductor: Ernst Märzendorfer.
Sets: Max Röthlisberger.
Costumes: Charlotte Flemming.

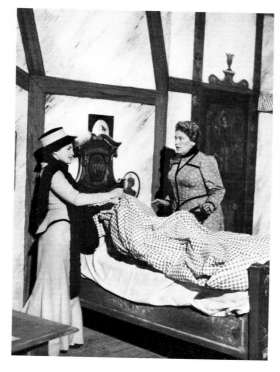

(Bavarian folkdancers); they also dance along with one of the waltzes. Peasants in traditional folk-costumes mingle colourfully with the winter-sports enthusiasts.

Frau Storch dances with the Baron, and when they've got their breath back exclaims: 'I've had enough! I've not had a good dance like that for a long time...' After a few flattering remarks from the Baron: 'Madam, you dance as lightly as a feather...' the two again dance a waltz. The curtain falls.

Christine is of course wearing a local 'dirndl' dress at the ball, which means that now she must make a very quick costume change. All her scenes require her to wear elegant and fashionable clothes.

The ball scene—with its eating, drinking and smoking, and sausages and beer consumed at long tables in comfortable, cosy corners—offers plenty of opportunity for stage business, for clever intermingling of local traditional costumes with winter-sports gear; the year is about 1907–8. Although short, this scene must, like the tobogganing scene, be so skilfully detailed that the atmosphere is convincing.

Scene IV: a furnished room in the Notary's house. Christine enters quickly with the Notary's Wife. She has been enquiring about a room for Baron Lummer and is now explaining the situation to the inquisitive Notary's Wife: 'You know, my husband, who is always at his work—he's so terribly hard-working—has al-

ways said to me, if you ever find a nice companion to go off with for a walk or some sport—this Baron Lummer, you know, is the son of old friends of my parents in Linz!'

Her torrent of words reveals that her flirtation has made her feel guilty. The Notary's Wife adopts an air of knowing complicity but is soon set to rights. Christine then gives the maid, who has accompanied her, strict instructions to use a damp cloth in all the drawers in the room 'for hygienic reasons', and before she goes admonishes the Notary's Wife, who is now insulted and unsure of herself: 'My husband always says I'm the incarnation of a doctor, and you can see how well he is. Goodbye!' The Notary's Wife is left speechless; any suspicion of possible infidelity on the part of the Hofkapellmeister's wife has been entirely quashed.

The next transformation takes place during a very short interval. The room, to be used again in the seventh scene, has to be reconstructed, in all its details, as rapidly as possible.

Scene V: the house of Frau Christine Storch. The dining-room. Christine is sitting by the lamp and is re-reading for the umpteenth time an almost finished letter to her husband. In it she tells him that she has met the Baron, but, on the principle that attack is the best form of defence, she has also written: '... a companion of rare suitability for your poor wife whom you have always neglected so much.' Satisfied with was she has written, she says: 'That's good. That's what

he should hear! The wife whom you have always neglected so much!'

For the letter scene, as for the following monologue and the scene with the cook, Strauss alternated speech with recitative accompanied by short orchestral comments. Thereby he achieved what he was aiming at: total comprehensibility of the libretto.

The Baron arrives and helps to check the household accounts. He turns down an invitation to dinner, which slightly annoys Frau Storch. She waits for a conversation to develop and, when it does not, turns to the newspaper, giving him a section of it. Then she asks about his studies and he, sensing an opportunity, says how hard-up he is. She advises him to seek a scholarship, offers her husband's aid and talks glowingly and effusively of his generosity and helpfulness. The Baron cannot get a word in edgeways and is finally bidden farewell in the most endearing fashion with an appointment for a rendezvous the next day.

Christine is alone, day-dreaming a little: 'A handsome man . . . and young, too—now here I am, alone again—my dear husband—he is so

good, so loyal—these long, lonely evenings—one can grow quite sad . . .' She sinks deeper and deeper into her own thoughts, accompanied by an aria-like interlude from the orchestra. The curtain falls.

Scene VI: the Baron's room at the Notary's house. The Baron is on his own and rather cross about his unrewarding visit to Frau Storch's house. He considers the possibility of leaving. The he reconsiders: 'Should I not perhaps make a proper declaration of love?—But then she is capable of answering with a hymn of praise to the old cripple, her husband!' He is unexpectedly disturbed by a pretty girl, a *Skihaserl* (a 'ski-bunny'), who is then equally rapidly despatched after the evening's rendezvous has been arranged. The Baron then decides to write to Christine: 'the first and last attempt', he says somewhat cynically to himself. As he is writing, the curtain falls.

Scene VII: the Storch's dining-room. Outside, snow is falling heavily.

Christine holding the Baron's letter, is almost bursting with outrage: 'He wants a thousand marks! Is he mad? What's he thinking of? A

Cuvilliéstheater, Munich, 1960 The game of *skat* is disturbed by a telegram from Frau Storch, which her husband is reading distractedly. *Left:* Hermann Prey; *at the table:* Friedrich Lenz, Max Proebstl, Karl Christian Kohn and Hans Hermann Nissen. Producer: Rudolf Hartmann. Conductor: Joseph Keilberth. Sets: Jean-Pierre Ponnelle.

Cuvilliéstheater, Munich, 1960 and Gärtnerplatz Theater, Munich, 1975

Above: Sleigh scene in two different productions. *(left:* Cuvilliéstheater, 1960; *right:* Gärtnerplatz Theater, 1975).

Below: Final tableau *(left:* Cuvilliéstheater, 1960; *right:* Gärtnerplatz Theater, 1975).

Cuvilliéstheater: Sets: Jean-Pierre Ponnelle. Producer: Rudolf Hartmann. Conductor: Joseph Keilberth. Gärtnerplatz Theater: Sets: Hermann Soherr. Producer: Peter Kertz. Conductor: Bernhard Conz.

thousand marks! . . .' The Baron then enters, curious about the effect his letter has had. First he has to let the maid dust off his shoes and then hears her say: 'That is absolutely out of the question!' The disppointed Baron is then reproached for his tactlessness, and there is embarassment on both sides. The maid brings in a letter addressed to the husband. On reading it Christine utters a piercing scream. The startled Baron then learns the contents of the letter: 'My darling, please send me two more tickets for the opera tomorrow. See you afterwards in the bar as usual. Your little Mieze [= pussy] Maier.'

Frau Storch is beside herself and the Baron disappears quickly. She writes out a telegram to

her faithless husband and orders the maid to pack everything ready for immediate departure.

The scene changes quickly to Scene VIII: the child's bedroom, lit by a single candle. Christine is sitting on the bed, crying and bemoaning her fate. The boy tries to defend his father, wanting to stay with him, until he finally bursts into tears as well and is then tucked up in bed. The boy's mother puts out the candle and leaves: 'Oh, what a poor deserted woman am I!' Here Act I ends.

This sentimental eighth scene evoked the not unjustifiable criticism that the action had taken too serious and tragic a turn. Above all the stage direction: 'She kneels, praying, at the foot of the boy's bed' was attacked as tasteless. When *Intermezzo* was put on during the Zurich *Festwochen* it was suggested that the scenes should be grouped differently and that there should be two intervals, a suggestion which Strauss was not disinclined to accept in his later years. But the alteration did not produce the improvement expected, and it was only by injecting a slightly ironic atmosphere into the scene in the boy's bedroom (the woman somewhat excited, the boy slightly cheeky and secretly amused at the whole incident) that the heavy sentimentality was overcome and the audience showed amused appreciation.

Thereafter the piece has continued to be presented in two parts. The second part contains a smaller number of scenes but despite—or perhaps because of—the fact that settings from the first part recur along with the new ones, it is no less difficult to put on. The basic concept behind the technical stage effects, no matter how varied it may be, must be to satisfy every demand that the piece makes: the constant and rapid scene changes, carefully considered division of the stage into 'flat' settings or those with 'depth', and the atmospheric lighting effects, necessary to support the comedy's elegant, cheerful undertone.

ACT II

Scene I (9th setting): the *skat* party in the Commercial Councillor's house. A comfortable, well-appointed living-room, with modern paintings and bronzes.

The skat-players are seated at the card-table and chat about the absence of Hofkapellmeister Storch. The Commercial Councillor makes plain his disapproval of the Hofkapellmeister's wife. Storch enters, enjoying the relaxed atmosphere. 'Oh, a little game of skat is such a delight, the only form of relaxation you can find after music!' He plays a game and in conversation defends his wife, who is repeatedly criticized by the Commercial Councillor.

A maid brings Storch a telegram which he reads. He is shocked by the contents, which his friends then learn: 'You know Mieze Maier. We are parted forever!' Stroh, a colleague of Storch, is familiar with the name and makes satirical, ironic comments. Storch becomes agitated and leaves the party abruptly. After an embarrassed pause the others resume their game. Curtain.

In 1925, shortly after the première in Dresden, I put on the piece for the first time in the Landestheater at Altenburg, where skat was a popular game. I had great difficulties with this scene, because I was unfamiliar with the game and wanted to stick to the given stage directions. It turned out that Strauss, a skat-player himself, had not wanted to portray the game correctly because he found this too boring. In Dresden the producer, Alois Mora, had already been compelled to make various changes to put the matter right and the publishers later issued a special sheet of corrections for the skat scene which was then sent round to the various theatres.

The characters in the skat scene are so clearly outlined that it is a pleasure for the producer to round off something that has already been so ably sketched.

Change to the Scene II (10th setting): the Notary's office.

Christine Storch is appropriately dressed for the 'serious' occasion in sombre clothes. She explains to the astonished Notary that she wants a divorce. He suspects that the young Baron is the cause, but she angrily denies this, showing him the letter to her husband. The Notary refuses to do anything before knowing all the circumstances. Frau Storch is insulted and leaves, saying: 'There are other notaries!'

After a stormy musical interlude the scene changes again. Scene III (11th setting): in the Vienna Prater; a thunderstorm.

Herr Storch, armed with an umbrella, is walking up and down, almost in despair, trying to find an explanation for all this. His colleague Stroh appears, and guiltily tells him that Mieze Maier had written to *him!* She had got the addresses wrong.

Robert is furious and orders Stroh to go to his wife and clear up the affair at once. He, for his part, must stay behind to complete a business deal.

A rapid change to Scene IV (12th setting): Christine's dressing-room, which is in the wildest disorder, with cupboard doors and drawers open.

Frau Storch and Anna are hastily packing. Frau Storch is also considering whether it was right for her to send the Baron to Vienna to make enquiries about the affair. She is almost hysterical and very trying to her two servants. A telegram arrives and she responds dismissively: 'What, again? I think this must be the tenth. I don't even open them any more.' Anna asks if she can open it and the request is granted: 'Wretched mix-up with my colleague Stroh. He arrives tomorrow with all necessary proof to correct matters. Your innocent, highly delighted

Robert.' Christine reads the telegram herself, but remains doubtful: 'Wretched mix-up—Stroh—Storch—Stroh—Storch—Anna, do you think that's possible?' While she is still considering, Kapellmeister Stroh is announced. At first, she does not want to see him, but then allows herself to be persuaded: 'All right, bring the scoundrel in!'

Change to Scene V (13th setting): the dining-room. The breakfast table is laid. It is a bright winter's morning.

The preceding orchestral interlude illustrates Herr Storch hurrying back (we can feel the relief and impatience of the husband as he leaves the train and is brought to the house in a sleigh drawn by galloping horses). His wife is about to rush towards him when she stops suddenly: 'No! no! Not so forthcoming! Let *him* dance in here! I have upset myself enough already!' She conceals her pleasure by adopting a reserved, wounded air. Her nonplussed husband, who wants to embrace her, is told off and lectured about the sufferings he has caused her, albeit now past. He repeatedly tries to treat the whole matter as a dead issue, but she remains stubborn: 'Now I've seen everything!' The dialogue continue in this manner until Herr Storch, tired from his overnight journey, finally 'explodes' and leaves in rage. His wife is somewhat taken aback by this outburst of anger and slips into a tragic mood: 'I knew it would end like this one day...!'

The Baron enters triumphantly. He is just the right kind of 'lightning conductor' that Christine needs at this moment. She makes ironic comments about his reports on Vienna and Mieze Maier, and, on hearing that her husband has returned, the Baron leaves hurriedly in confusion. The husband returns just in time to catch a glimpse of him as he departs: 'Who was that, then?' His embarrassed wife answers: 'That was the young Baron I wrote to you about.' She explains that the whole affair was harmless, finally coming to the heart of the matter: 'That is, until he asked me for a thousand marks!' Storch roars with laughter.

Nothing now stands in the way of a reconciliation, which develops with a broad, expansive aria-like duet. It ends at the breakfast table in the brilliant winter sun. In a production by Peter Kertz at the Gärtnerplatz Theatre, this 'bourgeois comedy' came to a harmonious close with the little boy coming in to join his parents.

Despite the fact that *Intermezzo* has been performed less frequently than other Strauss operas, the development of its stage-design and manner of presentation has been very clear. It has been freed from the excessive autobiographical emphasis of its early productions and has given delight to a wide public.

Die ägyptische Helena
('Helen in Egypt')

After an interval of several years Strauss and Hofmannsthal once again decided to work together. They returned to the legends of ancient Greece, which they had abandoned after *Elektra*. Initially their intention was to create a cheerful work with a gently ironic touch, but things turned out differently. In 1928, shortly before the première, Hofmannsthal wrote of the period in which the work took shape:

> Since 1920, some of the material—a group of figures—had been reflected in my imagination—glittering and intangible, like half-hidden, running water. This was precisely the story told in this work, the homeward journey of Helen and Menelaus... The night when the Greeks entered the burning city of Troy, Menelaus must have found his wife in one of the burning mansions and carried her out of the city between the collapsing walls. This woman, his beloved abducted wife, the most beautiful woman in the world, had been the cause of these terrible ten years of war, of this plain littered with dead, and of this fire. She was also Paris' widow and the friend of ten or twelve other of Priam's sons who were now all either dead or lay dying. She was thus also the widow of these ten or twelve young princes! What a situation for a husband to face!

Hofmannsthal then remarked that curiosity could also act as inspiration for a dramatic work. Greek chroniclers and poets, he pointed out, had been very reserved in telling this part of the story. They alluded to the possible intervention of higher powers. Hofmannsthal's interest in this obscure gap in the legend remained unsatisfied. His curiosity prompted him to do his own research, and to try to make mythical and poetical sense of the few accepted but confusing versions of the legend that exist. For example, according to Book IV of the *Odyssey*, Telemachus, the son of Odysseus (who had not yet returned home from the war), arrives in Sparta searching for his father. There he finds Helen and Menelaus alive and well. But how can that be on the basis of the story so far—the Trojan war with its thousands of deaths, the sack of Troy and Menelaus' vow of vengeance? This story is indeed confirmed in her own suavely sophisticated manner by Helen, who by all accounts was now more beautiful than ever.

Hofmannsthal rightly said: 'How modern this is! How close to the story-telling style of our own time! But involuntarily one asks oneself, what had happened in the meantime? What can have happened that this marriage reverted once more to a life of peace and togetherness in the sunlight?'

He referred to Euripides' play *Helen,* which contained the idea of a phantom, a second Helen—that is, an Egyptian Helen:

> But the force of my imagination could not leave the matter alone. The episode of the married partners returning together turned over and over in my mind. What awesome events could have occurred between them which ultimately led them to become reconciled? The entire story seemed so mysterious; only magic could have solved it...

Two or three years later Hofmannsthal showed Strauss the result of his work on the Helen legend. The composer, glad to be once more back in Antiquity, immediately recognized that this was material for an opera. He had at first felt that the opera would have to end after the peaceful reunion at the end of Act I, the triumph of the world's most beautiful woman. But Hofmannsthal, drawing on the version of the legend which spirits the couple away to Egypt, introduced psychological subtleties, such as Helen's willingness to commit herself and her willingness to die. The effect of this poetic elevation was to make the story more interesting, but also more complicated.

For even without Hofmannsthal's embroidery of the legend the audience would need to

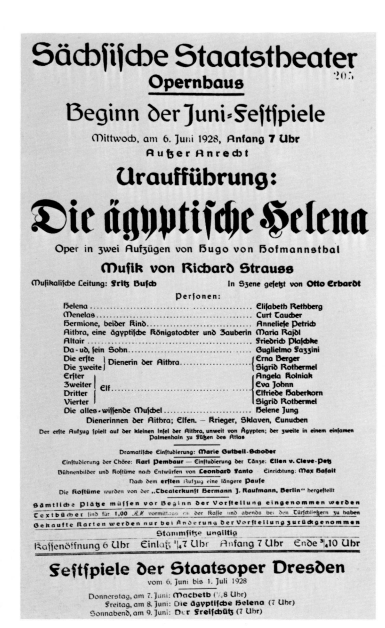

Staatsoper, Dresden, 1928
The première was held once again
in Dresden. In place of Maria
Jeritza, whom composer and librettist had planned for the title
role, Elisabeth Rethberg sang
with great success. The tenor Curt
Taucher made a good Menelaus
and Maria Rajdl an interesting,
lithe Aithra. Sets and costumes
were by Leonhard Fanto; the producer was Otto Erhardt, who
mastered the style of this difficult
opera brilliantly; the conductor
was Fritz Busch.

be acquainted with the causes and course of the
ten-year Trojan war. This is fundamentally
different from *Elektra,* where even someone unfamiliar with the fate of Agamemnon can, from
the stage action alone, immediately grasp the essence of the terrible tragedy.

So is *Die ägyptische Helena* another opera only
for a discerning audience? Perhaps. However,
the fact is that the librettist and the composer renewed their collaboration with a legend whose
ambiguity is of timeless interest, and they worked together on it harmoniously from the very
beginning.

As work progressed, the initial idea of writing
a comic opera based on Greek legend changed.
It is almost as if the demi-goddess Helen herself

had taken control and, in Hofmannsthal's words
and Strauss's music, created a luminous ode, like
the diamond-studded sea glimpsed on a sunny
day at Cape Sounion. If one lingers awhile before such a vista, or immerses oneself in the pure
light of the Hellenic world, one undoubtedly
gains a greater understanding of the opera.

Act I, above all at the close, radiates this overwhelming sense of light. Act II is not so
straightforward. The original version of this act
proved to be so perplexing that corrections were
made soon after the first performance. This became known as the 'Viennese version' of Clemens Krauss and Lothar Wallerstein. However,
even this revised version was not entirely satisfactory, so a second revision, seen at Berlin and

Munich, was made by Krauss and the present writer. This involved making some cuts and further tightening the plot; it is the version generally used today. One important feature of this version is that the first act is divided into two parts.

Hofmannsthal places the action in a chamber in the palace of Aithra, a sorceress and mistress of the sea-god Poseidon. All the dramatic events to come—a storm, the rescue of Helen from a shipwreck and so on—are related by the *alleswissende Muschel* (omniscient Sea-shell).

This presents the first major problem. Hofmannsthal described the Sea-shell—which knows everything that happens at sea—as something between a newspaper and the radio. We must remember that, at the time that the work was being written, radio was relatively new; an on-stage microphone and loudspeaker for the Sea-shell would be a new stage contrivance. However the electronic device proved unsatisfactory; it produced a strange new sound and the voice was distorted. Different solutions were sought, but the scene remained boring and largely incomprehensible until the entrance of Menelaus and Helen.

The 1935 version, seen first in Berlin and developed in Munich in 1937, transposed the opening of the act to a terrace in front of the palace, where the broad, glittering sweep of the sea could be seen. The Sea-shell at the edge of the steep coast concealed the singer (as far forward as possible), who could then sing her part clearly and without a loudspeaker.

Let us now look at the action of the opera in the Munich revised version. Light spills on to the narrow rocky terrace from the palace entrance to the right. In the centre of the set we see the giant Sea-shell, and behind it the vast ocean. Aithra comes out of the palace. She is impatient, for she is awaiting the arrival of the Ruler of the Sea for a banquet. The servants try to calm her, and so does the Sea-shell which, however, gives her nothing but oracular information. Aithra is angry, but shows interest when the Sea-shell reports the approach of a ship. She learns that a man wants to kill a woman and that the woman is the famous Helen of Troy. In order to save her, Aithra conjures up a terrible storm with the aid of the spirits of the air under her command. The ship founders; Menelaus, far from killing her, saves Helen, the

Staatsoper Dresden, 1928
Helen's chamber, presented clearly and straightforwardly. The architectural style is Baroque, with freely ornamental additions.
Producer: Otto Erhardt.
Conductor: Fritz Busch.
Sets: Leonhard Fanto.

Bayerische Staatsoper, Munich,
1928
Design by Leo Pasetti for Act I.
The open view on to the sea (so
important to the action) is very
beautiful and the Sea-shell is well
positioned against the mighty
central pillar.
Producer: Kurt Barré. Conductor:
Hans Knappertsbusch.

Bayerische Staatsoper, Munich,
1928
The first performance in Munich
came shortly after the Dresden première. The sets were by Leo Pasetti, who used his gifts as a painter
to great effect. The design shows
the Pavilion in Act II.

wife he has found again after so many years; Aithra calms the storm and withdraws again to the entrance whence she surveys the scene.

The advantages of the revised version are clear. The events at sea—the storm, the shipwreck, the movements of the group of Elves—which were previously presented as narrated details, can be followed visually. Also the explanatory comments of the Sea-shell (not transmitted through a megaphone or loudspeaker) make the whole scene, with its impressive and detailed musical structure, a captivating prologue to the events that follow.

It is clear, too, that presenting the action in the manner described makes the task of the producer more difficult. But the revisions, as also those to Act II, were necessary for the sake of comprehensibility, particularly in order to understand the psychological development of the main characters. As early as 1924 Hofmannsthal recognized the special position which *Helena* occupied in his entire œuvre. He wrote to Strauss:

Although you will not be spared here the necessity of having to search once more for a

new style (since one can never rest on one's laurels), certain features of what you have done can in future be regarded as vested and indefeasible qualities. This is the real point of artistic development and in this sense one can speak of a master above all, learning and growing through what he has learned.[1]

Strauss always paid attention to wise comments such as these. No clearer example could be given of the manner in which Hofmannsthal stimulated and encouraged his collaborator.

Hofmannsthal paid close attention to details: 'May I say this about Act II of *Helena:* Aithra's speech on page 23, "Helena, ich lache", is there for one purpose only, namely to give you the words for a small trio. If you do not intend to use it for that purpose, it is better to leave out these nine lines of Aithra's...[2]

It was probably Strauss, the practical man of the theatre, who, in another letter from the same period persuaded Hofmannsthal to reconsider the role of the Sea-shell in Act I: 'In order to clear the Sea-shell entirely of all trace of obscurity, I have hit upon the following device. The Sea-shell (an immense triton shell) lies on a stand in an alcove. Whenever the Sea-shell is supposed to sing, a mermaid with green hair and bluish cheeks appears in the veiled and sparsely lit alcove behind it, so that this vocal part comes properly and clearly out of a human mouth. The shell after all has to provide the actual exposition.[3]

This solution clearly also raised problems. The staging of the work after the première made plain the difficulties and the need for those changes which were made in the revised version.

Work on the opera progressed smoothly, with Strauss endeavouring to adhere to Hofmannsthal's stylistic advice. The composer was in the best of moods, because he had shaken off the tiresome burden of running the Vienna Opera.

But by Act II he was in difficulties. He wrote on 1 June 1925:

With *Helena* I've been stuck for a long time at the entrance of Altair and can't make any progress. I want to give the whole thing the pure sublimated style of Goethe's *Iphigenie,* and it is therefore particularly difficult to find, for this entrance of the sons of the desert, the kind of music that still sounds sufficiently characteristic to one's ears in 1925 without degenerating into the so-called realism of *Salome* or even the eccentricities of today's modernists who only hear with American (I don't want to insult the Negroes) ears.[4]

Bayerische Staatsoper, Munich, 1928
The final scene of Act I from the Munich performance already referred to, with Elisabeth Ohms (Helen) and Fritz Fitzau (Menelaus).
Producer: Kurt Barré. Conductor: Hans Knappertsbusch. Sets: Leo Pasetti.

Hofmannsthal replied: 'Your present struggles with *Helena* I understand very well, only too well. For each time it is the unity of style which is at stake.'[5] He then recalled interruptions that had occurred during the composition of earlier works: 'Twice in the course of your composing career you have come to such a deadlock at the entrance of a new character that you almost abandoned the work: the first time before the arrival of Clytaemnestra [in *Elektra*], the other time over Bacchus [in *Ariadne*]—strange that you should have forgotten this.'[6]

He went on to provide some further guidance: 'Only let us have none of the cheap "orient"-effects of present-day music. I have not introduced a single geographic conception which does not belong to ancient Greece! Atlas, Egypt, Libya—they are all mentioned in Pindar and Aeschylus.'[7]

Hofmannsthal then suggested possible cuts in Act I, the draft of which was already finished. The cuts were gratefully accepted by Strauss. But in regard to Act II he remained sceptical and bided his time. The objections which he raised with Hofmannsthal elicited the following reply from the poet, contrasting *Helena* with *Elektra*—and it would be hard to imagine a more telling elucidation:

The action of *Elektra* leads darkly and massively up to terrible murder; how could that be reconciled with this ethereal, fairy-tale-like first act, which barely touches upon the dark side, and takes its origin from an almost comic intrigue? If *Elektra* might be compared to a taut chain of heavy, massive iron links, *Helena* is a festoon of interlaced lyrical wreaths... and stylistically it has had the result that not a single prose scene remains in Act II. The prose scenes, by interrupting the flow of the music, had a retarding effect.'[8]

Hofmannsthal repeatedly sought to make Strauss keep to the lofty, hymn-like style, which he believed to be appropriate. I first understood how difficult this must have been when I had to produce the work for the first time after its première and thus encountered Act II in its original form. I still remember clearly the qualms I had when Altair and his entourage entered, and during the following scene with the Eunuchs before the feast of the desert prince. It was impossible to avoid seeing embarrassing parallels with Karl May* and everything associated with the hymn-like quality of Act I seemed to have been eclipsed. Later many of the unimportant secondary characters were eliminated from the action, which in the end produced a tighter effect and greater clarity. None the less many practical experiments were needed before the work gained even a degree of the stylistic unity which mattered so much to Strauss.

The Egyptian adventure (scene 2) begins with the entrance of the two main characters, Helen and Menelaus. Helen, who has just been saved from drowning, is immediately in control of the situation—she knows that her husband wants to kill her; however, her first concern is with her hair, which she rearranges in front of a mirror. Menelaus is confused; he sees the shining palace; Helen invites him to be seated at table where a meal has been laid; he refuses, trying to compose himself and to resist her air of superiority. Aithra observes both of them and intervenes when Helen is threatened with serious danger. She summons her Elves of the moon, and the noise of a battle distracts Menelaus. He runs after an apparition of the dead Paris: 'Do the dead walk here, calling out and

---

* German author of Wild West stories particularly popular with children. Many of his stories have been filmed and are still performed regularly in an open-air setting with Wild West trappings: horses, coaches, etc.—*Translator's note.*

Staatsoper, Hamburg, 1928 ▷
The Hamburg Opera was also among the first theatres to put on this work. Three famous names can be found in the cast: Maria Hussa (Helen), Gunnar Graarud (Menelaus) and Rudolf Bockelmann (Altair).
Producer: Leopold Sachse (the director-general of the theatre). Conductor: Egon Pollak. Sets and costumes: Willy Davidson.

Salzburg Festival, 1933 ▷▷
The first re-working of the piece by Lothar Wallerstein and Clemens Krauss, who were producer and conductor at the Salzburg Festival performance of 1933, was known as the 'Vienna version'. Sets and costumes were designed by Alfred Roller and his assistant Robert Kautsky. The cast, which included the best names from the opera world of the day, helped ensure that the production was a major success.

Bayerische Staatsoper, Munich, 1928
Leo Pasetti's design for Aithra's costume.

seeking to be struck down again?' He storms out after the apparition and Aithra reveals herself to Helen (scene 3): 'You are in my house, Helen, and I will save you. I am your friend.' She restores Helen to her full beauty and has her servants take her into the palace. Menelaus returns, still deeply confused and with many psychological blocks, as we call them today. He imagines that he has just killed Paris and Helen; the Elves laugh mockingly. Aithra approaches him, and with the help of the servant girls hands him a drink of forgetfulness brewed from lotus seeds. With this she begins her great deception of Menelaus. She tells him that the gods sent an airy spirit, which resembled Helen, to Troy, while the real Helen, his wife, was innocent, having been held for nine years in a fortress on the distant slopes of Mount Atlas. The sorceress has increasing success in fooling the doubting husband, who then follows her into the palace to find his wife.

The stage darkens; the two characters slowly depart; a new scene begins: with increasing radiance, magic rays of light fall on the bed where Helen rests, revealing her dream-like beauty.

The music for this transformation, which rises to the highest fortissimo, is of sufficient length for the transformation to be completed by the time the E major pianissimo is reached. The technical aids that can be used are either a turn-table or—more suitable here—a mobile platform which can be manoeuvred in from the side. The important point is to make the transformation truly magical. The lighting which accompanies the transformation plays a central role; and nothing must be allowed to distract attention from Menelaus as his hesitant steps, his confused astonishment, gradually lead him into the situation conjured up by Aithra.

Helen awakes; in whispers, Aithra quickly tells her of the deception of Menelaus: 'On the slopes of Atlas stands a fortress, there she lay and slept.' Menelaus does not dare embrace the woman who is now offering herself to him. She tries in vain to entice him and asks Aithra to spirit them away to a place where no one knows the name of Troy. The sorceress acts swiftly: 'At the foot of Mount Atlas lies an oasis, there I shall erect a magic pavilion for you.' Menelaus' half-conscious resistance disappears; he thinks of his daughter Hermione, and comes to Helen's arms.

Aithra spreads her dark magic cloak and the couple disappear from sight. This final sequence shortly before the close of the act is like a new scene which develops gradually from the hymn-like vocal texture. The cloak must unfold into a gigantic expanse, and its semi-transparency must convince the audience of its lightness. This is no 'flying Persian carpet' but a great stage spectacle like the storm or the transformation of Helen's chamber at the beginning.

A note here for the producer: during the expansive lilting cantilenas the singers may adopt familiar empty operatic gestures. I am always concerned about this. This is a danger in all arias, of course, since after a while the meaningless waving of hands can become extremely boring. The singers must therefore find a measured style which matches Strauss's music and Hofmannsthal's poetry, although this is certainly not easy. The producer must take particular care in positioning the accompanying groups of Elves, spirits and servants clearly and distinctively. The complicated stage sequences inevitably make great demands on the stage-hands.

Act II leads us into a bright desert landscape, to the 'magical pavilion' at the foot af Mount Atlas created by Aithra. Helen recalls the previous evening's passion in a song of triumph and gratitude. Menelaus lies sleeping at her feet: 'Under my wing he fell asleep, as my treasure I guard him, sparkling in the golden pavilion, as my treasure above the lustrous world.' With these words the radiant Helen expresses her happiness, believing that she is now free of all problems.

Struggling with dim memories, Menelaus awakes; he resists Helen, whom he believes to be only a strange magical figure. Helen attempts to draw him to her, and searches in the chest for the potion which Aithra had given her. The crooked dagger which once belonged to Paris falls at Menelaus' feet, and he at once recalls—or so he believes—having killed Helen. He turns her away from him: 'Siren of the air, do not come near me! Do not stretch out your arm! Away! He who encounters anything so terrible must resist the temptation to tangle with it.'

Helen angrily realizes the imperfections of the spell cast by Aithra, throws away the potion, and decides to attempt to overcome Menelaus' resistance by confronting him with the truth.

A desert prince, Altair, approaches in procession and interrupts Helen and Menelaus. Helen first believes that they are being attacked and calls Menelaus to her side to protect her. Then she realizes that the prince is paying her homage, with oriental magnificence and costly presents. The prince is immediately dazzled by Helen's

Salzburg Festival, 1933
Helen (Viorica Ursuleac) on her couch at the end of Act I.
Producer: Lothar Wallerstein.
Conductor: Clemens Krauss. Sets and costumes: Alfred Roller and Robert Kautsky.

Staatsoper, Berlin, 1935
Design by Ludwig Sievert for Act I, which for this performance was divided into two scenes (see text). The unobscured view to the sea allowed the storm and the sinking of the ship to be shown.
Producer: Rudolf Hartmann.
Conductor: Clemens Krauss.

Staatsoper, Berlin, 1935
From the same performance: the pavilion in Act II, very sketchy and unrealistic.
Producer: Rudolf Hartmann.
Conductor: Clemens Krauss.
Sets: Ludwig Sievert.

173

beauty and desires her. His young son, Da-ud, is equally captivated by the irresistible charm of 'the most beautiful woman in the world'. Menelaus is painfully reminded of Troy, of Priam's sons, of Paris. He sets off on a gazelle hunt, using weapons given him by Altair and accompanied by Da-ud, who prior to the hunt has dedicated his young life to Helen and is consumed by jealousy of Menelaus. The encounter with the Arab prince and his family helps Menelaus to solve his problems not by discussion but by working them out in action. Helen is troubled because she is unable to restrain her husband, who—under the influence of Aithra's stupefying potion—is drifting back and forth between his real and imaginary memories.

Aithra hurries in, accompanied by her servants. She wants to prevent the potion of recollection—which is also hidden in the chest—from being given to Menelaus because it could endanger Helen. But Helen, sure of the course she must take, herself takes the fateful vial from the trunk. She wants to know the truth, and if death is to be her fate, seeks it at Menelaus' hand.

Altair, the desert prince, interrupts the scene. He has returned secretly to fetch Helen for himself. The servant girls report on the progress of the hunt, which they are observing. With horror they relate that a fight has suddenly broken out between Menelaus and Da-ud, and that Da-ud has been killed. Altair ignores everything and says to Helen: 'Tonight I shall prepare a feast for us two and for no other!' He roughly

tries to embrace her, but is prevented from doing so by the arrival of the procession of mourners with the body of Da-ud.

Helen takes the sword which killed Da-ud from Menelaus, who stands in front of the dead man trying to clear his thoughts from the confused memories which fill his mind. Altair looks on, planning an attack, and then stealthily withdraws. Da-ud is carried off and Menelaus, still believing he has killed Helen, determines to follow her into death. For her part, Helen makes a major decision and offers him the death potion he desires: 'Yes, may it bring enlightenment to both you and me.' Menelaus goes with his slaves into the pavilion to dress 'for the last journey'.

Then, despite Aithra's warning that it will bring about her death, Helen and the servant girls solemnly prepare the potion of recollection which will lift Menelaus out of his confusion; with determination and courage she follows the path she has chosen. Menelaus returns and drinks the potion she hands him, believing it to be the death potion—and in a flash remembers everything. He reaches for his sword: 'Who is that before me?' He wants to kill her, and Helen says, smiling: 'Aithra! He is going to kill me!'

But Aithra's magical powers are exhausted and she calls on the god Poseidon, to assist her: 'Helen, live! They are bringing your child!' These words penetrate to the deepest layer of Menelaus' consciousness. He lowers his sword: 'Dead yet alive! Alive yet dead! I see you as no mortal man ever saw his wife!'

Bayerische Staatsoper, Munich, 1964
Set by Helmut Jürgens for Act I. The experience gained from previous productions was put to good use by the designer and producer. The style of the production aimed at a freer development of the drama.
Helen: Inge Borkh, a strong and personal interpretation. Menelaus: Fritz Uhl, who brought austere, convincing expression to the part. Producer: Rudolf Hartmann. Conductor: Joseph Keilberth.

With an embrace and in hymn-like phrases Helen and Menelaus forgive one another and are reunited in admiration and newly awakened love. Aithra is happy and freed from all anxieties. Then, in a treacherous attack, Altair and his slaves seize the newly reunited couple and threaten to have Menelaus killed. Aithra has to intervene one last time. Armed warriors sent by Poseidon are outside the pavilion. Altair is disarmed and taken prisoner. Now Aithra leads into the triumphant finale: 'Helen! See, they bring your child!' Hermione, her daughter, who is still a child, turns to Menelaus: 'Father, where is my beautiful mother?' He takes her to Helen: 'Oh, my lucky child, what a mother, indeed, do I restore to you!'

The scene concludes with a prayer-like invocation sung in unison by Helen and Menelaus:

Gewogene Lüfte führt uns zurück,
heiliger Sterne segnende Schar!
Hohen Palastes dauerndes Tor
öffne sich tönend dem ewigen Paar!

('May favourable winds and benedictory hosts of holy stars lead us back; may the stout portal of the Great Palace resound as it opens before the eternal couple.')

Modern taste allows us to dispense with the embellishments originally demanded by the closing scene, such as white horses. These were splendid, but also distracting. They did nothing to help the audience get the real point of the work. In this closing scene, Hofmannsthal's fertile imagination leant too much towards 'Baroque' theatre. This has had the effect of making it extraordinarily difficult to give proper emphasis to the opera's spiritual content and to make it comprehensible in its Classical context. In spite of the various attempts made by producers to solve the problems of *Die ägyptische Helena,* a satisfactory solution has so far been elusive and one is still searching for a view of the opera that might hope to evoke the magnificent vista from Cape Sounion over the bright expanse of the Aegean.

Arabella

'Well, have you any idea who we really are?...' asks the clever, pretty Arabella of the man who wishes to marry her. She is the elder daughter of the former cavalry officer, Count Waldner, and by means of marriage to a rich man she is aiming to rescue the family from their present financial ruin. This is the situation in which we first meet the group of characters conceived by Hofmannsthal.

Strauss had been repeatedly asking him for a libretto similar to *Der Rosenkavalier,* a comic opera which would give him the chance to make use of the riches which his musical genius still had to offer in this field. The poet at first delayed, but in 1927 (on 1 October), after years of deliberation and prompting on Strauss's part, Hofmannsthal put forward a dramatic sketch, set around 1860, *Der Fiaker als Graf* ('The Coachman Count') as a possible basis for such an enterprise. In November 1927 he wrote: 'The characters of this new comedy for music are cutting their capers under my very nose, almost too obtrusively. The spirits which I summoned for your sake now refuse to leave me alone.'[1]

The process of creation had begun. At first Strauss was very critical, niggling about the characters (Arabella, Mandryka) and repeatedly making counter-proposals, with the result that Hofmannsthal had to be both patient and ingenious in commending his ideas—which he believed in passionately—to the composer.

Hofmannsthal had such a vivid conception of his characters that he even began to put forward suggestions about casting famous singers in the various roles. As a connoisseur of fashion, he also took an interest in the costumes at this early stage. (Strauss and he were continuously interrupted by anxiety about the final casting for the role of Helen; they wanted Maria Jeritza, the *prima donna assoluta* who sang the first Ariadne, but ultimately failed to secure her.)

At first Strauss was not entirely happy with the figure of Arabella. In December 1927 Hof-

mannsthal described her thus: 'The main character is a female one: Arabella, the elder of two sisters... this time she is not a woman but a young girl, a thoroughly mature, wide-awake young girl, conscious of her strength and of the hazards she runs... an entirely modern character...'[2]

Strauss wanted to bring the mother, Adelaide, more into the foreground, but Hofmannsthal remained very firm: 'The mother is definitely still a young and very pretty woman, and I had already thought of her as a little bit in love with her daughter's admirers herself... but to involve her in serious scenes of love and resignation, to make her a sort of a sham Marschallin, to introduce a kind of 'quotation' of the Marschallin's fate—no, for God's sake not that...'[3]

Hofmannsthal energetically rejected Strauss's suggestions on this point. He also declared the *Fiakerball* ('Coachmen's Ball') in Act II to be of secondary importance, more a background feature, and continued: '... this touch of the ballroom atmosphere, and at the same time of an animated, pulsating crowd, all that matters is this flash of a dance rhythm now and then, while the foreground is entirely given over to *parlando* and to sentimental-lyrical mood. The kind of dances people would in fact have danced around 1860 were waltzes, waltzes above all...'[4]

This indicated the direction of the music to Strauss, but it created problems for staging. Even today Act II sometimes does not quite come off. We will return to this problem in discussing the opera's production.

In the summer of 1928 Strauss was impatiently asking for information about Act II, and was also trying to gain an overall impression of the work. He was not fully satisfied with Act I either: 'At present I can't really do very much with that somewhat disjointed first act, especially as the title part is still rather sketchily treated...'[5]

This engraving by Rudolf von Alt of St. Stephan's Cathedral evokes the atmosphere of nineteenth-century Vienna, the world of *Arabella.*

However, intensive cooperation led to a splendidly cohesive Act I, which made Strauss very happy. Creative understanding developed and ripened between composer and librettist. Neither of them could have known that *Arabella* would be their last joint project. Yet a letter from Strauss on 3 July 1928 seems to indicate a sense of premonition: '... I find we understand each other better every year. A pity such good, continuous progress towards perfection must come to an end some day...'[6]

Strauss now wanted to do some intensive work on the figure of Mandryka, whose importance for the style of the whole work had been stressed by Hofmannsthal.

Now certain of Strauss's understanding, Hofmannsthal was overjoyed and again drew a comparison with *Der Rosenkavalier:*

Vienna under Maria Theresa—and the Vienna of 1866!... the atmosphere of *Arabella*, quite close to our own time as it is, is more ordinary... these figures are tangled up with a rather vulgar and dubious Vienna... For Mandryka above all this pleasure-seeking, frivolous Vienna, where everybody lives on tick, is the foil; he is steeped in his world of unspoilt villages, his oak forests untouched by axe, his ancient folksongs. With him the wide open spaces of the vast half-Slav Austria enter Viennese comedy, carrying into it a breath of totally different fresh air; that is why I was so delighted when, with your sure artistic instinct, you saw the figure of Mandryka as the key to the whole piece...[7]

The two collaborators became increasingly immersed in the draft and did not permit other matters to distract them. They had established a happy, close intellectual rapport of a kind they had seldom experienced before. It was based on honesty, criticism and self-awareness. In view of Hofmannsthal's early death, and with the hindsight of the intervening decades, a letter he wrote to Strauss on 26 July 1928 takes on the quality of an almost premonitory summation of their artistic relationship:

Let me now try and say something in all modesty. One of the strong points of your judgment about my writing and one reason why I can always take this judgment most seriously is that you are an artist but obviously not a poet, not a librettist; thus you are free in the most naive way from all the literary prejudices, preferences, fashions and so on of our time. I, in turn, am a non-musician and a stranger to musical tastes and education, but at the same time almost frighteningly free from ephemeral judgments, scales of value

Sächsische Staatstheater
Opernhaus

24?

Sonnabend, am 1. Juli 1933

Anfang 7 Uhr

Außer Anrecht

Uraufführung

Arabella

Lyrische Komödie in drei Aufzügen von **Hugo v. Hofmannsthal**

Musik von **Richard Strauß**

Musikalische Leitung: **Clemens Krauss** a. G.　　　　　Inszenierung: **Josef Gielen**

Künstlerischer Beirat für Regie und Vortrag: **Eva Plaschke-von der Osten**

Personen:

Graf Waldner, Rittmeister a. D.	Friedrich Plaschke
Adelaide, seine Frau	Camilla Kallab
Arabella ⎱ ihre Töchter	Viorica Ursuleac
Zdenka ⎰	Margit Bokor
Mandryka	Alfred Jerger a. G.
Matteo, Jäger-Offizier	Martin Kremer
Graf Elemer ⎱	Karl Albrecht Streib
Graf Dominik ⎰ Verehrer der Arabella	Kurt Böhme
Graf Lamoral ⎰	Arno Schellenberg
Die Fiakermilli	Ellice Illiard
Eine Kartenschlägerin	Jessyka Koettrik
Welko, Leibhusar des Mandryka	Robert Büssel
Djura ⎱ Diener des Mandryka	Rudolf Schmalnauer
Jankel ⎰	Horst Falke
Ein Zimmerkellner	Ludwig Eybisch

Begleiterin der Arabella. Drei Spieler. Ein Arzt. Groom. Fiaker. Hotelgäste. Kellner.
Ballgäste: Hilde Schlieben, Gino Neppach, Peter Pawlinin, Damen und Herren der Tanzgruppe

Ort: Wien — Zeit: 1869

I. Akt: Salon in einem Wiener Stadthotel
II. Akt: Ein öffentlicher Ballsaal
III. Akt: Offener Raum mit Stiegenhaus im Hotel

Chöre: **Karl Maria Pembaur**

Dekorative Ausstattung: **Leonhard Fanto** und **Johannes Rothenberger**

Trachten: **Leonhard Fanto**. — Technische Einrichtung: **Georg Brandt**

Längere Pause nach dem zweiten Aufzug

Sämtliche Plätze müssen vor Beginn der Vorstellung eingenommen werden
Textbücher sind für 1,00 ℛℳ vormittags an der Kasse und abends bei den Türschließern zu haben
Gekaufte Karten werden nur bei Änderung der Vorstellung zurückgenommen

Kassenöffnung 6 Uhr　Einlaß 6¼ Uhr　Anfang 7 Uhr　Ende geg. 10¼ Uhr

Staatsoper, Dresden, 1933
The stormy history of the events leading up to the première is recorded in the text. After the departure of Fritz Busch, Clemens Krauss was brought in from Vienna to conduct the first night. With him came Viorica Ursuleac (Arabella) and Alfred Jerger (Mandryka), both of whom scored major successes. Leonhard Fanto designed the sets, together with Johannes Rothenberger; Josef Gielen was the producer and showed himself to be a shrewd delineator of character.

etc. My appreciation of music might almost be called barbaric, but still, with great attentiveness and with the sensitivity of an artist, I listen and try to get right inside all music presented to my ears by an orchestra, by a piano or by a gramophone, whether Beethoven or Lehár, a scene from Verdi or one of yours, gipsy music or *L'Après-midi d'un Faune* ... And somehow ... I do know what it is all about ...'[8]

Their mutual candour was very valuable for the work in progress. Strauss made many suggestions, prodding Hofmannsthal on; Hofmannsthal responded but was not afraid to defend and explain his text. This process went on through the summer. On 6 July 1929 Strauss laid down the endings of the various acts:

'1st Curtain: Arabella.
2nd Curtain: Mandryka.
3rd Curtain: Arabella—Mandryka.'[9]

Hofmannsthal followed these suggestions, and then on 10 July 1929 wrote a short, heartfelt letter to Strauss—his last, for on 15 July he suffered a stroke and died. He never received Strauss's telegram of the 14th: 'First act excellent. Many thanks and congratulations. Devotedly Yours, Dr. Richard Strauss.'[10]

Act I begins with the cheerful sound of sleigh bells; the vitality and somewhat frivolous atmosphere of the Vienna of 1860 is charmingly evoked, not least by the pretty Countess Arabella.

We are in the drawing-room of the Count's suite in one of the city's elegant hotels; Count Waldner, with his wife and two daughters, knows how to put on appearances, even though he cannot really afford to; as a retired cavalry officer and passionate gambler, he has lost everything. But he is not a con man, and does not wish to cheat and deceive—it is simply that he consistently believes in a miraculous transformation of his fortunes in the same way that his still attractive wife, Countess Adelaide, bases her own quest for happiness on the prophecies of a *very* famous fortune-teller.

The first scene opens with a delightful ironic joke. The fortune-teller is sipping coffee with the impatient Countess; the cards are laid out on the table before them. The fortune-teller already knows a good deal about her client and begins her act with a well-tried routine: 'The blonde girl ... the great forest ... a letter ... a complication because of another admirer ... further financial losses because of your father's card-playing, etc., etc.' The Countess is fascinated, and by her reactions provides the necessary cues for the fortune-teller to continue, including the admission that the boy Zdenko, present in the room, is really a girl, the sister of the much-admired Arabella. The fortune-teller is now well away and gives her fantasy free rein; the Countess promises her the very last piece of jewellery she possesses if the rich admirer from afar really appears and everything does come true.

And indeed it *does*. But initially Zdenka, the younger sister, is left behind alone with all the unpaid bills and the final demands. She is the only one in the family who is worried about the situation; she is troubled by the ever-growing debts, by Arabella's indecisiveness, and by her own passionate love for Matteo, a young officer in the Rifles. Matteo persists in trying to court Arabella, who, in turn, feels sorry for him and wants to help him. Forging her sister's handwriting, Zdenka sends love letters to Matteo as if they were from Arabella. She daily accepts flowers from him on her sister's behalf, and the love-lorn officer moves into the same hotel just to be close to Arabella. He is not well off and has

to live on his army pay. He is consumed with jealousy of Arabella's three permanent admirers, the three young Counts with whom the beautiful, spoilt girl flirts, revelling in the expensive presents they send her. But what about marriage? Which one should she choose? Matteo, whom she thought she once loved, is now *passé*, an affair of the past, and his constant presence is beginning to get on her nerves. She has no idea about the correspondence being carried on by her younger sister.

Matteo enters the Count's drawing-room quickly and secretly: he finds Zdenka alone, demands a new letter from Arabella, threatens suicide and disappears again. Zdenka is at her wits' end with worry. By nature she is highly-strung (a trait inherited from her mother), and searches desperately for a solution.

Then, after a skilful and tense build-up, Arabella enters. She has just come back from a walk. She takes her leave of her chaperone (a poor elderly creature who has been earning herself—not without difficulty—a few guilders) and turns to Zdenka.

Staatsoper, Dresden, 1933
Three further designs for Dresden by Adolf Mahnke. As always, the work by this designer was well suited to the requirements of the piece. The solution adopted for Act II is particularly stylish, and an appropriate venue for intimate personal encounters. The ball can be glimpsed in the background, through the glass doors, but it never intrudes or distracts.
Act III, with its staircase, is less happy; none the less, it has a great deal of atmosphere. These designs were apparently made at about the time of the première, but it is not certain whether or not they were actually used.

Act I.

Act II.

Act III.

The two sisters enjoy a warm and open relationship with one another, despite their very different natures, and so Arabella freely tells Zdenka what she thinks of each of her admirers. Her father has set *Faschingsdienstag* (Shrove Tuesday) as the deadline of his ultimatum: by then she must decide which of her admirers she will marry. Most probably she will choose the Hungarian Count Elemer who would best provide for her. It would not be a marriage of love. But she admits to Zdenka a secret yearning, a young girl's dream: *'Der Richtige* (the right one)—if there is such a man for me in this world—will one day stand before me, and will

Nationaltheater, Mannheim, 1933
Design for Act II by Eduard Löffler. It has little ballroom atmosphere and hardly any sense of intimacy for the dialogue scenes, so
it presents a difficult problem for
the producer.
Producer: Richard Hein.
Conductor: Philipp Wüst.

Nationaltheater, Mannheim, 1933
Design for Act III by Eduard
Löffler. It presents too few alternatives for the different scenes,
which take place almost simultaneously, and restricts the producer's freedom.

Opernhaus, Cologne, 1934
Design for Act III by Otto Reigbert. The steep staircase hardly helps Arabella's important final entrance. All in all the set has a cramped appearance, but it does contain one or two well-characterized details.
Producer: Walter Felsenstein.
Conductor: Fritz Zaun.

look at me and I will look at him, and there will be no doubt and no questions, and I will be happy and obedient as a child!'

Zdenka listens enraptured to the romantic notions of her sister, who then tells her of whom she had seen that very morning: 'You see, there was a strange man... tall, in a fur travelling-coat. And behind him there was a hussar—just a stranger from Hungary perhaps, or from Wallachia.' Arabella would like flowers from him. Zdenka is horrified; she gives her sister the bouquet from Matteo, but is brushed aside.

The Hungarian Count Elemer, who looks not unlike the man she met that morning, arrives to take Arabella out for the sleigh ride in the Prater which they had arranged earlier. He presses his suit forcefully, aware of the fateful nature of the ball to be held that evening. 'And this evening at the Coachmen's Ball I shall be your master!' Arabella deflects his passion and sends him away, but says she will be down in half an hour because she loves driving in the sleigh with beautiful horses. She looks forward to the trip with child-like delight.

Zdenka re-enters and is told of the sleigh ride. She is to accompany her sister as groom. Then from the window Arabella catches sight of the stranger who has so captivated her imagination.

He is standing in the street in front of the house... and then moves on.

The two sisters' parents arrive at the same time: the mother emerges from her room after the fortune-telling session, and the father returns to the house in the foulest of tempers.

The two girls leave. Count Waldner tells his wife of his latest gambling losses and explains that he has written in vain to several regimental comrades asking for money: 'Not a reply from one of them, that is a hard blow.' He recalls with a smile the tale of an eccentric old Croesus he'd once known who would freely squander his money—gloriously and senselessly—when it was matter of a pretty girl. He had written to him too. '... I appealed to his magnanimity and enclosed a picture of Bella—in the steel-blue dress with swans' down trimming. I thought: perhaps he will come here, fool that he is, and marry the girl! Countess Adelaide is horrified at the idea (an old man!) but the father states categorically that he can think of no other solution. Her suggestions about what to do, which smack suspiciously of work, he rejects decisively, including her final, prophetic comment: 'Has there never yet been a marriage for love in the highest of noble houses?'—a remark which he contemptuously brushes aside. Left alone he peruses several letters and final demands: 'I am not in a position to wait any longer! ... I shall have to turn to the courts...'

Feeling deeply sorry for his wife and his daughters, he rings for room service and orders a cognac, only to be told by the waiter that nothing more is to be served to Room 8 until outstanding bills have been paid. This news is a severe shock and when the waiter announces that he has a visitor, Waldner denies that he is in, fearing that it must be a creditor. He then takes a closer look at the visitor's card and discovers the name Mandryka. The waiter returns to say 'The gentleman urgently requests', and immediately behind him Count Mandryka enters, followed by his hussar valet. Waldner, preparing to give a hearty welcome to this old regimental comrade, instead sees a young man before him whom he does not know. He turns out to be the nephew of Uncle Mandryka, who in the meantime had died. In the course of the conversation which ensues, Mandryka albeit hesitantly, tells of his inherited wealth, of a hunting accident and of the fact that he (instead of the uncle) has fallen in love with Arabella's picture.

And now, amazingly—for the cards did not lie—he asks for the hand of the young girl and shows the stunned Count the large amount of money he has obtained from the sale of a wood, for he wants to have unlimited funds available for the bridal procession into the Imperial City of Vienna. Rightly interpreting the avaricious look in Waldner's eye, the young Count provides him with several thousand-guilder notes—but of course the seasoned poker-player Waldner tries to bluff: '... it's just that my banker is travelling; I will return it to you by this evening at the latest'. He accepts the notes nevertheless and is almost beside himself when the suitor withdraws. He must get to the gaming tables immediately; he leaves the disconcerted Zdenka behind, and repeating Mandryka's generous phrase *Teschek* [old chap] help yourself', he races from the room. Zdenka is again disturbed by Matteo, who has returned for Arabella's letter. She promises to give it to him that evening and arranges to meet the lieutenant at the Coachmen's Ball, the climax of Fasching (Carnival).

Arabella enters, dressed for the sleigh ride, and tells Zdenka to hurry; although Zdenka is furious that she has to go, she leaves to change. Arabella once more reconsiders her position. She just cannot imagine herself as Countess Elemer; the stranger has turned her head completely. But in anticipation of the ball she cheers up; Zdenka comes back dressed as a groom and goes off with her sister for the sleigh ride. This concludes Act

I, on which one important production comment must be made.

The hotel is not a cheap guest-house of doubtful repute but one of the decent old family hotels. It is therefore mistaken to turn it into a dubious establishment where rooms can be 'rented by the hour' and so forth. Matteo, the serving officer, lives there; the three Counts visit Arabella there; and the seasoned gambler Waldner is well aware what he must do to keep appearances, even though he is unable to pay the hotel bill or to find the means for his daughters' fashionable dresses. He plays for high stakes and for that he needs a luxurious setting. Besides, Count Mandryka, somewhat suspicious by nature, would never visit the woman of his choice in a house of doubtful reputation.

Act II, with its difficult dramatic construction, presents the Shrove Tuesday Coachmen's Ball held each year for the coachmen's best clients, notably officers and the aristocracy. But it is a popular social function, which one cannot attend in uniform. That is important for Matteo, who along with his fellow officers has to wear evening dress. The officers mingle with the good-humoured coachmen and their wives and daughters, as well as with aristocratic families who are 'doing the coachmen the honour'. Fiakermilli (Coach-girl Milli) was at one time intended to be more than just a passing character, and was based on a real historical Viennese figure. Unfortunately Hofmannsthal did not make her a significant counterpart to Arabella, no matter how much Strauss pressed for such dramatic conflicts in the opera. Hofmannsthal's death prevented them from undertaking a joint revision, as they had of Act I. (Act III above all suffered from this fact.) The weak ending of Act II was one of the main reasons for fusing the second and third acts, a point we shall return to later.

With the exception of two chorus appearances, the scenes in the *Fiakerball* act are restricted to very few characters; the ball itself remains a backdrop; the waltz music is in the foreground only for short periods; everything is focussed on the first meeting of Arabella and Mandryka.

Arabella's parents present her to her suitor and retire. The intensity of feeling on both sides is clearly evident in their first conversation, which begins hesitantly and develops awkwardly. The duet ends with their betrothal and first shy kiss. Arabella requests just one more hour of freedom to take leave of her youth—that is, to bid farewell to her three fond admirers and to dance one last waltz. Mandryka agrees but stays

Bayerische Staatsoper, Munich, 1943
Strauss greets his leading lady, Viorica Ursuleac, on stage.

at the ball, already assuming his role as protector.

With the entrance of the spirited Fiakermilli, the three counts and other groups, the ball moves into the foreground for the first time. As the 'Coachmen's Herald', Milli declares Arabella to be Queen of the Ball with a polka-like couplet and then, with a yodel, leads the assembled company into a waltz, with Arabella and her partner (wherever possible, one of the three counts) taking the lead. Mandryka does not take part; Countess Adelaide appears, impatient and hopeful, and is overjoyed when Mandryka confirms the engagement. At the same time Matteo and Zdenka arrive on the scene. Matteo is embittered and upset: 'How she forgets me in the ecstasy of her beauty!' Zdenka is anxious and tries to calm him. These two scenes, which are played simultaneously, are each of the greatest importance and they must both be fully understood; also they must be played separately in such a way that the scene with Zdenka and Matteo cannot be seen by the Countess. At Mandryka's news, the Countess is overcome with joy: '... my son, my friend', and goes to fetch her husband. Matteo and Zdenka leave quickly. Count Waldner, who has been fetched from the card-table, is in radiant mood as he embraces his future son-in-law and Mandryka orders a celebratory supper.

Waldner, feverish to continue his gambling, hurries back to the cards.

Challenged by Mandryka, Adelaide now revels in being able to enjoy things to the full again after such a long time. The bridegroom packs off his servants with various orders, and then, as the waltz music rises in intensity, walks—or dances—with the overjoyed Countess into the ballroom. At the same time Arabella dances in with Count Dominik on the other side of the stage. It is a nice effect when for at least a few bars mother and daughter are seen to be in the same lively mood. Arabella takes her leave of Dominik, her childhood friend and first admirer: 'But the right man for you, that was not I; and you were not the right one for me...' Dominik, perturbed, has to leave because the rumbustious Count Elemer begins his conversation with his beloved Arabella. She has shown a sympathetic attitude towards him on many occasions, and he would have been the solution, if it were not for... Elemer senses the situation immediately and is insanely jealous: 'Become my wife! Who is there in the world who can prevent it!' But his words are no longer of any avail, and he leaves angrily. Then comes the third admirer, Lamoral, the youngest of the three. His half-shy, sentimental admiration for her has gained him a warm sisterly affection in

Städtische Bühnen, Nuremberg, 1952
A scene from Act II. A simple and appropriate solution. The details are well characterized.
Producer: Rudolf Hartmann.
Conductor: Alfons Dressel.
Sets: Max Röthlisberger.
Costumes: Margret Kaulbach.

Arabella's heart. As a farewell token he receives a kiss and it is with him that Arabella dances the last great waltz of her youth.

Here the ball can once again flood into the foreground (a musical repetition became an integral part of the Munich version). Into the finale come Mandryka's servants to lay the table for supper, and with them the hotel waiters.

Matteo and Zdenka have observed Arabella's dance, and now they step into the foreground. The lieutenant is in despair, enraged by jealousy; Zdenka hesitates, but then, making a clearly difficult decision, shows him a letter which apparently comes from Arabella.

Once again the various scenes merge into one another: Mandryka enters the room and inspects the laid table. Here Matteo and Zdenka must be separated from Mandryka by a pillar, screen, or similar object. Mandryka unintentionally witnesses the following scene: first Matteo refuses to accept the letter, afraid that Arabella will take leave of him; Zdenka presses him to take it, as it contains a key. Matteo asks what the key is for and Zdenka, now almost beside herself with excitement, says it is for Arabella's room, and that Arabella is excepting him there: 'You should go home—she will come in a quarter of an hour.

The key fits the room next to hers.' Zdenka runs off, followed by the confused Matteo.

Mandryka, hearing this traitorous conversation, angrily chases off after his servants. He is filled with doubts and disappointment. His thoughts oscillate between a half-hope that what he heard may be a misunderstanding, and deep distrust.

His musings are interrupted by the turbulent entrance of Fiakermilli and her cheerful entourage. They ask him if Arabella is with him. One of his servants brings him a letter which he then reads: 'For today I bid you good night, and return home. After tomorrow I am yours—a small "a" in place of signature.' He is enraged but forces himself to appear cheerful. He drinks heavily, sings, dances, grabs hold of Fiakermilli, and, at heart deeply distressed, pulls her to him and kisses her.

He invites the assembled company to help themselves to champagne and they all carouse with wild abandon until Adelaide, called by Count Dominik, appears on the scene. Shocked by Mandryka's behaviour, she summons her husband. In the argument that follows Count Waldner puts on a show of paternal dignity and the dispute ends with everyone concerned re-

Metropolitan Opera, New York, 1955
Set for Act II, with good opportunities for the performers' entrances. The symmetrical arrangement of the set produces a slightly stiff effect. The doorways to the ballroom next to the staircase are a good feature.
Producer: Herbert Graf.
Conductor: Rudolf Kempe.
Sets: Rolf Gerard.

Staatsoper, Hamburg, 1955
Design for Act II by Rudolf
Heinrich. A beautiful view into
the ballroom; the decoration is
superb kitsch. The separation of
the foreground is a good idea.
Producer: Rudolf Steinboeck.
Conductor: Leopold Ludwig.

solving to return to the hotel in order to obtain a much-needed explanation from Arabella. Mandryka, too, accepts this decision, after first inviting the people at the ball to accompany him as his guests.

The close of this act in the original version—with the extended 'coloratura yodel' by the Fiakermilli—remained weak. The same was true of the introductory music for Act III which portrays the love scene between Zdenka and Matteo. There is just not the same sense of conviction about this music as there is, say, in the introduction to the first act of *Der Rosenkavalier*.

Strauss was always very critical of his own works. He agreed without hesitation to a fusion of the second and the third acts (with abridgements of Act III) when this was suggested by

Clemens Krauss for a new production of the work at Munich in 1939. This was successful. Strauss took the view that the three-and-a-half-minute orchestral piece between the two acts which effected the transition was more appropriate than a full introduction.

However, the new version imposed considerable new demands on the producer. The sets for the two acts now had to be changed within three minutes or so. Even with technical aids such as stage platforms and so on, this set-change remained a difficult technical operation. It was effected with admirable skill at the old Prinzregenten Theater in Munich. The various sections of the set—constructed as separate 'trolleys'—were so built that they could be very swiftly manhandled. These transformations were timed to a split second; they always worked superbly, and were the pride and joy of the technical director, Emil Buchenberger.

The setting for Act III is the hotel foyer, at night. The first to enter is Arabella, who is just returning home. Just before that we see Matteo stealthily leave a room in the Count's suite and hurry along the corridor. Arabella is still uplifted by the strains of the last waltz which she can hear in her mind, and stands for a few moments in the foyer, moved by happy thoughts of the past and future.

Matteo, perhaps in search of a drink, appears at the top of the stairs and is thoroughly taken aback to see Arabella—whom he has, so far as he knows, just left in her room—standing before him, dressed as if to go out.

The confrontation which follows between the two of them is the first of a hectic sequence of somewhat contrived encounters and dialogues. One has the feeling Hofmannsthal's guiding hand is lacking, and that Strauss's musical invention is strained. Certainly, the potentially explosive events follow one another in rapid tempo, but they lack that inner conviction apparent in the exemplary first act. A producer has to use all his skill to make the development of the plot credible and clear. The difficulties begin with the encounter between Matteo and Zdenka, who is over-excited after her bold deception, the act of a hot-blooded girl caught in a web of contradictory emotions, and driven to make a gift of herself.

One singer in the role of Matteo once came to me during a rehearsal and said that the whole episode simply was not credible. The differences in the figures of the two singers playing Arabella and Zdenka led him to remark that Matteo—although not exactly brimming over with intelligence—would have to be a complete idiot not to notice this difference, even in the darkest room. In reply I merely referred to the accustomed readiness of the audience to believe in the developments of the plot which take place offstage and which are briefly reported. Matteo, in particular—a key figure—should be played by a singer who is also a first-class actor.

So is Act III unsatisfactory? No, it is not; for with the final meeting between Arabella and Mandryka—the now famous duet—Strauss created one of the most beautiful scenes in recent operatic literature. The melodic quality of his music overrides the confusing impression left by the previous events.

Metropolitan Opera, New York, 1955
Set for Act III by Rolf Gerard. A hotel foyer with the entrances distributed rationally, rather un-Viennese in appearance.

Salzburg Festival, 1958
Arabella (Lisa della Casa) and
Zdenka (Anneliese Rothenberger)
in Act I. An attempt to give the
set a freer form was not, in fact,
an improvement. The ornamentation over the doors is a questionable touch. The acoustics were
not helped by the absence of a
proper ceiling.
Producer: Rudolf Hartmann.
Conductor: Joseph Keilberth.
Sets: Stefan Hlawa.
Costumes: Erni Kniepert.

Salzburg Festival, 1958
Reconciliation scene in Act III.
This photograph does not show
the full impact of the staircase but
does indicate the expressive capabilities of the two singers, Lisa
della Casa and Dietrich Fischer-
Dieskau. The superb costumes
were by Erni Kniepert. All in all
this production's attempt at
breaking new ground (in Act II
especially) remained no more than
an experiment.

Bayerische Staatsoper, Munich,
1959
Lisa della Casa in the role that
brought her so much success. The
press referred to her as 'Arabellis-
sima'.

Munich Festival, 1959
Dietrich Fischer-Dieskau in the
final scene of Act II. Here the
audience is well prepared for the
descent into total inebriation at
the end of the scene.
Producer: Rudolf Hartmann.
Conductor: Joseph Keilberth.
Sets: Helmut Jürgens.

Maggio Musicale, Florence, 1961
Act II. The set is original and un-
conventional in its arena-like
shape. There are many useful entrances, but little intimacy for the
dialogues.
Producer: Frank de Quell.
Conductor: Heinz Wallberg.
Sets: Emanuele Luzzati.

To sum up: the embarrassing encounter between Arabella and Matteo fails to clarify the
situation. They are interrupted by the return of
Countess Adelaide, who is followed by Mandryka. He catches sight of his supposed rival
Matteo and orders his immediate departure.
Arabella has no idea what is going on and tries
to explain, but Mandryka cuts her off brusquely.
Count Waldner demands an answer from his
daughter and the latter, not aware of having
done anything wrong, for her part turns to Matteo and asks him to say something: the confusion grows, challenges to a duel are heard, until
suddenly, with a cry of 'Papa, mama...' Zdenka
appears on the stairs. Pushing her way through
the group of guests, she rushes down the stairs
into the foyer. Quite beside herself, she says that
she wants to throw herself into the Danube.
Arabella and her mother immediately suspect a
link with the other events: a solution to the
problem seems close. The older sister leads the
sobbing Zdenka into Matteo's arms. Mandryka,
deeply ashamed of himself, asks Zdenka's
parents that her hand be given in marriage to
Matteo; everything ends happily. Adelaide takes
Zdenka upstairs; the weapons are put away and
Count Waldner goes off with his friends for a
game of cards. Mandryka remains behind, after
Arabella, too, has gone up to her room. The
night porter extinguishes the lamps; Welko,
Mandryka's hussar escort, takes Arabella a glass
of water she has asked for.

In the half-darkness of the foyer, Mandryka
tortures himself with self-reproaches until he is
enchanted and freed from his torment by the re-
appearance of Arabella, who slowly comes down
the stairs in the moonlight carrying the glass of
water. In bringing Mandryka the water Arabella
is following a custom of his homeland which he
has told her about. This is an inspired symbolic
gesture of forgiveness. Mandryka takes her into
his arms: 'As truly as none shall drink from this
glass after me, so you are mine, and I am yours
for eternity!' The sound of the glass being
smashed underlines Arabella's answer: 'And so
we are betrothed and united for suffering and
joy, and for pain and forgiveness!'

The première of *Arabella* was once again entrusted to Dresden. Fritz Busch, musical director after Ernst von Schuch, was forced to withdraw because of the new Nazi government. Clemens Krauss, who arrived as guest conductor
from Vienna, took his place as conductor at the
first performance on 1 July 1933. Viorica Ursuleac from Vienna sang the part of Arabella,
and Alfred Jerger that of Mandryka. Leonhard
Fanto from Dresden designed the sets and costumes, and the producer was Josef Gielen.

The new Strauss opera was performed at a historical turning-point. On the one hand, traditional opera enthusiasts in Dresden stressed the
festiveness of the occasion; on the other, the
Nazis claimed this production as their own cultural achievement. The composition of those

Munich Festival, 1968
Scene from Act II. The set has successfully been opened out, with a view directly into the ballroom. The women's costumes were a sensational success. It was not difficult to develop the action and to separate off the dialogue scenes.
Producer: Rudolf Hartmann.
Conductor: Heinrich Hollreiser.
Sets: Herbert Kern.
Costumes: W. F. Adlmüller.

Deutsche Staatsoper, Berlin, 1976
Set for Act II by Wilfried Werz. A freely conceived solution with many—almost too many—period details in the curtains, etc. The entrances and seating arrangements are well positioned.
Producer: Erich Witte.
Conductor: Otmar Suitner.
Costumes: Christine Stromberg.

Munich Festival, 1968
Probably the most beautiful solution ever for the staircase in the hotel foyer. It is elegant and dominates the scene: the 'staircase of fate' for Arabella and Mandryka.

members of the audience who assembled after the première reflected the new circumstances. *Arabella* was given a festive première, albeit the last; once again bygone glories were revived.

Hofmannsthal's delineation of the characters in *Arabella* is quite masterful. The sequence of scenes in Act I is a dramatic success in terms of comedy, and offers rich possibilities for the characterization of all the roles. The more the producer works like a film director, and the nearer the characters are to modern sensibility, the easier it is for the audience to believe in them and empathize with them. The figures must be given life with no sense of caricature. The period in which they live must also be conjured up with visual precision. Small cameo parts, such as those of the room-service waiter, the hussar valet, Welko, the head waiter in Act II and so on, can be deftly sketched.

The design for the set calls for a sure sense of taste. Nothing should be exaggerated or ironically emphasized so as to distract the performers from their task. One very positive aspect of the fashion for nostalgia is that it has revived a serious historical interest in the interiors of earlier decades. Efforts are thus made to discover unsuspected beauty and interest in the visual taste of other times than our own, such as that when art nouveau was all the rage. The Vienna of 1860 had its own particular charm, above all in the fashion of that day.

The profusion of *Arabella* productions throughout the world has led to engaging variations. The pleasure one experiences when admiring the stage-designs of these productions lies in the recognition of detail, just as it does when looking at an engraving or drawing from the same period.

Die schweigsame Frau
('The Silent Woman')

◁ A 'ship of the line': the frigate
Victory, built in 1765. It was in a
ship similar to this one that Sir
Morosus spent his life as a sailor.
(Model from the Deutsches
Museum, Munich.)

Hugo von Hofmannsthal's successor, Stefan
Zweig, who was born in Vienna in 1881, began
his collaboration with Richard Strauss in 1932
when he wrote the libretto of *Die schweigsame
Frau* for him.

Zweig himself provided a detailed and informative account of his first meeting with Strauss
(in *Die Welt von gestern: Erinnerungen eines
Europäers*), at least part of which deserves to be
quoted:

This was the first time I had co-operated
with Richard Strauss. Up to then Hugo von
Hofmannsthal had written all his libretti,
from *Elektra* and *Rosenkavalier* onwards, and
I had never met Strauss personally. After
Hofmannsthal's death Strauss let me know
through my publisher [Kippenberg] that he
wished to start a new work and asked if I
would be prepared to write the libretto for
him. I fully appreciated the honour of such a
request...

I immediately said I would and at the very
first meeting suggested *The Silent Woman* by
Ben Jonson as a subject for an opera. I was
pleasantly surprised that Strauss accepted all
my suggestions so quickly and clear-sight-
edly. I had never suspected he would display
such keen artistic comprehension, such an astonishing knowledge of dramatic problems.
Even as I explained the material to him he
shaped it in dramatic form and—all the more
remarkably—adapted it immediately to the
limits of his own capabilities, which he assess-
ed with an almost uncanny clarity. I have met
many artists in my life but never one who
showed such an unwavering objectivity
towards himself...

With his gift for observation, Zweig captur-
ed Strauss's character exactly, just as he was later
to describe so accurately his work with the composer and the latter's attitude to the difficulties
of life as an artist under Hitler.

After the sad loss of Hofmannsthal, with whom he had worked for many years, Strauss found in Zweig, who was Jewish, a congenial collaborator. He fought hard to maintain an association which began fruitfully, but his efforts were all in vain. We shall come back to this point later when examining the inspiration which Zweig provided for Strauss's subsequent works, right up to *Capriccio*.

In his notes Zweig mentioned the way Strauss worked and the way he spoke. His first impression was that the composer's appearance had an air of bourgeois rectitude about it, but then he added:

One glance at his eyes—those bright, blue, forcefully radiant eyes—and one immediately sensed a magic power behind this bourgeois façade. They were, perhaps, the most alert eyes I had ever seen in a musician, not demonic, but somehow clairvoyant; they were the eyes of a man who knew exactly what he had to do...

When Hitler came to power in January 1933, the vocal score for our opera *Die schweigsame Frau* was virtually ready and Act I just about orchestrated. Only weeks later came the strict order to German theatres not to present works by non-Aryans or those in which Jews, however remotely, had been involved... I assumed, as a matter of course, that Richard Strauss would abandon all further co-operation and begin another project with someone else. Instead he wrote asking what was the matter with me; on the contrary, he said, I should now start preparing the libretto for his next opera, because he was already working on the orchestration. He would not dream of letting anyone forbid his working with me; and I must say quite openly that he maintained a comradely loyalty towards me throughout this whole affair as long as he could...

The première of the work came about because of Strauss's tenacity, and the composer even succeeded in getting his librettist's name on to the theatre programme against all resistance. But then, as Zweig writes: 'Suddenly after the second performance there came a bolt from the blue. Everything was cancelled and the opera was banned in Dresden and throughout Germany... Strauss had again written to me, pressing me to start work soon on the libretto for a new opera and stating his personal attitude all too frankly. This letter fell into the hands of the Gestapo...'

That was the end for the time being of *Die schweigsame Frau* which received only occasional

Sächsische Staatstheater
Opernhaus

Montag, am 24. Juni 1935

Anfang **6** Uhr

Außer Anrecht

Uraufführung

Die schweigsame Frau

Komische Oper in drei Aufzügen

Frei nach Ben Jonson von Stefan Zweig

Musik von Richard Strauß

Musikalische Leitung: Karl Böhm   Inszenierung: Josef Gielen

Personen:

Sir Morosus	....	Friedrich Plaschke
Seine Haushälterin	....	Helene Jung
Der Barbier	....	Matthieu Ahlersmeyer
Henry Morosus		Martin Kremer
Aminta, seine Frau		Maria Cebotari
Isotta		Erna Sack
Carlotta	Komödianten	Marion Hundt
Danuzzi		Kurt Böhme
Farfallo		Ludwig Ermold
Morbio		Rudolf Schmalnauer

Chor der Komödianten und Nachbarn

Ort der Handlung:

Zimmer des Sir Morosus in einem Vorort Londons

Zeit: etwa 1780

Chöre: Karl Maria Pembaur / Tanz im dritten Akt: Werner Stammer

Bühnenbild: Adolf Mahnke   Einrichtung: Georg Brandt   Trachten: Leonhard Fanto

Pausen nach dem ersten und zweiten Akt

Krank: Liesel von Schuch, Hermann Kutzschbach, Horst Falke

Sämtliche Plätze müssen vor Beginn der Vorstellung eingenommen werden

Textbücher sind für 1,00 R.M vormittags an der Kasse und abends bei den Türschließern zu haben

Gekaufte Karten werden nur bei Änderung der Vorstellung zurückgenommen

Einlaß 5¼ Uhr   Anfang 6 Uhr   Ende geg. 9¾ Uhr

Staatsoper, Dresden, 1935
Adolf Mahnke designed the sets for this première, which once again took place in Dresden, and the costumes were by Leonhard Fanto. Maria Cebotari was unforgettable in the main role; Strauss once referred to her as a 'stroke of luck'. An excellent production by Josef Gielen.
Conductor: Karl Böhm.

performances abroad, in Zurich, Prague and Milan. This explains the work's relatively late appearance on the German stage.

After the death of Hugo von Hofmannsthal, Strauss had not believed he could continue with his work for the stage, but with Stefan Zweig he experienced a period of unexpected happiness. Everything proceeded smoothly and in perfect harmony. He composed steadily and without interruption. The change in political circum-

Teatro alla Scala, Milan, 1936
The Italian conductor Gino Marinuzzi was a great admirer of Strauss and in 1936 put on *Die schweigsame Frau* at La Scala. The set, which had few nautical touches, was by Mario Cito Filomarino.
Producer: Lothar Wallerstein.

Salzburg Festival, 1959
The Salzburg production of 1959, with Hilde Güden as Aminta and Hans Hotter as Morosus, included several amusing details of Morosus's previous naval career. Teo Otto designed the witty and elegant set, and the costumes were by Erni Kniepert. Günther Rennert, who was especially fond of the piece, was the producer and Karl Böhm conducted.

stances did not affect his creative work and he was perhaps more cheerful and relaxed than he had ever been on any other project.

This long opera was completed between November 1932 and 20 October 1934. The première had been planned with Fritz Busch and Alfred Reucker in Dresden, but then disruptions from outside began. The heads of the production staff had to be replaced; the conductor was Karl Böhm, the producer Josef Gielen, and Adolf Mahnke was responsible for the sets and costumes. The work was staged for the first time in Dresden on 24 June 1935.

Strauss deserves our admiration for completing *Die schweigsame Frau* in a remarkably short time. At seventy he still displayed unbroken creative power, and he was able to close his mind to the increasingly threatening and unpleasant events that were going on around him. Nothing could destroy his joy in his work. This is astonishing because Strauss was certainly aware of the difficulties which would face his librettist. But he wanted to defy these difficulties and to continue his fulfilling and agreeable collaboration with Zweig; he did not want to lose Zweig as he had Hofmannsthal.

In this he failed: the cool-headed writer, who saw the future more clearly, thanked Strauss for his courageous support but voluntarily decided to forego any further joint professional association with him. He even suggested the man who, he thought, could most suitably take his place and to whom he handed on all the plans he had developed for new works. It was thus that Joseph Gregor was to become the third librettist to work with Strauss.

Against this background, there is a fateful air about *Die schweigsame Frau* which stands in contrast to the unfettered music and the content of the comedy. Despite an ecstatic première, the work made slow progress in other theatres. Everyone knew of the depressing circumstances in which it had been written. Dark shadows hovered over all the jollity, and they still have not entirely been dissipated.

The plot is simple and treats a motif often found in comedy: the story of a man who hates noise and upon whom a dastardly trick is played. A great deal then transpires before the tormented Sir Morosus—the unfortunate victim of youthful exuberance—can finally sigh in relief:

Oh how beautiful music is.
But, oh, how much more beautiful it is when it stops!

Zweig's libretto is freely based on Ben Jonson's comedy *Epicoene, or the Silent Woman* (1609).

After a sprightly overture, which Strauss called a pot-pourri, the curtain opens on to the large drawing-room of Sir Morosus, a former admiral. Items in the room point to his naval career. The doors and windows are specially sound-proofed with curtains, blankets and sacking. The action of the play is set around 1780.

The housekeeper Zimmerlein, an old widow, is dusting when the Barber (Schneidebart; in Jonson, Cutbeard) enters. He has come to shave Sir Morosus. But instead of announcing him, the garrulous old widow tries to make him convince Sir Morosus that he should marry her. The Barber is enraged and shouts at her, until suddenly Sir Morosus rushes in from the bedroom and beats the housekeeper out of the drawing-room.

Schneidebart's sympathetic, flattering comments are countered by a long, lively complaint by Sir Morosus about the noise in the city: 'Fiddles and flutes, trumpets and drums, rumbling and mumbling, scuffling and carousing, jingling and bungling; never, never does it cease; in house and alleyway, never is there peace.'

The Barber agrees, *speaking:* that is, there is no recitative but a free dialogue, which according to Strauss's instructions the orchestra has to follow.

Morosus continues to complain about the bells and the chatty housekeeper until the Barber advises him to throw the 'old dragon' out and to take in a quiet, obedient young woman. The old man comments: 'Yes, what a good idea,' but he cannot believe the Barber's assertions that he knows many suitable girls. Then a thunderous knock at the door startles them both, and noises are heard. Morosus runs for his stick with which to chastise the intruder, who then forces his way into the room—it is Henry Morosus, a long-lost nephew whom Sir Morosus has missed a great deal. The old man becomes calm and happy. He immediately offers his heir a place to stay and every amenity, but Henry has something else on his mind: 'I am not alone... they are waiting below... namely... namely... my troupe...'

Sir Morosus is delighted, imagining a troop of soldiers, and is therefore bitterly disappointed when he discovers that Henry means a troupe of operatic performers led by Maestro Cesare Vanuzzi. Henry admits that he, too, has become a singer and Sir Morosus is outraged: 'A Morosus who sings is no Morosus. You will leave this troupe immediately.'

Henry pleads with him and presents his wife Aminta. Morosus is now beside himself with rage, disinherits Henry and curses the opera

Bayerische Staatsoper, Munich,
1962
Helmuth Jürgens marked out the
stage area with only a few prominent details. The various complications of the plot could then
develop freely.
Producer: Hans Hartleb.
Conductor: Heinz Wallberg.

singers. There is a furious argument. Morosus
calls for silence, repeats that he is casting Henry
out and orders the Barber to bring him a quiet,
taciturn girl *immediately*—he wants to marry at
once and leave everything to her. He tells the
troupe to leave and runs off in a fury, seeking
peace—peace at last for once in his life.

The theatre troupe remains behind, offended
by this outburst. Then they plot revenge. The
Barber calms them down, defends Sir Morosus
and advises moderation. He tells them of the
captain's wealth and of the treasures in his cellar:
sixty to seventy thousand pounds 'in good bars
and round ducats'.

Accompanied by an ensemble from the singers, who have adopted an attitude of awe and respect, the cunning Barber attempts to persuade
Henry to be sensible and to reconcile himself
with his uncle. Aminta is willing to sacrifice her
own interests and leave Henry, but the latter de-

clares his unchanging love for her and shows no
wish to leave the opera troupe. Everyone is moved by this, and he is kissed, embraced and praised
as a good comrade.

The Barber is slightly aggrieved and comments: 'Very righteously intended, young master, but such a shame that all the rectitude in this
world is mainly stupidity, because you are letting a fine sum of money slip through your
fingers!' Then he bemoans the difficulties involved in finding a silent girl for Sir Morosus by
the next day. He asks the female members of the
troupe, Isotta and Carlotta, but their heads are
only full of practical jokes. Suddenly the Barber
is struck by a flash of inspiration. He explains to
the nonplussed actors that he is thinking of or-
ganizing a bogus marriage, with Aminta playing
the bride and the other parts—vicar, notary,
witnesses, relatives—distributed among the
members of the troupe. Strauss showed im-

mense Rossini-like virtuosity in the uproarious finale ('Curing this fool will be especial fun') to this first act.

At the start of Act II Sir Morosus is donning his dress uniform with the help of the housekeeper. He then chases the gossipy old woman, who still has her eye on him, out of the room.

The Barber arrives and announces that he has found three candidates, but calls on Sir Morosus to show them special consideration and tenderness because all are inexperienced maidens. Aminta, Carlotta and Isotta—all three cleverly disguised—enter. The Barber first presents Carlotta: 'This girl of pure innocence comes from the country, the only child of simple farmers...' She speaks in dialect, behaves somewhat idiotically, and is rejected.

Isotta is introduced as an impoverished noblewoman and boasts of her upbringing and education: 'She speaks Latin, Greek, Hebrew and Aramaic as if they were her mother tongue... and she plays the lute...' By this time Morosus has already heard enough and when Isotta

swamps him with a flood of 'educated' talk, begs the Barber to free him from her presence.

Finally, Aminta, posing as a decent middle-class girl, immediately pleases the old sea-dog in search of a wife. She plays her part masterfully and Sir Morosus is determined to marry her at once. The Barber is told to fetch the vicar, the notary, etc.

Morosus remains behind alone with Aminta, who calls herself 'Timidia'. This scene evokes a great deal of sympathy for Morosus. Even Aminta begins to feel strongly drawn to the old gentleman, before slipping back with difficulty into her comédienne role.

The Barber, who is controlling the whole affair, brings in the vicar (Vanuzzi) and the notary (Morbio); these experienced actors play their parts with conviction; the Barber and Housekeeper act as witnesses. Then together with the 'married couple' they sign the register.

Peace is disturbed by the entrance of a gang of loud-mouthed sailors—the rest of the opera troupe in disguise. They are led by Farfallo, who makes a speech to the assembled company in

Teatro Colón, Buenos Aires, 1968
Leni Baur-Ecsy designed a spacious variation with a delightful array of naval memorabilia. But the design changed considerably when constructed as the actual set.
Producer: Ernst Poettgen.
Conductor: Otmar Suitner.

Teatro Colón, Buenos Aires, 1968
Final form of the set by Leni
Baur-Ecsy.

which he pays homage to his 'former commandant'. Morosus tries in vain to disown the
honour—the sailors claim they were part of the
crew on board his old frigate and have come to
celebrate his marriage. The old admiral is enraged and tries to eject them, but to no avail. Farfallo throws open all the doors and windows and
calls in the whole town. The neighbours enter,
and the enraged master of the house is held back
bodily until he capitulates in the face of all the
hellish noise around him and sinks exhausted
into an armchair. On behalf of Morosus the
Barber then invites the whole crowd to the
nearest inn. Even the vicar (Vanuzzi) and the
notary (Morbio) are thankful for the suggestion
and leave with him.

Morosus is again alone with Aminta, who
earlier on had needed a good deal of encouragement and persuasion to continue with the deception. She is sorry for the harassed old man:
'Oh, if only you had chosen another for such
games! I feel so sorry for him, the poor, good
man.'

At this point it is not only Aminta/Timidia
who is on the verge of a fateful decision. The

audience, too, experience ambivalent feelings.
Up to now the piece has been a somewhat acer-
bic, boisterous jest. Suddenly there is a pensive
hiatus in the action. What has Morosus done to
deserve such harsh disruption of his existence?
Must he really be punished in such a hurtful way
simply because he wants peace and quiet and is
angry at the company Henry is keeping?

There is a danger that Aminta and the other
members of the opera troupe will appear as un-
sympathetic and cruel characters. Aminta does
after all feel a degree of sympathy for Morosus;
but it is easy for the singer in the role to fall into
the trap of overemphasizing the characters' ne-
gative traits. She must allow the true, kind-
hearted Aminta repeatedly to show through her
adopted personality, or else the comedy will
change its nature and become tragi-comedy.

At the Dresden première the unforgettable
Maria Cebotari ideally solved this difficult task.
Her graceful charm during the entire prank
enabled her to retain the audience's affection.

None the less Aminta *does* have to rage. With
a fortissimo high C she begins to scream, with
the result that Morosus almost collapses in

fright. She behaves like a power-hungry fury who wants to change everything (and that means everything) and makes insane demands —all at breakneck pace. She wants a coach, horses, servants, her own domestic orchestra, singers, dancers—too late does Morosus recognize what kind of person he has married: 'Oh, what a fool am I! What a seasoned fool! What a devil have I got mixed up with in my folly!'

The raging tantrum is Aminta's way of blotting out her pangs of conscience. She begins to destroy the furnishings in the room along with Morosus's beloved collection of marine objects. The admiral, at the end of his tether, falls at the feet of Henry, who re-appears (this time in his own clothes again), and begs to be liberated from this 'female Satan'. Henry begins to argue with Aminta, who defends herself, until he drags her bodily into the next room.

Morosus is in despair: 'Henry, you know I was never a cowardly man... I have fought in seventeen battles... but I can do nothing against her! She'll finish me off, Henry...'

His nephew shows him a way out. The following day he will fetch the Lord Chief Justice and an advocate and have the marriage dissolved. Morosus, in a touching display of gratitude, asks Henry to watch over him while he sleeps and to protect him from this she-devil. Henry takes the exhausted old man to the bedroom and the door is then locked from within. Henry fetches Aminta from the next room and they embrace.

Following the alarming turbulence of the previous scene, the act now settles back into a magically lyrical close, with the young couple in an embrace, and—out of sight—the weary admiral with one desire, sleep.

Aminta gives voice to what must be regarded as the motto for the preceding scene: 'Oh God, the poor old man; how unwilling did I do him harm! Even at the height of my delivery I wanted to treat him kindly. Would that everything will work out well, so that I'll be able to show how fondly I cherish him.'

Once again we hear the voice of Morosus. The admiral wants to reassure himself that Henry is keeping watch. Only after the latter has replied does he sink into longed-for sleep with a murmur: 'Thank you! Thank you!' which mingles with the couple's kiss as the curtain closes.

Act III is difficult to link to the sensitive lyrical close of the last act because it picks up where the apparently crazy Aminta left off—with the brutal transformation of the whole house: the moving of furniture; a new spinet; a squawking parrot; the entrance of a singing teacher (Henry) and an accompanist for the spinet (Farfallo). Aminta starts to sing an aria by Monteverdi, is praised and corrected by Henry, who then sings a duet with her.

Morosus comes rapidly out of the bedroom, begging for mercy; but they sing on. To add insult to injury, the tormented admiral is also showered with triumphant recriminations by the Housekeeper, the parrot squawks: all hell is let loose. The scene is interrupted by the Barber who announces that the Lord Chief Justice will be arriving very shortly. Morosus breathes a sigh of relief and asks the Barber to negotiate with Aminta, who rejects all offers that are made and is obstinate until His Honour and the two Notaries are announced. Morosus leaves to don his full-dress uniform.

Vanuzzi enters pompously as the Lord Chief Justice, escorted by the 'advocates' Farfallo and Morbio. The actors, who are alone to start with, remove their heavy wigs and dance a little; but in a flash they resume their disguises and austere demeanour as Morosus re-enters, this time in his robes of state.

In this scene there is a lengthy series of negotiations caricaturing legal pedantry. Aminta declares her objections, and Henry in disguise finally appears as a witness, testifying that he had slept with Aminta. Crying, she admits this to be true. Everything seems to have been solved. But once again there is a delay: this time it is Farfallo who raises an objection. Here Morosus really does collapse. He does not want to listen to anyone or anything any more; he throws himself on his couch and covers his ears.

The Barber realizes that the comedy has gone far enough and calls for quiet. Henry and Aminta throw off their disguises and approach the couch. They explain everything and ask for forgiveness. The others also reveal themselves and Morosus realizes that they have made a fool of him. The rage that consumes him is then transformed into grandiose Falstaffian laughter at his own behaviour and at the comedy that has been perpetrated so successfully. He is also overjoyed that he has survived everything. He orders wine; the actors drink, dance with the Barber, pay their respects to Morosus who has been cured of the disease of marriage, and then withdraw at his request. The object of their exuberance, now freed, remains behind with the young couple, lights his favourite pipe and says: 'Oh, I cannot describe how well I feel. Peace, just peace, ah!'

This then is the content of the comedy which inspired Strauss to a profusion of lively ensembles with high-spirited music, and also to ly-

Bayerische Staatsoper, Munich, 1971
Rudolf Heinrich created some remarkable figures for the 1971 production: for example, Henry as a cavalier and Sir Morosus in full-dress uniform.

Staatsoper, Hamburg, 1971
Ekkehard Grübler designed the set, which had many humorous touches. Rudolf Steinboeck was the excellent producer.
Conductor: Marek Janowski.

rical scenes of exquisite 'Straussian' beauty. Musical ideas abound on every page of the score. In it Strauss demonstrated an undiminished delight in composition.

The question remains whether too much is not being asked of the audience by the renewal of tumultuous high jinks in Act III, and whether tightening the dramatic structure would not help to counteract a certain wearisome effect. None the less the work in its entirety is so masterful, and achieved in such a virtuoso style, with an elegance worthy of Rossini, that admiration and awe must surely overcome all objections.

Richard Strauss fought hard to persuade his librettist to continue their collaboration, but Stefan Zweig was equally stubborn in wanting to bow out to avoid further complications. As late as 17 June 1935, that is, shortly before the première, Strauss wrote:

My dear Herr Zweig,

Your letter of the 15th has thrown me into despair. This Jewish obstinacy! And one is then supposed not to become anti-Semitic! ... Do you think I have ever let myself be prompted to take any action by the thought that I am a 'Germanic' being (perhaps, qui le sait?)? For me there are only two categories of people: those who have talent and those who don't. For me the 'Volk' only exists at the moment when it becomes an audience, and whether that consists of Chinese, Upper Bavarians, New Zealanders or Berliners is a matter of complete indifference to me...'

On 28 June 1935, a few days after the première, Strauss reported on its success and once again implored Zweig:

Once and for all, please, please work through for me the two pieces which you conceived on your own: 1648 [Friedenstag] and the comedy—but without Gregor whose co-operation on them is strictly rejected. I won't compose any disguised operas! Texts conceived by Zweig I will compose only under the one title: Zweig. Let what happens after that, please, be my worry. In the Dresden performance the little Cebotari was quite simply perfect! If for the première one can find such a performer to play such an exceptional role (how long did I wait and still wait for one for Salome!), then the future can be faced with composure. So 'up and away'! I'm waiting...

But this was all to no avail. The Stefan Zweig-Richard Strauss chapter was over almost before it had begun.

The task of the producer in *Die schweigsame Frau* can readily be deduced from the description of the work's content.

The numerous splendid comic roles in the work are a gift to talented actors, and the producer is likewise confronted with a multitude of ideas. Much will depend on his skill at keeping the swirl of life on stage under tight control and, with great precision, maintaining a light and apparently effortless touch on stage.

Attention has already been drawn to the dangers inherent in the part of Aminta. The work must not end with the audience feeling merely pity for Morosus. Sympathy must also be maintained for the young couple and the other members of their troupe.

Producing *Die schweigsame Frau* is both gratifying and challenging. Since its brilliant première, staged by Josef Gielen, good productions have been put on by Günther Rennert and others.

As for the sets, the stage instructions offer plenty of scope: 'a broad untidy room with many indications that a former seaman lives there: model ships, flags, guns, anchors, skeletons of fish, tackle. Particularly noticeable is the fact that all the doors are covered by thick curtains or sacks.'

Adolf Mahnke designed the première. He and his successors have shown virtuosity and imagination in the images they have presented us with. However, visual exaggeration distracts the audience, just as much as extravagance of production, when the intention should be to present the opera in a farcical setting where the basic mood is one of high-spirited fun.

The new National Socialist cultural policy, which made it impossible for Stefan Zweig to continue his artistic collaboration with Richard Strauss, meant that the composer had now lost his second librettist.

Once again the seventy-year-old Strauss was deeply depressed about the future, because he felt there was much music still left in him, music which was crying out for form and expression. Stefan Zweig had been the only one since Hofmannsthal who had proposed interesting projects. These were now still-born, since Zweig steadfastly refused to work under the prevailing conditions, no matter how hard Strauss searched for a way out. Unselfishly Zweig proposed Joseph Gregor as his successor, to whom he passed on the ideas he had sketched out, without wanting in any way to enter the limelight himself. Strauss stubbornly resisted collaborating with Gregor. He respected him as an expert on the theatre and as a human being, but he could not see him as poet. 'I cannot use an enthusiastic philologist. I must have a real poet and a creative man of the theatre,' he wrote on 24 May 1935 to Zweig.

Nevertheless, with considerable apprehension, he did begin to work with Gregor, turning to the draft of *The Peace of Westphalia* which had been preoccupying him. Gregor was faced with a difficult task. Strauss was in a very nervous and irritable frame of mind. It is remarkable how Gregor was able to put up with the often vehement criticisms of his work, how he was not discouraged and how his admiration for Strauss never wavered. Gregor nevertheless grew into his task, finding for *Daphne*—his second work for Strauss—beautiful, poetic words about which more will be said later.

First, work was begun on a drama about war and peace, the basic ideas of which have roots way back in *Guntram*. In opposition to the dangerous international tensions, Strauss wanted to utter a clearly understandable warning. In his own country that warning went unheeded: the terrible years that followed showed how sorely it had been needed.

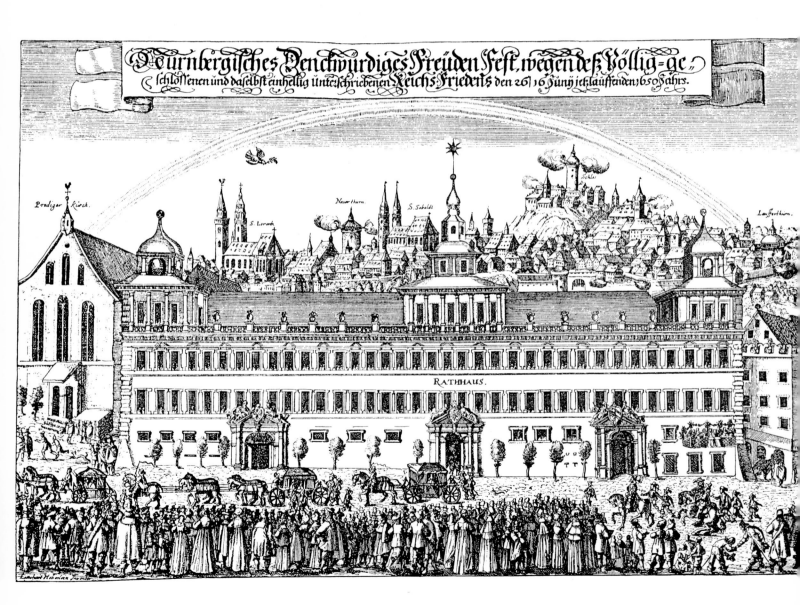

Nürnbergisches Denckwürdiges Freuden Fest, wegen deß Völlig-ge-
schlossenen und daselbst einhellig unterschriebenen Reichs Friedens den 26/16 Junÿ jetzlauffenden; 650 Jahrs.

RATHHAUS.

Friedenstag
('Armistice Day')

On 21 August 1934, a year and a half after Hitler became Reichschancellor, Stefan Zweig wrote to Richard Strauss:

> In the meantime I am writing to you about that festal elevated one-act piece: I have thought a great deal about it and would like to propose the basic outlines of a plan for it. I should like to summarize three elements: the tragic, the heroic and the human, which would culminate in a Hymn to the Reconciliation of all Peoples and to the grace and mercy of creative action. But I should also like to exclude emperors and kings completely, and set it in an anonymous atmosphere.
>
> Let me outline the scene:
>
> Time: the thirtieth year of the Thirty Years' War. Place: inside a citadel. A German fortress is besieged by the Swedes. The Commandant of the fortress has sworn not to let his men fall into the enemy's hands alive. The Commandant of the besieging forces has sworn to show no mercy. Terrible deprivation exists in the town below the citadel. The Mayor beseeches the Commandant to surrender the fortress. The people force their way in; all manner of voices of urgency, fear and famine are directly personified (individual voices, amorphous crowd scenes). The Commandant does not relent. He has the people, who curse him, forcibly ejected. Then alone with his officers and soldiers he declares that he can no longer hold the fortress. But rather than surrender he is prepared to blow it up. He gives everyone the opportunity of going down into the town and asking for mercy from the enemy. As for himself, he will not do this. There follow individual scenes (short but each one highly accentuated). Some go, some stay (depending on their character).
>
> Among those who remain behind: a heroically tragic mood.
>
> Religious scene: the wife of the Commandant appears. He orders her to go without saying what he intends to do. She guesses what he is planning. Powerful scene. She does not try to dissuade him because she is aware of his oath. But she does not go. She stays with him (this as a lyrical element) in order to die with him.
>
> Preparations for blowing up the citadel. Final farewells. Everyone embraces. The slow fuse is released and ignited. Complete silence.
>
> Then—the report of a cannon. All leap up, startled. The Commandant suspects an attack. The slow fuse is extinguished. They are happier about dying in open combat. There is, though, no second cannon report. They wait, surprised, unsettled. A further moment of tension.
>
> Then a bell is heard in the far distance from a neighbouring village. A second bell sounds in another village. Then (still in the far distance) a third bell is heard. The sound of trumpets. It is announced that a parliamentarian is approaching with a white flag. Then more and more bells are heard. And suddenly from below there comes a cry: peace. Peace has been concluded. More and more bells ring out with the jubilation of the people (off stage). The parliamentarian appears. Peace has been concluded in Osnabrück. The enemy Commandant requests that the peace may be welcomed. Agreement. Scene of awakening. The bells continue to ring, flooding the entire scene like the sound of organs.
>
> The enemy Commandant appears. Both men stare grimly at one another. Each had sworn to destroy the other. The tension gradually ceases. They approach and shake hands. They embrace.
>
> The people stream in, and cheer the Commandant. He gives a speech: everyone must set to work. Reconstruction and reconciliation. All for all. Individual voices express agreement. One class after another takes up the refrain. And from this, step by step, the great

Contemporary representation of the festival held in 1650 in Nuremberg, where peace was concluded after the Thirty Years' War. Negotiations had taken two years from the armistice to the formal conclusion of peace.

National-Theater

München, Sonntag den 24. Juli 1938

Uraufführung:

Friedenstag

Oper in 1 Aufzug von **Richard Strauß**
Text von **Joseph Gregor**
Musikalische Leitung: **Clemens Krauß**

Inszenierung: **Rudolf Hartmann**   Bühnenbild und Kostüme: **Ludwig Sievert**

Kommandant der belagerten Stadt		Hans Hotter
Maria, sein Weib		Viorica Ursuleac
Wachtmeister		Georg Hann
Schütze		Julius Patzak
Konstabel		Georg Wieter
Musketier	von der Besatzung	Karl Schmidt
Hornist		Willy Merkert
Offizier		Emil Graf
Front-Offizier		Josef Knapp
Ein Piemonteser		Peter Anders
Der Holsteiner, Kommandant der Belagerungsarmee		Ludwig Weber
Bürgermeister		Karl Ostertag
Prälat	der belagerten Stadt	Theo Reuter
Frau aus dem Volke		Else Schürhoff

Soldaten des Kommandanten der belagerten Stadt und des Holsteiners
Stadtobere und Frauen aus der Deputation an den Kommandanten, Volk
Ort: In der Zitadelle einer belagerten Stadt
Zeit: 24. Oktober 1648

Chöre: Josef Kugler — Chorverstärkung: Mitglieder des Münchener Lehrergesangvereins

Munich Festival, 1938
The *Friedenstag* première in Munich had both a historical significance, on account of the political situation, and a particular one, because this was the first première that Strauss granted to his native city.
Producer: Rudolf Hartmann.
Conductor: Clemens Krauss. Sets and costumes: Ludwig Sievert.

chorus is built up in which all the tasks and achievements of the peace between nations are celebrated, in terms of each separate class, and which unfolds into a powerful finale: the hymn to the community of peoples.

That would be my plan. Now it is always possible to describe the idea of peace between nations contemptuously as pacifist, if one wants to, but here it seems to me that it is entirely linked with the heroic. I would leave everything anonymous, giving no names, either to the town or to the Commandant; each should be only figurative, a symbol and not an unique individual entity.

Zweig presented this first draft to Strauss, and also suggested that he hand it on to someone else. Zweig recommended Rudolf Binding 'so that you can be spared all forms of trouble and the accursed politics of the matter'.

Ultimately it was Joseph Gregor who developed Stefan Zweig's sketch. In his recollections he made little reference to Zweig's original draft, but in *The 24th October 1648*, as the work

was originally called, he followed the ideas of the first draft closely, above all in regard to the final hymn which was to be the crowning glory of the piece. The character of the Italian was a new invention—and a beautiful one with its lyrical quality; his song at the beginning blossoms like a flower on a heap of rubble. Gregor commented that he heard the song in the South Tyrol during the First World War. Strauss recognized immediately that it could serve as a contrast to the soldiers' rough milieu.

The collaboration between Strauss and Joseph Gregor took time to develop. Gregor had to put up with many sharp criticisms, but each time patiently started from the beginning again under the composer's directions. Because Strauss had to cease corresponding overtly with Stefan Zweig, he sent news to him at secret addresses with false signatures. Stefan Zweig took similar precautions, signing himself 'Morosus' and using Joseph Gregor as go-between. Vienna was still free and the two were able to conduct extended discussions about the work that was

Munich Festival, 1938
Design by Ludwig Sievert. The
impressive, spacious fortress was
clearly conceived with the final
scene in mind. It gave great scope
to the producer.
Producer: Rudolf Hartmann.
Conductor: Clemens Krauss.

Munich Festival, 1938
This scene shows the mediating
role played by the woman be-
tween the two hostile Comman-
dants. Viorica Ursuleac between
Hans Hotter *(left)* and Ludwig
Weber *(right)*.
Producer: Rudolf Hartmann.
Conductor: Clemens Krauss. Sets
and costumes: Ludwig Sievert.

Staatsoper, Dresden, 1938
Adolf Mahnke solved the problem
of the upper part of the set by
means of back projection, which
disappeared in the final scene,
revealing open sky.
Producer: Max Hofmüller.
Conductor: Karl Böhm.

Staatsoper, Dresden, 1938
The final set, designed by Adolf
Mahnke, created a liberating,
open effect, with plenty of space
for the chorus.

Nationaltheater, Weimar, 1938
Design by Robert Stahl. A lively
and vigorously painted set, well
suited to the action.
Producer: Rudolf Hesse.
Conductor: Paul Sixt.

Opernhaus, Breslau, 1938
Hans Wildermann took a somewhat more austere approach to
the citadel. All the practical requirements seem to have been allowed for, but it is not obvious how
the final scene was dealt with.
Producer: Heinrich Köhler-
Helffrich. Conductor: Philipp
Wüst.

emerging. Strauss and Gregor referred to it as 'our friend' because Strauss's correspondence was under strict surveillance.

In one of the last letters which Strauss wrote directly to Zweig (31 October 1935) he reported as follows on the work he was putting into *Friedenstag* ('Armistice Day'):

For weeks I have been engaged almost exclusively with the composition, but it does not want to turn into music of the kind I must demand of myself. The entire material is just a little too ordinary—soldiers—war—famine—medieval heroism—dying together—it just does not really suit me, for all the goodwill I can muster.

We should recall that Strauss replied to Zweig's very first draft with a counter-proposal that the Commandant's wife should be brought into the foreground by means of a love affair and that the piece should end with her husband's suicide. Clearly Strauss had missed the female element which dominates almost all his works. But the idea of a woman as a heroine in the military sense did not appeal to him. Stefan Zweig did not take up Strauss's suggestion; he wanted clear and sharp contours, and this was also the approach taken by Joseph Gregor.

The letters just referred to also contained comments on Gregor's draft for *Daphne* and the direct request:

Don't you yourself want to do something else for me? *Coelestina* and 'poi le parole doppo la musica?'... In my last years of life I should still like to have some enjoyment from my work, even if I then simply put it in my drawer without comment—as I have already mentioned in one of my letters to you. My legacy! *Friedenstag* is too strenuous and tiresome a piece—Gr's verse has no depth and without music is only nice-sounding and superficial. I am sending this letter from the Tyrol and I ask you too not to send any letters to me across the German border because all of them are opened! Sign yourself, please, as Henry Mor. I shall sign as Robert Storch.

Shortly before this, on 6 October 1935, Strauss had written to Gregor from Garmisch:

I have now re-worked the second half of *Friedenstag* as well and I don't believe that I will ever find music for it. These aren't real people: The Commandant and his wife, they're on stilts... Our friend probably feels this too!... I have now established a sense of distance between myself and your otherwise so valuable work. But as it stands today, it is not for me.

He requested Gregor to re-work the entire piece again, and to send it to their mutual friend (Zweig) so that it could be subjected to 'merciless criticism and the most thorough revision',

Städtische Bühnen, Nuremberg, 1939
Design by Heinz Grete. The fortress-like setting is strongly emphasized by the embrasures.
Producer: Willi Hanke.
Conductor: Alfons Dressel.

Staatsoper, Berlin, 1939
Design by Emil Preetorius. Fine
arrangement for the entrances
from below. Sombre , menacing
atmosphere.
Producer: Wolf Völker.
Conductor: Clemens Krauss.

Teatro Fenice, Venice, 1940
Emilio Toti designed his set in the
style of the great Italian Baroque
stage-designers. The final scene
seems to have been built into the
set.
Producer: Corado-Pavolini.
Conductor: Vittorio Gui.

he was to 'ask for diligent (critical and productive) collaboration'.

Strauss was trying to force things to the point where Stefan Zweig would after all take over the libretto himself. In November he did manage to get the most important scene rewritten, the meeting between the two Commandants. Progress on *Friedenstag* was very slow. Gregor responded to all of Strauss's criticisms, which the composer laconically justified by saying: 'I am sorry, of course, that I have hurt you: but then the surgeon's saw also hurts without an anaesthetic...'

Gregor felt hurt, but not as a result of the discussions about *Friedenstag*; rather from Strauss's abrupt rejection of his (Gregor's) first version of *Daphne*. The composer had spoken of 'badly imitated Homeric jargon' and 'banalities of *Weltanschauung*'.

We should not be surprised that *Friedenstag* and *Daphne* became intertwined in their creators' minds. Both these one-act pieces were intended as two parts of a single evening's programme. Besides—and this was more important—Strauss needed another project to balance the tough material of the war opera; he longed

for his beloved Antiquity to allow him to compose easily. The fact that he was constantly working away at other plans and ideas may have been due to a growing awareness of his age— and also to an awareness of the powers he still possessed. He was driven forward by a creative restlessness which led him to work unrelentingly on *Friedenstag*, *Daphne*, *Die Liebe der Danae* and *Capriccio* all at the same time. Old plans reappeared: *Coelestina* and *Semiramis*, the latter accompanying him through the decades like a recurring theme.

At last, in December 1935, Gregor was able to relax. 'The ending is magnificent, many thanks!', Strauss wrote to him. And at the beginning of 1936 he commented: 'Happy New Year! *Daphne* is promising—if the two major characters succeed—to become an excellent piece. Congratulations!'

The libretto work on *Friedenstag* was now complete, so that they could devote their joint efforts entirely to *Daphne*.

On 24 July 1938 *Friedenstag* was presented at the Nationaltheater in Munich together with the ballet *Die Geschöpfe des Prometheus* ('The Creatures of Prometheus'), using Beethoven's

Munich Festival, 1961
Munich presented a new production of the work with a good cast at the Prinzregententheater in 1961. The public reaction was reserved and cool.
Producer: Rudolf Hartmann.
Conductor: Joseph Keilberth.
Sets: Helmut Jürgens.

Munich Festival, 1961
This sketch by Helmut Jürgens
reproduces his spatial concept of a
stage: an attempt to manage without any realistic details.
Producer: Rudolf Hartmann.
Conductor: Joseph Keilberth.

music. *Daphne* had its première a little later in Dresden, where *Friedenstag* was also to have had its first performance..

It was Clemens Krauss who caused the two pieces, originally planned as a single evening's programme, to have separate premières. Strauss acceded to his request and entrusted *Friedenstag* to Krauss, since he had a high regard for him as a conductor and this was the first time that he had submitted a new work for performance in his home town, Munich. From 1937 on, when Krauss took over the running of the National-altheater, the relationship between him and Strauss deepened; increasingly the influential man of the theatre had guided the creative plans of the composer. Strauss was living in Garmisch, and often went to the opera in Munich.

As chief producer of the theatre I naturally came into close contact with Richard Strauss, who frequently discussed with me problems re-lating to the stage work or direction of his pieces.

We frequently talked about the preparations for *Friedenstag*. When Strauss was in a talkative mood he was happy to discuss his plans with the close circle of colleagues associated with his work.

Staging the première of *Friedenstag* at Munich also meant that Strauss had conluded peace with his home town, against which he had borne a grudge for many decades.

I particularly recall the frequent conversa-tions we had about shaping the final scene. In his preparatory exchange of ideas with Gregor,

Strauss had once written: 'the tower sinks out of sight'. In this way, not only the final hymn but also the optical effect was to express the atmosphere of liberation. I was worried by the idea of the tower sinking or disappearing (as it did in the otherwise beautiful production at Dresden) because, in my view, this effect was too baroque and magical, and impossible to reconcile with the realism of what had gone before. First, I argued, there was the fortress with its cannon, muskets and gunpowder store, all readily believable dangers, and then suddenly things were by no means as serious: the stage caused them to disappear and the theatre became a concert platform. One night we were discussing the matter on the way back to the Hotel Vierjahreszeiten

after a rehearsal. Strauss stopped at the corner where for many years he had bought his beloved 'Papyrus' cigarettes (in a famous shop owned by Dora Weid) and thought for a moment. Then he said: 'We'll have to discuss this with Krauss.' And that is what happened. Krauss agreed with my views and the set-designer Ludwig Sievert found a solution which convinced the composer and virtually everyone else.

Joseph Gregor, who seldom came to Munich, tended towards the Dresden idea. But from the many conversations I had with him, particularly later about *Daphne,* I gained the impression that Gregor's imagination, so far as the stage was concerned, was not particularly well developed. The very different theatrical instincts of Gregor

Munich Festival, 1961
The spacious stage area allowed for a convincing finale, in which the producer grouped the performers in oratorio style.
Producer: Rudolf Hartmann.
Conductor: Joseph Keilberth.
Sets: Helmut Jürgens.

and of Strauss continued to assert themselves. My relationship with Gregor remained somewhat distant and aloof, partly because of suggestions which I made in connection with the performance of *Daphne*. The great authority on the theatre, who accepted every criticism of his work by Strauss, was very sensitive to comments from others. 'But that's for *me* to say', was his indignant reaction on one occasion to a proposal I put forward.

The Munich Festival of 1938 had as its climax the embattled première which the public took to their hearts with great enthusiasm. There was equally open disapproval in official places, though in Dresden there was an amusing exception. The stage-designer, Leonhard Fanto, had given Mutschmann, the official adviser to the Reichsstatthalter (governor), the *Friedenstag* libretto to read. Strauss reported the story to his wife in a letter (placed at my disposal by Dr. Willi Schuh of Zurich) dated 9 December 1936: 'The official adviser was highly enthusiastic about this "highly political opera libretto: this is what we need". Children! You see, I'm always up to the minute. Since *Salome* it's always been the same!'

The final version of the plot can be presented very briefly.

The location:

A circular hall in the citadel. A walkway encircles the hall at a man's height and includes loopholes. A staircase leads to the upper floor of the fortress, another leads down into the depths. Massive medieval walls everywhere, newly manned because of the war. A gaping hole in the wall has been superficially repaired with wood and stone. Guards are sitting at a large oak table: weather-beaten soldiers in leather jerkins and helmets. They sit there motionless. One cannot see if they are asleep or simply numbed with tiredness and privation. On the table: pewter jugs but no mugs. The fire at their backs throws a dim light on them. They are surrounded by mighty weapons: muskets, swords, 'double-handers'. A few have taken off their breast-plates. Day is breaking. The first sign of dawn appears through the loopholes, blending strangely with the dull glow of the dying fire.

The old Sergeant of the Guard is checking on the various sentries. A young Private expresses sympathy for the peasants in the countryside, but meets with no understanding from the Sergeant, who can think only in military terms, and of his duty. The light voice of a young Piedmontese rings out; he sings a popular love song from his homeland. The soldiers are aroused from their weary numbness and they, too, think back over their dreams and memories. The individual characters are sharply defined. They talk of peace without knowing what it is. Finally, they sing a soldier's song together and this calms the atmosphere.

From outside the citadel voices can be heard crying: 'Hunger!' A crowd approaches. The Sergeant of the Guard suspects a rebellion, gives the alarm and observes with consternation that the lower gates are being forced open.

An officer comes from below to announce the Mayor and the Bishop as leaders of a deputation; they then approach.

The Commandant appears above, dominating the scene with great authority, carrying a document in his hand. The Mayor describes the privations of the people and requests that the fortress be handed over to the enemy. The Commandant refuses, referring to the Emperor's orders and to his duty as a soldier. The Bishop underlines the mayor's entreaties, but in vain.

A wounded officer from the Front interrupts the negotiations. He announces that there is no more ammunition and requests release of the supplies held in the tower below. The Commandant rejects this too. He reads the Emperor's letter with its irrevocable order. The people despair, begin to mutiny and to threaten. The Commandant, greatly shocked, gives notice that he will make an announcement at noon. He promises that an important signal will be given, at which all the gates are to be opened. With this the deputation and the crowd are reassured, and return to the town. The Commandant for his part appears changed by his decision. He orders the soldiers to scatter all the gunpowder there is around the lower tower and calls for a slow-burning fuse.

The soldiers realize what he intends to do; they are shocked and appalled. The Commandant speaks to each of them individually, giving each of them the chance to go down into the town and save themselves. The Sergeant of the Guard, the Constable of the Citadel, and the young Private want to stay with him. Others go or are undecided. The Commandant dismisses the young Piedmontese with his thanks. He had brought the Commandant the letter from the Emperor through enemy lines. After ordering: 'To work! The powder kegs! And fire!' the Commandant goes up the staircase. The hall is empty.

Maria, the Commandant's wife, enters. She has come up from the town and cannot understand why there is such a deathly hush in the ci-

Munich Festival, 1961
Design by Helmut Jürgens. An attempt to condense the set to fit a normal theatre.
Producer: Rudolf Hartmann.
Conductor: Joseph Keilberth.

tadel. She thinks of her beloved husband, of the past, and dreams hopefully of the future.

The Commandant's stone-faced expression and the noise from the lower part of the tower tell her what her husband intends. He wants to send her back into the town, but she decides to stay and die with him.

The soldiers return in sullen submission. The Sergeant of the Guard follows the Commandant's orders and lights the fuse.

Then amidst immense tension a cannon report is heard, then another and yet another. The Commandant believes the enemy is attacking, the soldiers breathe a sigh of relief and prepare to defend themselves. The fuse is extinguished. But outside nothing happens. There is a tense stillness and then the sound of a bell can be heard in the distance, followed by another. After that more and more bells can be heard ringing out, a sound that has not been heard for a long time. The Officer storms in and announces that the enemy is approaching with white flags. The mayor and the deputation arrive as well and speak of peace.

The Commandant refuses to believe them: 'The will of the Emperor was that I should hold out here, that I should be victorious!'

Enemy troops approach; the Lutheran Holstein Commandant enters, radically altering the situation. The enemy Commandant reports the conclusion of an armistice at Münster; the people outside are jubilant. The citadel Commandant suspects a trick, pulls Maria to him and starts to move towards the Holstein Commandant with his sword. Maria throws herself between the two enraged men, calms them and finally her husband gives way. He throws down his weapon and embraces his former opponent.

Led by the jubilant voice of Maria, the final chorus of liberation begins. The stage gradually fills with more and more people, white flags appear everywhere—peace has arrived.

At the beginning of the powerful *allegro maestoso* we find the following instruction: 'The walls open, the tower sinks out of sight. Sunlight penetrates the scene, everything is one swaying mass of people.'

Remember: the stage is a mass of people and the tower is supposed to sink out of sight—an almost impossible demand. In Dresden, Adolf Mahnke came up with the technically excellent solution of *projecting* the upper part of the set which was then able to disappear without trouble. Suddenly the sky over the structures which remained and over the chorus was clear and bright. We have already referred to the problems associated with the tower's disappearance on account of the highly realistic events that preceded it. In Munich Ludwig Sievert found a different solution. The crowd which poured into the citadel opened and destroyed all hatches and doors. The citadel was then illuminated by the sun from all sides and was transformed, but it still existed.

Soon after *Friedenstag* we learnt the horrors of war for ourselves and came to know what destruction and need really meant. It appears that as a survivor one has to feel the rubble under one's feet if one is to be able to rejoice after the danger has passed.

At the 1961 Munich Festival I ventured to put on a new production of *Friedenstag* which, despite all the criticisms of it, is a fine opera. Together with Helmut Jürgens I attempted a solution which from the start avoided any sense of crass realism and which was determined by the concept of the concert-like finish and by parallels with *Fidelio*. This produced several good scenic improvements, but was not totally satisfactory. A symbolic game with war? The public had experienced everything themselves; the opera could not hope to approximate to reality.

Friedenstag was, in an ideal sense, an appeal to men's political conscience (in so far as it exists), but the warning came too late; in the modern world the opera seems fated to have historic rather than immediate significance.

If Richard Strauss were still alive, perhaps he would have erected a second monument in his park. Not a 'Marterl' imbued with humour, but, in the midst of the silent mountain pines, a grave for that human Utopia: eternal peace.

We have referred in detail to the task of the stage-designer. The producer's problems are basically twofold: to establish an overall style linked to the solutions found for the set design and to create a continuous characterization for the well-defined figures in the libretto, and thus removing any unnaturalness (stiltedness, as Strauss called it) from the two main *dramatis personae*, Maria and the Commandant, whose words are so highly charged. Control and direction of the crowd scenes call for the normal skills that any producer might be expected to have.

Daphne

Although work on *Daphne* proceeded at the same time as *Friedenstag*, I do not wish to go into details of its composition because the end result is something unique in the œuvre of Richard Strauss. It is more than an opera in the usual sense and also more than the 'bucolic tragedy' it is called in the sub-title. It symbolizes the composer's passionate affirmation of the world of Antiquity, and is an act of homage to it.

Gregor's basic idea for the opera had appealed to Strauss from the beginning and he applied himself to it fully—forming, shaping, changing, searching for perfection. Again and again he urged the use of the elevated language which was so essential to him, making the following comment on the work's ending: 'Everything distracting must go—it is the tree alone that sings.' With that he achieved a poetic distillation of the spirit of Antiquity. The musical conception triumphs over the verbal; in this opera symphonic music intones a prayer of the most personal kind. In a letter of 20 May 1937 Strauss wrote to Gregor precisely outlining the shape of the finale, which he had discussed in detail with Clemens Krauss:

On Sunday Clemens Krauss was here and we have agreed that after Apollo's farewell song there should be no human figures on the stage except Daphne—no Peneios, no soloists, no chorus—in short, no oratorio: that would weaken the effect. During Apollo's final song Daphne rises slowly, looking at him in astonishment and moving away from Leukippos' body. After Apollo has gone she starts to follow him but, after only a few paces, she stops as if rooted to the spot and then—in the moonlight but completely visible—the miracle of her transformation is fulfilled: with the orchestra alone! At most Daphne can say perhaps a few words during the transformation itself, words which spill over into a kind of stammering and *wordless* melody! But perhaps not, it depends! At any rate, right at the end, when the tree stands complete, she sings a further eight bars of the laurel-tree motif—but in natural tones without words!...

And this—with only a few minor variations—was the final form of the last scene.

As has already been mentioned, Clemens Krauss had an increasing influence on Strauss's ideas and I was often present at their deliberations. After *Friedenstag* it was *Daphne*, and even more so *Die Liebe der Danae*, that gave Krauss, the experienced man of the theatre, occasion to suggest practical advice to Strauss. Even in his old age the composer listened to criticism, and remained self-critical.

As by far the youngest person present at these conversations, my role was partly that of the 'third man', the listener, and partly that of someone directly involved when it came to technical details of production; I can recall how Krauss would sometimes grab a piece of paper and a pencil to explain a scene. Strauss on the other side of the desk would do the same, and then both would give up again after only a few strokes, Krauss saying: 'I can't draw!' Here I was able to help. Small sketches made in this way to clarify a point were later passed on to the stage-designers (Sievert or Gliese), who would be working on a plan or model. These conversations—profound and valuable—always took place in a harmonious atmosphere; there was never any irritability or aggressiveness. However, in them both men sometimes expressed doubts about the ability of the librettist, Gregor. The latter knew, of course, that Krauss, the conductor, was acting as an adviser, and it cannot have been easy for him then to have to carry out the revisions or implement the new ideas given him by Strauss. But as we have already mentioned, Gregor excelled in this work and profited from criticism; of the three libretti that he wrote, *Daphne* is arguably the most complete in itself and his best.

For *Daphne*, Richard Strauss drew on the classical masters and their interpreters for his inspiration. He particularly loved Bernini's statue *Apollo and Daphne* in the Borghese Gallery, Rome.

This is the story of the 'bucolic tragedy' of *Daphne.* The action takes place near the hut of Peneios, a fisherman, on the river of that name. We see a knot of olive-trees and a stony river bank. The sun's last rays are fading. To the right the landscape rises towards Peneios' hut. In the background we can envisage the river. Completing the scene is the massive shape of Mount Olympus. We hear sounds associated with large flocks of sheep: shouts, bells ringing, pushing, shoving, dogs barking, and, amidst all this, a mighty Alpine horn.

The First and Second Shepherds meet on stage. The older one tells his much younger associate about the forthcoming Festival of the Blossoming Vine—the festival of the god Dionysos and of the mating season, the greatest event in the life of a shepherd and his flock. Other shepherds join them, receive instructions and go off to their animals. From below come the strains of their solemn evening song.

Daphne, daughter of Penios and Gaea, listens to the song and then joins in: 'Oh, stay, beloved day. You tarried long, so stay, stay forever!'

Above all else the girl, still a child, loves light and the sun. She is afraid of the Dionysiac abandon of the forthcoming festival. A tender girl, she feels herself at one with the young tree which she planted as a child, at one with her environment of flowers and trees.

Peneios, the fisherman, and his wife, Gaea, are to be seen as deities of lesser rank: he personifies the river, the life-giving element of nature, and she embodies the fruit-bearing earth. Daphne, the girl who loves flowers, to whom everything animal-like is alien, should be seen as belonging to the tree nymphs of the valley, which is situated at the foot of Mount Olympus, the seat of the highest gods. The shepherds and shepherdesses are simple people of the surrounding countryside, which for them signifies life and home.

After Daphne's song—which is in F sharp major, the silvery key of the finale—Leukippos, her childhood friend, runs out from behind the tree where he has overheard what the daydreaming girl was saying. Courting her, he recalls the days of their youth and childhood; but he also wants more—he desires to possess his former playmate completely. She fends him off and remains behind alone.

Her mother, Gaea, comes out of the house, having heard the last few words Leukippos spoke. She talks earnestly and admonishingly to her daughter: 'When you contradicted your friend so forcefully, and turned him away on the day of the festival . . . I grew worried, Daphne.'

Sächsische Staatstheater
Opernhaus

Sonnabend, am 15. Oktober 1938
Anfang **6** Uhr
Außer Anrecht
Uraufführung

Daphne

Bukolische Tragödie in einem Aufzug von Joseph Gregor
Musik von Richard Strauß

Musikalische Leitung: Karl Böhm   Inszenierung: Max Hofmüller

Personen:

Peneios	Sven Nilsson	Zweiter Schäfer Kleontes	Heinrich Tessmer
Gaea	Helene Jung	Dritter Schäfer	Hans Löbel
Daphne	Marg. Teschemacher	Vierter Schäfer	Erich Händel
Leukippos	Martin Kremer	Erste Magd	Angela Kolniak
Apollo	Torsten Ralf	Zweite Magd	Marta Robs
Erster Schäfer Adrast	Arno Schellenberg		

Schäfer, Maskierte des bacchischen Aufzugs, Mägde

Ort: Bei der Hütte des Peneios am Flusse dieses Namens

Chöre: Karl Maria Pembaur   Tänze: Valeria Kratina

Bühnenbild: Adolf Mahnke — Einrichtung: Georg Brandt — Trachten: Leonhard Fanto

Zum ersten Male

Friedenstag

Oper in einem Aufzug von Joseph Gregor
Musik von Richard Strauß

Musikalische Leitung: Karl Böhm   Inszenierung: Max Hofmüller

Personen:

Kommandant der belagerten Stadt		Mathieu Ahlersmeyer	Ein Piemonteser	Willy Treffner
Maria, sein Weib		Marta Fuchs	Der Holsteiner, Kommandant der Belagerungsarmee	Kurt Böhme
Wachtmeister		Sven Nilsson	Bürgermeister	der belagerten Stadt	Martin Kremer
Schütze		Rudolf Dittrich	Prälat		Willy Bader
Konstabel		Robert Büssel	Frau aus dem Volk		Christel Golz
Musketier	von der Besatzung	Ludwig Ermold			
Hornist		Hermann Greiner			
Offizier		Arno Schellenberg			
Frontoffizier		Rudolf Schmalnauer			

Soldaten des Kommandanten der belagerten Stadt und des Holsteiners, Stadtobere und Frauen aus der Deputation an den Kommandanten, Volk

Ort: In der Zitadelle einer belagerten Stadt   Zeit: 24. Oktober 1648

Chöre: Karl Maria Pembaur

Bühnenbild: Adolf Mahnke — Einrichtung: Georg Brandt — Trachten: Leonhard Fanto

Nach der ersten Oper eine große Pause
Beginn des „Friedenstag" ungefähr 8½ Uhr

Sämtliche Pläne müssen vor Beginn der Vorstellung eingenommen werden

Textbücher für Daphne 0.80 R.M., für Friedenstag 0.80 R.M. sind vormittags an der Kasse und abends bei

Staatsoper, Dresden, 1938
As originally planned, the première of *Daphne* in Dresden linked this one-act work with another, *Friedenstag.* The programme proved too long, so *Daphne* was later usually presented on its own and *Friedenstag* put on with another work. The cast of the first performance once again includes the best names from the distinguished Dresden ensemble.
Producer: Max Hofmüller.
Conductor: Karl Böhm.
Sets: Adolf Mahnke.
Costumes: Leonhard Fanto.

Staatsoper, Dresden, 1938
Costume sketch by Leonhard Fanto for the shepherds' festival: a
male dancer as a Faun and a female dancer as a Maenad.

Staatsoper, Dresden, 1938
An impressive sketch by Adolf
Mahnke for the première. A well-
designed arrangement.
Producer: Max Hofmüller.
Conductor: Karl Böhm.
Costumes: Leonhard Fanto.

Two Maids bring in festival garments for the daughter of the house, but Daphne rejects everything. She wants to stay as she is and hurries off into the house.

Gaea, deep in thought, watches as she leaves: 'How distant you are from me, Daphne, my daughter. One day the gods will lead you back, back again to the earth.' She, too, goes into the house. The two Maids remain behind, making mocking comments and joking about Daphne's modesty, and sadly remarking on the jewellery and festive dress which she will not wear. They discover the unhappy Leukippos and wickedly persuade him to disguise himself in Daphne's dress: 'Love through cunning!' Leukippos agrees to the plan and follows the maids who laugh high-spiritedly.

Peneios and Gaea come out of the house, and the shepherds arrive from the valley below. The fisherman welcomes everyone and turns towards Mount Olympus upon whose heights he can still see the last rays of the sun. He greets the god of light, Phoebus Apollo, and dreams of his own lost divinity. He invites his 'brothers', the gods, to the festival, wishing to drink and laugh with them again as he used to do. In the strange bluish grey twilight the shepherds are frightened and crowd closely round Gaea. Peneios' laughter echoes from every direction, and red lights flicker from on high. A figure appears: it is Apollo, disguised as a cowherd, with bow and arrows. Calm returns and the 'cowherd' tells of his herd, which has broken away from him and has gone to graze by the river. Peneios is a little disappointed and Gaea makes fun of the look on his face: 'Now see whom you have attracted to your festival: sweaty farm-hands, frightened cows and a rutting steer!'

The Shepherds burst into laughter with relief. Peneios interrupts them and invites the newly arrived guest to the festival, ordering Daphne to look after him and bid him welcome. Peneios and the Shepherds go down to the river, Gaea re-enters the house, and Apollo is alone. He is ashamed of his lie and calls himself a rutting beast. The light, meanwhile, has changed completely, to an unearthly moonlight. Daphne appears with a shawl and a cloak.

Apollo is overcome by her appearance, believing her to be his sister Artemis who has come to punish him. Daphne—always child-like and natural—pours water over the stranger's hands and wraps the cloak around him. It envelops him like the blue of the firmament. Apollo speaks of the day's longest journey (the day of the summer solstice) and of the symbol of the blossoming vine, and then completely en-shrouds Daphne in the deep blue cloak. He kisses her for a long time; she pulls back in confusion from his embrace and the voices of the shepherds can be heard mysteriously below: 'Dionysos, give us ecstasy, give us love!' Daphne is deeply moved by the evocative sounds and by the stranger's words but does not seek to understand. Everything is a mystery to her—Leukippos, the festival, and the strange cowherd.

The festival begins: a red glow flares up, with flickering torches appearing from all sides. Apollo picks up his weapons, kisses the bowl and throws it aside. Shepherds with torches appear from every point of the thicket; Peneios is at their head and some of them are masked. At the same time a procession of women carrying amphorae and bowls on their heads appears from the side of the house.

Gaea leads the way with a basket of fruit. The two processions meet on stage. Daphne runs to Gaea's side while Apollo withdraws to join the men.

Peneios opens the festival with a dedication: 'Dionysos blossoms everywhere along the river's godly reach, so that one day from this love there may flow to us: his blood, his wine!' The Shepherds take their places and are served by the women. They eat, but they do not yet drink.

In the première Margarethe Teschemacher sang the part of Daphne. Her costume was based on Botticelli's *La Primavera* (Florence, Uffizi Gallery) in accordance with the composer's wishes. Producer: Max Hofmüller. Conductor: Karl Böhm. Sets: Adolf Mahnke. Costumes: Leonhard Fanto.

Bayerische Staatsoper, Munich, 1939
The feast of Dionysos.
Producer: Rudolf Hartmann.
Conductor: Clemens Krauss.
Choreographer: Pino Mlakar.
Sets: Ludwig Sievert.

Bayerische Staatsoper, Munich, 1939
Set for the finale by Ludwig Sievert with Daphne transformed into a laurel-tree.
Producer: Rudolf Hartmann.
Conductor: Clemens Krauss.

Preparations for the Munich première, with *(left to right)* Ludwig Sievert, Clemens Krauss and Rudolf Hartmann looking at the model of the set.

Staatsoper, Berlin, 1939
First Berlin performance, with
Peter Anders (Leukippos), Maria
Cebotari (Daphne) and Torsten
Ralf (Apollo).
Producer: Wolf Völker.
Conductor: Robert Heger.
Sets: Emil Preetorius.

Staatsoper, Berlin, 1939
Design by Emil Preetorius. A
calm, classical landscape.

Alfred Roller's son Ulrich, who was killed during the war, produced this design with the assistance of Robert Kautsky in Vienna in 1943.

Staatsoper, Berlin, 1939
Maria Cebotari, one of the best interpreters of the role of Daphne.
Producer: Wolf Völker.
Conductor: Robert Heger.
Sets: Emil Preetorius.

A wild dance of the masked Shepherds begins, *allegro furioso*, which is directed towards the women. In a second phase, a train of girls appears, some lightly clad, bearing thyrsi; others, with veiled faces, drinking-bowls. They are followed by the disguised and unrecognizable Leukippos. After a short round dance by the girls, the men, wearing rams' masks, burst on to the scene and take possession of the Bacchant maidens. The chorus of shepherds is given wine by the girls with the drinking-bowls, and they accompany the action with wild calls and shouts.

Leukippos walks up to Daphne with his bowl. Her mother demands that she drink from it, and the two Maids who are watching make malicious comments. Daphne drinks from the bowl and follows Leukippos—whom she does not recognize—to the festival dance. Everyone's eyes are on the couple and the mood changes almost to one of a cultic rapture: 'Great are the gods, rich are their wonders! Dionysos! Dionysos!'

Apollo, standing at a higher level, suddenly breaks into a rage: 'This is a fearful insult to the gods.' The indignant Shepherds turn threateningly towards the man who has dared to inter-

Munich and Milan, 1942
Costume design for Apollo by Irmingard Prestel.

Munich and Milan, 1942
Design by Ludwig Sievert for the first performance at La Scala, Milan, which was sung in Italian by a house cast.
Producer: Rudolf Hartmann.
Conductor: Gino Marinuzzi.

Teatro Colón, Buenos Aires, 1948
Design by Hector Basaldua, successfully focusing on Daphne's transformation into a tree.
Producer: Josef Gielen.
Conductor: Erich Kleiber.

Städtische Bühnen, Nuremberg, 1942
Design by Heinz Grete. Daphne's tree is overshadowed by other foliage; the mountain, however, is well depicted.
Producer: André von Diehl.
Conductor: Alfons Dressel.

Staatsoper, Vienna, 1965
Costume designs by Rudolf Heinrich. *Left:* Leukippos (?); *right:* Daphne in the early scenes. The designs show considerable feeling for the character of the work.

rupt their festival and demand that he provide proof to back up his assertion. Apollo swings his bow, and suddenly the scene is darkened by a storm, there are lightning flashes and terrible peals of thunder. Confusion and alarmed indecision reign among the assembled company. 'The fertility rites have been ruined... Save us, save us!' Everyone runs off after their scattered herds, leaving Apollo, Daphne and Leukippos behind.

'Now to you, young fellow, who crept with impudent deceit to the festival of my divine brother and wanted to rob me of the glorious Daphne!' Leukippos throws off his disguise, courageously acknowledges what he has done and openly tries to woo Daphne. He suspects that his rival is not really a cowherd, and demands that the stranger reveal himself in his true identity. Daphne supports him in this demand. Apollo hesitates for some time, knowing full well that it means death for any mortal who catches sight of him as he really is. But then, ultimately provoked, he throws off his cowherd's disguise.

There is no instruction at all in the libretto about the manner in which this important new development is to be presented on stage. But the music at least is unmistakable in its expression. After Leukippos makes his final challenge: 'Purify yourself, false brother!' Apollo—with the threatening query: 'Truth?'—tranforms himself into his real, divine form. As often in Strauss's music where 'the gods' are involved, Apollo's declaration is accompanied by a solemn E flat major. The declaration ends in an radiant

Staatsoper, Vienna, 1965
Designs for Daphne and Apollo
by Rudolf Heinrich. Four productions of *Daphne* have been given
in Vienna. (1) In 1943 at the
Theater an der Wien with Maria
Reining as Daphne; sets: Robert
Kautsky; conductor: Karl Böhm.
(2) At the same theatre in 1950
with Annelies Kupper as Daphne;
conductor: Rudolf Moralt. (3) In
the rebuilt Staatsoper in 1965
with Hilde Güden as Daphne;
sets: Rudolf Heinrich; producer:
Rudolf Hartmann; conductor:
Karl Böhm; (4) In 1972 the same
decor was used for a fresh interpretation with Mimi Coertse as
Daphne; conductor: Horst Stein.

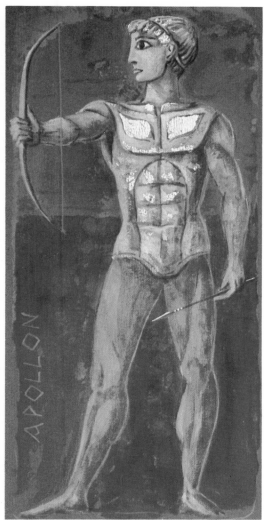

triumph: 'Rejoice, you gods; rejoice, all people and creatures: and see the Sun in me!'

Leukippos, overcome by powerless despair, curses the god Apollo, who raises his bow swiftly and shoots an arrow at him. Leukippos falls to the ground.

Though still dazzled by the harsh light of Apollo's transformation, Daphne can see her mortally wounded childhood friend and throws herself across his body. 'Daphne—my playmate—I dared to love you—and was struck down by a god.' With this final lament Leukippos dies. Daphne then utters a moving lament, which ends with the words: 'But I, unhappy Daphne, will cower in stillness and deep mourning at your feet, in profound humility, and wait...wait until they call me—the proud masters who have killed you and loved me.'

Throughout this great scene, and above all in Daphne's words, Gregor attained a power of ex-

pression which is reminiscent of Hofmannsthal. Here we find a linguistic intensity (which helped to inspire the music) of a kind he never achieved elsewhere.

Apollo observes the motionless Daphne, asks his brother Dionysos for forgiveness, and implores Zeus to forgive his transgression in interfering in the fate of humans instead of transcending them. But he also asks the lord of the gods for mercy, requesting that Zeus give him his beloved Daphne for ever as a flourishing tree, as the laurel of the gods.

Zeus grants his request. (Here the libretto offers no precise guidelines. But the music does, at figure 232 in the *forte* of the E flat major motif.) Apollo rises and dedicates the laurel-tree to the future task of providing crowns of victory for those who excel in peaceful competition.

Apollo disappears in complete darkness. Daphne struggles to her feet, wanting to follow him, but then stops as if spell-bound by a sudden flash of light. Her metamorphosis begins and she gradually changes into a tree. Her last spoken words accompany this mysterious process: 'People, friends, take me as a sign of undying love.' She can now no longer be seen. Her voice can be heard once more from within the newly created tree, but she utters no words, singing naturally like a bird. The golden light of the rising sun, coming from the direction of Mount Olympus, plays on the green leaves of the tree.

The atmosphere of the dawning day deviates here, quite deliberately, from the original instructions, where 'silver light' is mentioned. It was the subject of several conversations between Strauss and Gregor. The composer vigorously applauded the idea when it first emerged (Munich, 1941) and it was later accepted—albeit somewhat hesitantly—by the librettist as well.

In this context it is obvious that the union of light (Apollo) with the young tree (Daphne) should be visibly presented as a crowning glory and a conclusion. No scrims or other technical artefacts should detract from the effect.

Some years ago I wrote an article for the *Schweizerische Musikzeitung* on problems connected with the production and sets of *Daphne*. Some of my conclusions have remained valid and with the kind permission of the periodical's chief editor, Dr. Willi Schuh, I now quote from my article: 'Strauss once during a conversation gave a characteristic answer about the not inconsiderable technical problems a work can cause: "Yes", he said, "that is the producer's concern. I composed the work and have tried to express everything in the music, now the theatre must do its bit towards it."'

Because of his early encounter with Max Reinhardt *(Der Rosenkavalier, Ariadne)* Strauss expected great expertise from producers. As his own mastery of music continued to develop, he expected the same progress from those responsible for producing his works and designing their sets.

As work succeeded work Strauss showed an ever increasing interest in all aspects of their production. His artistic temperament made ever more demands, seeking to make the entire theatre join in the mood of expectant excitement which he always felt was essential. That meant that the staging was often driven along with impatience and the producer was left to work out the relationship between the characters without having the appropriate music available.

The setting for *Daphne*, an Olympian landscape, should be balanced between naturalism and stylization. The former is excluded by the strict unity of the whole, despite the 'feeling for nature' it contains, whereas the latter is excluded by the need to give credibility to the symbolic figures: on one hand the people, animals and plants which are rooted in their earthly functions and on the other, the gods who determine the unfolding of the entire action.

In keeping with Daphne's touching, unselfconscious existence and with her sunny, soulful, plant-like nature, Strauss did not provide any entrance music for her. Daphne is simply there, like the bushes, the flowers and the spring. One successful solution to this problem is for Daphne—who is on stage from the beginning—to rise out of the bushes, where she has lain hidden, as the shepherds' song begins to die away, and for her then to utter her words of yearning as the sun's last rays fade.

The lighting squences for this first scene are particularly important. For example, as Daphne expresses her words of yearning, the dying rays of sunlight touch her whole figure, her shoulders and finally just her finger-tips; later, the repetition of her words by the disguised Apollo reminds the audience and gives the first scene its sense of tender courtship.

As for the rest of the scene, the stage must not be darkened too early. Peneios, glancing up towards the peak of Olympus, gives us the lead: 'There is the sun, not yet dimmed! Not yet has Phoebus Apollo left us!' But after that the twilight descends quickly and from it the god in his cowherd's disguise suddenly emerges, accompanied by small flashes of light. At this point the sun's rays should no longer be visible as Apollo himself is the light and his entrance must occur without any distracting elements. He must appear suddenly and supernaturally, so throwing the shepherds into confusion.

Following Apollo's entrance the setting moves into twilight, but for the moment without direct moonlight. The ensuing encounter between Apollo and Daphne takes place in a hazy, unreal brightness. When Apollo puts on the broad blue cloak (as a symbol of the firmament) this causes an intensified glow of light which fills the whole stage: 'He envelops her firmly, so that she sinks completely into the blue of the cloak.' As Apollo kisses Daphne—who trembles with fear (E major chord, a characteristic sound in Strauss's music for an expression of love)—a mysterious darkness develops, from which can be heard the distant chorus of the shepherds with their solemn hymn-like song.

At the start of the festival the torches carried by the shepherds introduce a flickering reddish light for the important ritual dances. But there is no drinking until Gaea says: 'Drink, my daughter' as Leukippos, disguised as a girl, offers Daphne his bowl.

The festival comes to an abrupt halt as the enraged Apollo makes his dramatic entrance. The lights are extinguished and the storm summoned up by the god breaks out. In the following scene between Leukippos and Apollo, the god is still disguised as a cowherd (the blue cloak has been torn from him by the shepherds) but in clear contrast to his first entrance he should now be surrounded by a threatening magic glow. Pressed by Daphne and Leukippos, Apollo has

to reveal himself in his true form. The sense of the action can be made clear at this point if, as the hymn 'Jeden heiligen Morgen...' with its lustrous E flat major strikes up, Apollo shows himself to the two dazzled children of Man in his radiant form as god of Light. By exercising some skill, the cowherd can discard his costume in such a way that no pieces are left lying around on the stage where they could be seen. The brightness reflected from Apollo's golden armour is linked with a faint light on the peak of Mount Olympus which then gradually fades. Before Apollo fires his mortal arrow the stage should darken again quickly and sharply. The flight of the arrow from Apollo's bow to its target, Leukippos, can be represented credibly by

Bayerische Staatsoper, Munich, 1964
The feast of Dionysos with the performers skilfully grouped. The size of the tree had a detrimental effect on the final scene.
Producer: Heinz Arnold.
Conductor: Joseph Keilberth.
Sets: Helmut Jürgens.
Choreographer: Pino Mlakar.

233

the use of two flash cubes, Leukippos wearing one in his costume and setting it off himself. After he has fired the arrow, Apollo should leave the stage quickly in the darkness and should not be present at all during Daphne's lament. His feelings of remorse and pity—in themselves not emotions found in ancient Greece—then provide a convincing motivation for his later re-appearance, because he has to witness Daphne's final words.

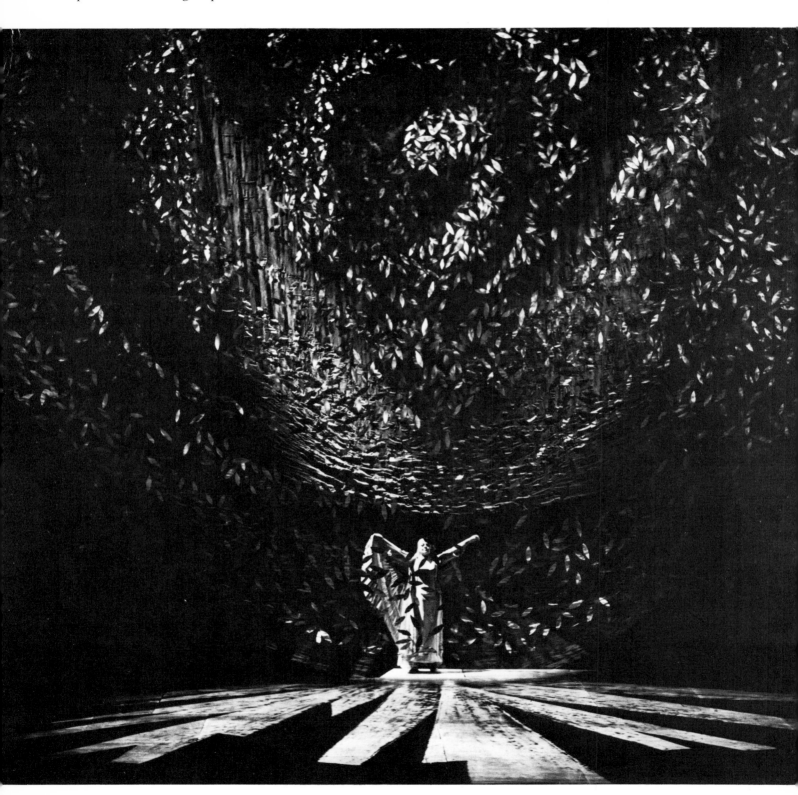

Strong light again strikes Apollo as he calls on Zeus and appeals for Daphne's transformation into a laurel-tree. Light must be used also to portray the granting of his request, after which he disappears again into the darkness.

Daphne's metamorphosis—which *is* visible—is a theme which has often been depicted in painting and sculpture. On stage it can be portrayed by resorting to various technical devices. The important thing here is that the young tree should grow tenderly and in a child-like fashion, so that Daphne herself remains recognizable while she is singing, and so that the new tree assumes a solitary position in the Olympian landscape. It should not be one tree among many but should stand out on its own by virtue of its very positioning. This means that careful attention should be paid to the effect of the setting as a whole.

As already mentioned, the portrayal of the final scene in Munich in 1941 deviated from the instructions in the libretto and was developed from the concept of the eternal union of Daphne with Apollo. The laurel-tree did not remain in the moonlight but was in the rays of the new morning sun, with Apollo's tender, sparkling sunbeams playing on the young leaves and branches which reached out tremblingly towards the light: an ideal union which conveyed a sense of spiritual exaltation.

Deutsche Staatsoper, Berlin, 1969
Final scene with a huge, symbolic tree.
Producer: Erich Witte.
Conductor: Otmar Suitner.
Sets: Gustav Hoffmann.
Costumes: Christine Stromberg.

The première in Dresden on 15 October 1938 was accompanied by the first performance of the one-act piece *Friedenstag*. This combination resulted in a very long evening which took place at a watershed in human affairs, on the eve of a new world war. The contrast between the two works was starkly emphasized: on one hand there was the warning in *Friedenstag*, which at that point had almost been superseded by events, and on the other there was the spiritualized, reconciliatory world of ancient Greece in *Daphne*; this too impressed the audience deeply and left it in a pensive mood. The première was no longer a rapturous operatic festival but an expression of desires and yearnings that seemed to have no place in the political climate of that time.

After that *Daphne* made its way on the stage alone, without any accompanying work in the same programme. For everyone who attended the première in Dresden the work left an indelible impression. With her light voice, the soprano Margarethe Teschemacher (who at Strauss's request wore a Primavera costume à la Botticelli) created a tender, moving Daphne and her performance served as a model for all her successors in the part. The wishes of the composer and librettist were carried out perfectly by the producer, Max Hofmüller and his stage-designer, Adolf Mahnke.

Die Liebe der Danae
('The Love of Danae')

In the Strauss archives at Garmisch there is a copy of a note in Strauss's hand relating to this opera, entitled 'History of the Opera *Die Liebe der Danae*. Written in 1946, it also deals with the staging of the première of *Die Frau ohne Schatten*, and reads as follows:

The splendid première of *Die Frau ohne Schatten* was held in Vienna on 10 October 1919. More or less successful performances followed in Dresden, Munich and Berlin. The work was somewhat misunderstood at first, and when it was presented at medium or smaller-sized theatres in Germany the straightened circumstances of the immediate post-war years were particularly disadvantageous and harmful to this difficult opera: skimpy sets and inadequate casting were barriers to comprehension of the work and restricted its success. The fate that had befallen *Die Frau ohne Schatten* made me determine—once *Die Liebe der Danae* was finished at the beginning of the last war (1940)—that *this* opera would only be released to the theatres two years after the peace treaty. I put the manuscript in my drawer and wrote the one-act piece *Capriccio*, which was then given its première in Munich.

In 1943 Clemens Krauss came to me and asked whether I would be willing to let Salzburg have the score of *Danae* for six performances as an extra celebration for my eightieth birthday, to be held in August 1944. After some hesitation I agreed to this as a reward to Krauss for his invaluable services in connection with my work and because I wished to hear a complete performance of the piece before my death. [Strauss's eightieth birthday was on 11 June 1944, and the war-time festival in Salzburg in August was under the artistic direction of Clemens Krauss.] After Salzburg, *Danae* disappeared from the stage.

Rehearsals began in Salzburg in July 1944, but not before Krauss had expended a great deal of energy in preparing the score and parts

and overcoming the many difficulties posed by the sets and costumes. Then a week before the première which had been arranged for 12 August, Dr. Goebbels cancelled the entire festival. [Dr. Goebbels was Minister for Propaganda and Culture in the Third Reich and at this time had called for 'total war'. Art in any shape or form lost its right to exist.]

None the less Krauss managed to keep the rehearsals going right up to the point of the dress rehearsal so that 'the composer could hear his work performed at least once'. This dress rehearsal, which was a very fine performance, was held on 16 August before an invited audience. (In the main the audience consisted of wounded or convalescent soldiers in uniform.)

Then everything was over and everyone dispersed. All the artists went into Herr Hitler's armaments industry and 1 September marked the end of a phase in German opera which had lasted almost two hundred years.

On taking my leave I promised the administration of the Salzburg Festival that they could have the première of *Danae* for 1945, but they did not even take advantage of this offer for the 1946 festival.

In October 1945 I was forced to leave my house in Garmisch because of the coal shortage and immediately the Stadttheater in Zurich, the Amsterdam Opera and the State Opera in Stockholm asked me to let them put on the première. My publisher and I considered the possibility of simultaneous premières at all three theatres on the same day, but because of the major technical difficulties involved we soon dropped this idea. In the meantime Schmid-Bloss, director at Zurich, repeatedly implored me to let the Stadttheater there have the première, but I could not make up my mind. The memory of the wonderful dress rehearsal at Salzburg renewed my desire to leave the performance to the administra-

This painting of Danae, ecstatically abandoning herself to the shower of gold, is a famous example of art nouveau by the Viennese artist Gustav Klimt (1862–1918). The combination of powerful eroticism and an almost musical handling of colour and form is close to Strauss's own treatment of the subject.

tion of the Salzburg Festival in the same form, with the same cast and the same director as for the dress rehearsal, and I let Clemens Krauss know this. But careful thought finally led me to abandon even this idea and to fall back on my very first resolve: the première should not take place until at least two years after the conclusion of peace.

Now, in 1945, catastrophe has befallen Germany and destroyed almost all the opera-houses; the country is occupied by the Allies, and the German borders are closed. This means that for the time being it has become impossible to hold a première in Salzburg before an international (and particularly the art-loving German) audience or before international music critics. The festival administration (and not just myself) must be concerned not to allow an admittedly unusual event such as the première of Richard Strauss's last opera to disappear like a puff of smoke without gaining some serious reaction. For this reason the première of *Danae* can wait until the festival is restored to its previous style, and a performance before the audiences that normally attend Strauss premières can be guaranteed, even if that means waiting until 1950 or 1955.

I promise that until such a time I will not give the première to any other theatre without reaching an understanding with Salzburg.
signed: Dr. Richard Strauss
Honorary Citizen of Salzburg
Co-founder of the Festival.
Baden (Switzerland), 8 December 1946.
Danae was not in fact Strauss's last opera, but it was his last stage work to be given a première, on account of the delays which he specified.

In accordance with Strauss's wishes, *Danae* was first performed on 14 August 1952 at the Salzburg Festival. The conductor was Clemens Krauss, the production by Rudolf Hartmann, sets and costumes by Emil Preetorius. Some of the singers of the main roles differed from those of the 1944 dress rehearsal.

Salzburg Festival, 1944 (dress rehearsal)
Scene from Act I. Jupiter (Hans Hotter) arriving on the golden ship.

Richard Strauss had died in September 1949 without of course seeing the première of this work. But he summarized his impressions of the dress rehearsal in a letter to Willi Schuh, giving a detailed description of the performance. In this letter we find the following passage, written in a mood of tense excitement and strongly influenced by the events of the day: 'It was really a "unique" event of the greatest cultural significance...' The mood of painful parting affected not just the composer but also all those, without exception, who had participated in the occasion and for whom the war thereafter had to take priority.

With the benefit of hindsight, and looking back on the experience of several new productions of *Danae*, it must be said that in its dramatic construction the work was not a success. As early as 1920 Hofmannsthal had drafted an outline of *Danae, or The Marriage of Convenience*. It had been his intention to write a 'cheerful mythology', but the original idea lingered only in the subtitle and in the more light-hearted scenes with the four Queens. The original outline became increasingly overlaid and overburdened with scenes of Wagnerian heaviness (especially in Act III). Both libretto and music quite lost the sovereign cheerfulness that had originally been intended.

Many attempts were made to produce a fundamentally new version and some of these fell back on the first drafts. On 2 January 1980 I spoke to Dr. Franz Strauss, the composer's son, in Garmisch about changes and the re-shaping of the work which I suggested would have to be undertaken and authorized by the Strauss family itself. However, Dr. Franz Strauss died on 14 February 1980. The intrinsic excellence of *Die Liebe der Danae* makes every effort taken on its behalf worthwhile.

It was Willi Schuh who drew Strauss's attention to Hofmannsthal's draft of 1920, which the composer had forgotten about. He thereupon gave Joseph Gregor the task of drawing up the libretto. Clemens Krauss was often asked by Strauss for his advice and took great interest in the progress of the work. The lack of unity manifested by the completed work can perhaps be traced to the many, often contradictory, ideas that went into it; the tense mood of the times, hardly conducive to art, also played its part in hindering the development of a graceful and elegant theme.

A letter from Clemens Krauss to Richard Strauss dated 28 July 1944 provides an eloquent and very moving account of the difficulties encountered during the preparations for the Salz-

SALZBURGER FESTSPIELE 1952

DIE LIEBE DER DANAE

Heitere Mythologie in drei Akten
mit Benützung eines Entwurfes von Hugo von Hofmannsthal
von Joseph Gregor

Musik von
RICHARD STRAUSS
OP. 83

Dirigent:
CLEMENS KRAUSS

Inszenierung:
RUDOLF HARTMANN

Bühnenbild und Kostüme:
EMIL PREETORIUS

Orchester:
DIE WIENER PHILHARMONIKER
CHOR DER WIENER STAATSOPER

DIE LIEBE DER DANAE

Heitere Mythologie in drei Akten
mit Benützung eines Entwurfes von Hugo von Hofmannsthal
von Joseph Gregor

Musik von Richard Strauß, op. 83

Jupiter	Paul Schöffler
Merkur	Josef Traxel
Pollux, König von Eos	Laszlo Szemere
Danae, dessen Tochter	Annelies Kupper
Xanthe, Danaes Dienerin	Anny Felbermayer
Midas	Josef Gostic
Vier Könige, Neffen des Pollux	August Jaresch
	Erich Majkut
	Harald Pröglhöf
	Franz Bierbach
Semele	Dorothea Siebert
Europa	Esther Rethy
Alkmene vier Königinnen	Georgine Milinkovic
Leda	Sieglinde Wagner

Vier Wächter, Chor der Gläubiger, Gefolge und Diener des
Pollux, Gefolge und Dienerinnen der Danae, Volk

ERSTER AKT
Thronsaal des Königs Pollux — Schlafgemach der Danae —
ein Säulenhof am Palaste — Hafen

ZWEITER AKT
Saal im Palast des Königs

DRITTER AKT
Landstraße im Orient — südliche Berglandschaft —
Hütte des Midas

---

burg performance of 1944. One should bear in mind that the artists—led by Clemens Krauss —were fighting with fatalistic idealism for what gave sense and meaning to their lives:

Only today have we gained some idea of when we shall be able to put on *Die Liebe der Danae.* Because of the bombing raids on Munich some of the carpenter's work was burned, also a number of pillars which were designed for the second act, along with several hundred metres of material which were in the dyer's shop awaiting treatment. There were also great difficulties in transporting things from Munich to Salzburg. We had to try to get the finished sections of the set over here in furniture vans powered by producer gas. The last load arrived only today. Tomorrow we will be able to take stock of what is missing and what we will have to remake. The painted drop-curtains for the three sets in the third act have been done in Prague and arrived here on schedule last week. The tailors in Munich had to stop working because, as you will know, they often had no electricity or light for days on end. Last week they took all the costume work they had started and all the material they still need to Salzburg, where they have set up shop in makeshift workshops.

Salzburg Festival, 1952
The programme for the première, which had been postponed until after the war. In accordance with the composer's wishes, the production staff was the same as in 1944, but the cast of singers had changed completely.
Producer: Rudolf Hartmann.
Conductor: Clemens Krauss. Sets and costumes: Emil Preetorius.

Salzburg Festival, 1952
Scene from Act III. In the desert.
Midas, the muleteer, and Danae,
now released from the spell of the
golden touch, are faced with
poverty, but are free to begin a
normal human life. In Emil
Preetorius's set the light colour of
the terracotta background produces a powerful effect.

All these interruptions mean that we could not adhere to the original date for the pre-mière.

The same letter was continued on 31 July 1944:

In the meantime a few changes have oc-curred, and events are following one after the other. An order from Minister Goebbels of 29 July has cancelled this year's 'Summer of Theatre and Music in Salzburg', which means that none of the events arranged will now take place. This puts us in a totally new situ-ation...

The rest of the story about the dress rehearsal of 16 August has already been described. Here now is an account of the plot of the work which was intended to be a 'cheerful mythology'.

The god Jupiter, who is for ever embarking upon new love affairs, is preparing for another conquest. He is tired of his previous loves, Se-mele, Europa, Alcmena and Leda. His interest has now been aroused by Danae, the beautiful daughter of the bankrupt King Pollux on the island of Eos. Having already taken on the forms of a cloud, a steer, Amphitryon and a swan, he is searching for a different manifestation in order to win Danae's heart. Danae is riveted by gold and riches, rather than by men. So Jupiter re-solves to transform himself into King Midas (whose immense fortune has caused amazement

Staatsoper, Berlin, 1952
Scene from Act II. Jupiter (Herbert Brauer) with his four former loves and the derisive Mercury. The producer at the Berlin première was Strauss's grandson (who has the same name as the composer).
Conductor: Leopold Ludwig.
Sets: Josef Fenneker.

Staatsoper, Berlin, 1952
Scene from Act II. Jupiter with his four former loves. Josef Fenneker created a set with a relaxed atmosphere. The decorative gathered curtains are typical of his work.

everywhere), so that he can then court her. To protect himself from the jealous gaze of Juno, Jupiter takes with him a 'poor muleteer', King Midas in disguise, who is to go to Danae as a messenger and to announce Jupiter as King Midas. The muleteer calls himself Chrysopher, 'bearer of gold', and in passing on his message from Jupiter he and Danae fall deeply in love.

ACT I

Throne room of King Pollux. Signs of previous wealth can be seen, but now everything is tattered, faded and in decay. The throne is only partly of gold, elsewhere it is grotesquely supported with bits of wood. Creditors are thronging before the open doors. Servants and guards are pre-

Teatro alla Scala, Milan, 1953
Set by Ludwig Sievert for the first scene of the Milan première. A fine design allowing great scope for the producer.
Producer: Margarete Wallmann.
Conductor: Clemens Krauss.

Teatro alla Scala, Milan, 1953
Transformation scene in Act I. The harbour; Jupiter's arrival. The sideways view of the ship is not entirely convincing, nor is the long landing-stage to the front. The pillars and the view to the sea are good, leaving ample space for the great final scene.

venting them from forcing their way into the room.

The angry crowd of creditors present their bills and credit notes, demanding payment in gold and cash.

The hard-pressed King Pollux appears, tries to appease the creditors, and explains his plan: he has sent out his four nephews—the kings of the island—with their beautiful wives Alcmena, Semele, Europa and Leda. They have taken with them a portrait of his daughter Danae and arrived at the fabulously wealthy court of King Midas of Lydia. Midas is now about to appear in the house of Pollux; his arrival has already been announced. Pollux pleads: 'Have patience for just one more day!' Then through his own ineptitude Pollux allows the gold throne, which up to now has been covered, to become visible. The creditors, at first surprised, then hurl themselves at it, fighting for possession of the golden emblems that adorn it.

Drop-curtain.

Danae's bedroom, darkened. A heavy golden rain is falling. Gradually we see the figure of Danae lying on her bed. The golden rain shower begins to ease off and by the time Danae awakes has disappeared completely.

Still drugged by sleep, Danae continues to imagine the brilliant vision of gold. But her servant, Xanthe, lying at her feet, sees only the night—Danae has obviously just been dreaming... The sound of a distant march (unusually in 5/4 time) heralds the return of King Pollux's four nephews.

Drop-curtain.

A pillared courtyard in the palace. In the background deep arcades can be seen which look out on to the sea through several rows of columns. King Pollux, his courtiers and creditors fill the courtyard, expectantly awaiting the four nephews and their entourage. The people crowd together in among the arcades.

The four Queens report on the journey, telling of failures, until in far-off Lydia King Midas showed enthusiasm for Danae's likeness and sent a golden branch as a 'greeting of love'. The creditors endeavour to gain possession of the gift, but Danae seizes it: 'Midas sent this to *me*!' In the ensuing chaos a cry from outside is heard: 'A ship! A ship!' They all run to the harbour to welcome Midas; Danae remains behind alone, shaking with anticipation. Midas (disguised as a muleteer) enters, greets Danae as 'the bride of Midas' whom he is to court as the latter's 'friend'. He calls himself Chrysopher, 'bearer of

gold'. He imparts the message entrusted to him by his king and presents Danae with a golden dress of honour which she puts on with the help of her servants. Danae is doubtful about the man she sees before her. 'You are the messenger? Not Midas—only Chrysopher?' Shouts of greeting are heard from outside as the two gaze into one another's eyes—Midas is not allowed to say what he is thinking, for he has to carry out the mission entrusted to him, although he performs his task of deception with immense reluctance.

While the curtain remains open, the scene changes to the harbour. Midas (still disguised as Chrysopher) leads Danae down to the harbour, the arcades moving back before them.

Soloists and chorus must now quickly re-enter for the following scene. (The baroque magic of moving arcades and golden figures of Muses conjured up by Midas may be found confusing by the audience.) Altering the sequence of scenes, as was first done in 1953 in Munich by Rudolf Kempe and Rudolf Hartmann, and again in the 1967 production (Keilberth/Hartmann), helped to improve the dramatic flow immensely. The story now went as follows: after the golden rain shower in Danae's bedchamber, the servant, Xanthe, then ran off-stage; the messenger, Midas in disguise, suddenly appeared before Danae, who was now alone. Midas imparted his message, presented the golden dress, and there was a change of scene, using the drop-curtain, to the major harbour set where in a sequence of events the return of the golden ship was enacted. This meant that the awkward double entrance of the chorus was done away with and a finale with a major climax helped to create a credible unity.

The crowd is now beside itself with excitement as Jupiter disembarks from the ship in the guise of King Midas, glistening like gold. The four Queens, aware of whom they really see before them, smile knowingly at one another. As Danae draws near to his golden radiance, she begins to suspect the truth, and falls fainting into the arms of her servant Xanthe. The messenger (Midas-Chrysopher) rushes to help her but a threatening gesture by Jupiter shows him his place.

ACT II

A magnificent chamber: a marriage bed in Pompeian style. The four Queens are adorning it with garlands of flowers. Recalling their own experiences of love with Jupiter they envy 'lucky Danae'. The god enters in his golden disguise

Munich Festival, 1953
The first time that the Bayerische Staatsoper in Munich put on this work at the festival was in 1953, when it presented a revised version, made as a result of the experience gained at the Salzburg Festival production. Helmut Jürgen's beautiful sets were perhaps too severe and economical for the nature of the piece.
Producer: Rudolf Hartmann.
Conductor: Rudolf Kempe.
Costumes: Rosemarie Jakameit.

and is greeted jubilantly: 'Jupiter-Midas, Midas-Jupiter, welcome!' His former loves know everything, and he has to warn them to be silent.

In the light-hearted scene that follows the Queens recall their own happy encounters with Jupiter and become jealous of Danae, since they themselves hope for new adventures. Jupiter is unsettled, and recalls, in an image of a gigantic shadow, his wife Juno, who keeps pursuing him. He explains why he has appeared to Danae twice—as the golden rain and as King Midas. The use of the muleteer as his double is to protect him from Juno's gaze.

When Midas the messenger enters, the four Queens—still longing for new encounters with Jupiter—leave the embarrassed and wearied god. Having got rid of them, Jupiter, irritated, comments disparagingly to the muleteer on his former loves. But he also jealously accuses his messenger of betrayal and threatens: 'Danae remains mine!' Then he reminds Midas of his ominous gift of the golden touch: 'Whatever you touch or take to your lips, whether it be dear to you or not, will turn to gold!'

He storms out of the room to call on Danae to make her decision. Here Midas has to leave the stage to don his golden armour. When he re-enters he appears as the king he really is, in the disguise which Jupiter had earlier adopted.

The marriage procession follows; Danae is led to the chamber by the four Queens. They make

Munich Festival, 1953
Scene from Act III. Jupiter bids
farewell to the four Queens.

246

Bayerische Staatsoper, Munich, 1967
There was a further new production in Munich in 1967, this time with costumes and sets by Jean-Pierre Ponnelle. The emphasis was placed on the work's 'cheerful mythology' and its irony, which forced into the background the heavier, Wagnerian qualities. This step proved successful and seemed capable of further development. Producer: Rudolf Hartmann. Conductor: Joseph Keilberth.

BAYERISCHE STAATSOPER
NATIONALTHEATER MÜNCHEN

Donnerstag, 4. Mai 1967

Neuinszenierung

Die Liebe der Danae

Heitere Mythologie in drei Akten mit Benützung eines Entwurfs
von Hugo von Hofmannsthal, von Joseph Gregor
Szenische und musikalische Einrichtung der Bayerischen Staatsoper

Musik von
RICHARD STRAUSS

Musikalische Leitung: Joseph Keilberth

Inszenierung: Rudolf Hartmann

Bühnenbild und Kostüme: Jean Pierre Ponnelle

mocking comments and lay claim to the 'Golden King' for themselves. But as they draw closer they recognize that they are mistaken and run off. Danae is left alone with Midas. Both want to know the truth, and to be free. Midas transforms the chamber into gold. Danae is ecstatic at the sight of such brilliance and the two embrace. The chamber is enveloped in darkness; thunder is heard. Midas calls out 'Danae, Danae!' A faint, dull light slowly illuminates the scene again, the only point of brightness being the golden statue into which Danae has been transformed.

Jupiter appears before Midas, who is in despair. (There are no details about what form Jupiter has now assumed—for Midas still has the golden garments! Some light will be shed on this by the summary of production problems at the end of this chapter.)

Midas and Jupiter call on Danae to decide between them. Jupiter offers the temptation of gold, but Midas offers her a human existence at the side of a muleteer. 'Choose, Danae, choose!', they both call. The golden statue speaks with difficulty: 'Midas... my love... stay close to me. I sense love—adieu, my dream!' The glistening gold begins to disappear, and the statue reverts to the enchanting form of Danae. In the darkness and the storm Midas and Danae (both of them now without any golden garments) hurry

away. An angry Jupiter is left behind alone. His monologue now departs from the general mood of the act, which hitherto has been one of an amusing comedy, and assumes an expansively dramatic, Wotan-like quality. The problems inherent in Act III are prefigured.

ACT III

A country road in the Middle East. Midas and Danae have just awoken beneath a group of half-dead palm-trees.

Danae endeavours to come to terms with the reality of her new situation. Midas helps her to recall what has transpired and relates how Jupiter, disguised as 'an old man in a burnous' approached him and said: 'What Man has never yet possessed in wealth, Midas, may it be yours! Hear this spell! Whatever you touch or take to your lips, whether it be dear to you or not, will turn to gold!' There was one condition: that, at the god's signal, each would exchange his identity for that of the other. And Midas had at all times to obey, otherwise he would lose the golden touch and the promised wealth. Midas recalls what has happened, how he courted Danae for Jupiter, how his love for her was suddenly awakened and how he argued with the god.

They have now truly found one another and embark on their new life together.

Drop-curtain.
A southern landscape; mountains and forests.
Jupiter enters, deep in thought. Mercury, Messenger of the gods, joins him. He relates mockingly how Jupiter's misfortune has caused laughter among the gods particularly in the case of Juno. Jupiter's four former loves, who have been called to this place by the mischievous Mercury, playfully greet the embarrassed Father of the gods. Jupiter, enraged, makes angry threats and tells them to go away. The women, however, fool him with flattery and calm him down. Jupiter then invites them to partake of a banquet which Mercury has conjured up. The avaricious women again try to seduce Jupiter but he takes leave of them for ever: 'Farewell! The god does not bear disappointment, disappointment of the last and final kind... and so he takes his leave of you and of the earth, which he loved in all its forms, loved above all as golden rain...'

The plot now departs once more from cheerful mythology as Jupiter, after an enchanting farewell banquet with the four Queens, resumes his role as Father of the gods. His last, vain love affair has made him melancholy and the resemblance to Wotan becomes increasingly evident.

The creditors then burst in on the scene, accompanied by the four Kings who have been searching for their faithless wives. Jupiter, called 'Midas' by the interlopers, feels ashamed of his deception. In a tight corner, on Mercury's advice he conjures up a golden rain shower which placates the demanding creditors. Everyone runs after the falling gold, moving towards the back of the stage. Mercury then cunningly tries to persuade Jupiter to undertake a new venture: to find Danae in her new surroundings and win her.

Drop-curtain

Inside the muleteer's hut. Everything is modest but orderly. A large divan, a low table with seats, many coloured hangings in oriental style. An old carpet serves as the door. Bright sunlight is streaming through the open window and through the curtain.

Danae is alone, and extols the contented happiness of her present life. Jupiter enters dressed as 'the old man in the burnous'. Danae recalls Midas' tale and is suspicious, but offers the stranger a drink of water.

Jupiter is unsettled by Danae's contentment and tries to re-awaken memories of her golden dreams. He succeeds only partially, before Danae reverts to her mood of calm security: 'See, I am in love!' The finale follows with Jupiter's farewell, which contains the tale of Maia, whom he loved—in itself a beautiful interlude—and Danae returns the golden brooch given her by Jupiter. This scene is somewhat drawn-out and contrived, and suggests more parallels with Wotan.

This final tableau emphasizes the need for a complete revision of certain scenes from the work. The act ends with Jupiter's departure and the imminent homecoming of the muleteer, whom Danae joyously rushes to welcome.

In a letter to Willi Schuh, written in 1945, I reported in detail on the production problems entailed in *Die Liebe der Danae*. Passages from this letter complement the outline of the plot just given: my comments relate to experience of the first dress rehearsal at the Salzburg Festival. Many of the points raised were later improved or solved in different ways in the new Munich productions of 1953 and 1967, but the problems themselves remained the same:

Some scenes took a great deal of hard work to shape, but others, such as Jupiter's comic encounters with his former loves, were magically easy right from the start. ... Against this, however, must be set the increasing difficulties which just seemed to pile up—partly because of the technical demands and partly because of wider considerations concerning the appearance of the actors, who constantly had to change their appearance. A solution was found for the difficult transformations into gold, to which the decor and costumes

Bayerische Staatsoper, Munich, 1967
Jupiter (Hans Günter Nöcker), hard-pressed by his over amorous former loves, finds it not altogether easy to resist their advances. Producer: Rudolf Hartmann. Conductor: Joseph Keilberth. Sets and costumes: Jean-Pierre Ponnelle.

Bayerische Staatsoper, Munich, 1967

These four sets from Acts II and III by Jean-Pierre Ponnelle are examples of settings constructed with a light touch and a sense of fun. They are an ideal background for the producer to shape the comedy.

made their own contributions. Emil Preetorius succeeded magnificently in capturing the mystical transparency of the events on stage in scene changes against a silken terracotta background which alternated with stylized Pompeian architecture. The incomplete stage directions had already given rise to serious misgivings during preparation of the overall production plan... To eliminate any lack of clarity, and on the advice of Clemens Krauss, I invited the librettist, Joseph Greg-

or, to visit us for a few days, which he willingly agreed to do...

The stage directions for the first act contain several details for Baroque-like effects which increasingly seemed out of place as the rehearsals proceeded and which were then done away with: for example, the ceremonial ballet called for in the third scene during the dramatically very important tale of the Kings and Queens. In the same scene, according to the stage directions, golden Muses were supposed to appear in the arcades (as they were gradually lit up), bearing the ceremonial garb intended for Danae. The multiplication of golden figures would have devalued the presentation of the 'robe of honour' to Danae. The Muses were left out and replaced by a small discreet group of women servants.

At the close of Act I the stage directions state that Danae faints into the arms of her companions. 'Jupiter stamps his foot, faint sounds of thunder.' On the basis of this somewhat lapidary formulation it was impossible for me to give the act the meaningful conclusion it required, particularly since the music at this point is broad and expansive and takes up a great deal of time. The solution of the problem came from the music: after her last, anxious question Danae takes a few hesitant steps towards Jupiter; he half turns towards her and under the influence of the 'golden radiance' which has suddenly come so close to her Danae falls into a faint (*f* preceding figure 117 in the score). Jupiter's stamping his foot and the accompanying distant sound of thunder express the god's triumphant hopes (Jupiter motif). In the following bars, Midas—forgetting himself, and drunk with love for Danae—approaches the unconscious girl but is ordered back into his place, as 'Chrysopher', by an imperious gesture from Jupiter. (Runs of fifths and *ff* shortly before the close.)

Much thought was devoted to the varying guises of Jupiter and Midas, who have to exchange roles. From the first act onwards these entrances are as follows:
1. Midas, simply dressed as the messenger;
2. Jupiter on the ship, dressed in golden attire as 'King Midas';
3. Jupiter enters the marriage chamber (Act II), still attired as the golden Midas.

Here the confusion begins. According to the directions on page 161, Jupiter takes off his golden disguise, giving it later to the muleteer (the fourth entrance). What is Jupiter to wear underneath this garment of deception? Should he—can he—appear at this point as a god? The prosaic doffing and donning of the golden attire destroys any mystery associated with the golden touch and removes from the climax of the second act any sense of uncanny forces at work when Danae is transformed into the golden statue.

A better solution is this: in the confrontation between Jupiter and Midas the god retains his golden attire, thus maintaining the deception that he is Midas and upholding his

control over Danae. The real Midas becomes a slave to the golden touch by which he is bound and which is to become a curse. Jupiter storms out and Midas—retreating before the approaching marriage procession—leaves the room. (In this way the audience still has in its mind's eye the image of Jupiter as a golden figure and of Midas as a simple messenger.)

At the point where the four Queens turn to the figure whom they believe to be Jupiter, Midas, now in the golden attire, appears again. (This is the fifth entrance.) The four Queens and Danae initially take him for Jupiter; so too must the audience—that is, until his voice reveals the deception.

The sixth entrance is 'Jupiter in an uncanny glow of light'. Again the question arises as to what appearance Jupiter should now assume. The golden transformations in the chamber and the transformations which Danae herself undergoes cause further problems, which become still more difficult in Act III. To start with Jupiter enters as a god— just as he was when he left the stage in Act II. But how should he look to the four Queens, who up to now have only seen him as the golden King Midas? Furthermore, Semele expresses the wish that her divine lover should reveal himself just once in his true form, a request which Jupiter refuses with great seriousness and emphasis. I pointed out this apparently insoluble contradiction to Gregor. In reply, he ventured that this other 'true form' should be taken to mean Jupiter as 'Zeus Cronion', a figure of ominous and fateful appearance to human eyes. On this basis the only logical solution was this: that in this seventh entrance Jupiter is in the same attire as at the end of Act II.

There are no instructions at all for the entrance of the angry creditors and the four Kings because, of course, Jupiter is addressed by them as 'Midas'—with the result that the only allowable circumstance for this scene is the appearance of Jupiter as the already familiar golden figure.

The cunning Mercury must help and provide the threatened Jupiter with the necessary articles of disguise (helmet, cloak) until the golden rain brings liberation.

The last scene in the hut (the eighth entrance) shows Jupiter as an 'old man in a burnous', where a change in make-up is *not* to be recommended.

A letter Richard Strauss wrote to me on 10 January 1945 contained echoes of the dress re-

Bayerische Staatsoper, Munich, 1967
Final scene of Act I. The messenger, Chrysopher (Midas: Waldemar Kmentt), wants to approach Danae (Maria van Dongen) but is turned back by Jupiter (Hans Günter Nöcker).
Producer: Rudolf Hartmann.
Conductor: Joseph Keilberth.
Sets and costumes: Jean-Pierre Ponnelle.

hearsal in Salzburg on 16 August 1944 where, for the first and only time, he was able to see and hear a production of his work: 'My life ended on 1 September (when German theatres were ordered to be closed). It would have been best if the exalted Muses on Olympus had called me to them on 17 August [the day after the dress rehearsal].'

Title-page of the vocal score drawn for the première of *Capriccio* by the Berlin artist Rochus Gliese; and a passage from the manuscript full score: the opening of the first scene, with Flamand's words: 'Bezaubernd ist sie heute wieder…' (How bewitching she is again today).

Capriccio

In writing about Richard Strauss's last stage work, personal memories crowd in upon me. I was drawn into the development of *Capriccio* from its inception; I learnt how intense concentration could make one forget the war completely and how a very special work like *Capriccio* could take shape and life from its librettist and composer. I can still recall the excitement of that period, and my love for this exquisite piece has endured: the number of times that I have produced it bears witness to that. At the very end of his life Richard Strauss called *Capriccio* his testament, and after his death I felt a sense of obligation to be executor of this testament by bringing the work to a wide public. After the Munich performance others followed in Dresden, Vienna, Zurich, Salzburg, Paris and London as well as at major German theatres. The work has a quality about it reminiscent of *Le nozza di Figaro*: pro-

ductions can be endlessly varied without wantonly altering the substance of the work.

The correspondence between Richard Strauss and Clemens Krauss, published in 1963 by Willi Schuh and Götz Klaus Kende, is very informative on the creative development of *Capriccio*.

Krauss was the fourth librettist, after Hofmannsthal, Zweig and Gregor, to work with Strauss. All four men were Austrian, or of Austrian origin, which is certainly no mere coincidence when one recalls the Bavarian Strauss's preference for Austrian literary resourcefulness. Their correspondence shows that the composer and librettist took immense pains over the opera. There were repeated discussions about the title. After considering various alternatives, they finally both agreed on *Capriccio; a Conversation Piece for Music*. Strauss described exactly what he wanted for the lighting sequences, the furniture

Bayerische Staatsoper, Munich, 1942
First sketch by Rochus Gliese, which at the producer's request was altered in many ways (positioning of the spinet, arrangement of the wall mirror, etc.). But the basic structural outline of the room, with the elevated rear section, was retained.
Producer: Rudolf Hartmann.
Conductor: Clemens Krauss.
Sets and costumes: Rochus Gliese.

and the musical instruments, and drew sketches to make his point. Krauss found work on the piece so gratifying that he soon suggested ideas for a new work.

Strauss set down his definitive attitude to *Capriccio* in a letter of 28 July 1941:

> As for a new opera, it can of course be agreeable to 'think about it'. But do you really believe that after *Capriccio*, or 'Fuge' [fugue] or the 'Muse' or the 'Muse Madeleine' or 'Erato' or ... something better or even just as good could follow? Is this D flat major not the best conclusion to my life's work for the theatre? After all one can leave only one testament!

News that Krauss was working with the composer at the same time as himself had been kept from Gregor; so it was with some pangs of conscience that Strauss gave Gregor the final text for his opinion. Gregor's reaction was justifiably critical, and revealed a sense of having been slighted. He soon, however, regained his composure and again took up the old draft for *Semiramis*, also proposing a new ballet, *Pandora*.

But *Capriccio*, whose plot runs as follows, was to remain as Strauss's testament.

In Paris, towards the end of the eighteenth century, a major argument broke out in cultural circles on account of the fundamental reforms to the hitherto accepted operatic style carried out so vigorously by Gluck the composer.

The date is 1775, and the topic of '*Wort oder Ton?*' (are the words or the music more important in opera?) is controversial even in the salon of Countess Madeleine, where it is hotly discussed. It will soon be the lady of the house's birthday and her brother is planning a series of artistic celebrations. On this particular afternoon various suggestions are being considered. Two favoured 'friends of the house', Flamand, a composer and Olivier, a poet, are hoping to crown the festivities with works of their own.

A string sextet composed by Flamand is just being played for the first time in the music salon. Both the composer and the poet are lovingly watching the Countess in the next room as she immerses herself totally in the music. The two friends realize that they are rivals for the affections of this highly educated and beautiful woman. La Roche, a theatrical producer, is also present, but he sleeps through the sextet. On waking he becomes involved in a conversational skirmish with the two friends. The hints of the differences of opinion that will emerge later are already evident. The Countess comes out of the music salon with her brother, the Count; she is almost tangibly excited by the music, leading

him to advise her, lightly but mockingly, that she should 'make a distinction between the work and the author' and not let her partiality to the handsome Flamand become too apparent. In reply, the Countess cheerfully reminds her brother of his dislike of music and preference for the spoken word—and above all of his lively interest in the beautiful actress, Clairon.

Returning from the hall that serves as a theatre, La Roche outlines to the Countess the festival programme which he has planned, and announces specifically that he will be putting on his own work, a grand '*azione teatrale* with the whole troupe'. A disagreement seems about to break out when the discussion is interrupted by the arrival of the actress, Clairon, whom the

Bayerische Staatsoper, Munich, 1942
The programme for the première gives the names of a carefully chosen cast which proved to be a most happy combination of players. Even the smaller roles (Servants, Prompter, Major Domo) were filled by first-class singers.
Producer: Rudolf Hartmann.
Conductor: Clemens Krauss.
Sets and costumes: Rochus Gliese.

Bayerische Staatsoper
National-Theater

Mittwoch den 28. Oktober 1942

Uraufführung
Capriccio
Ein Konversationsstück für Musik in einem Aufzug
von
Clemens Krauß
und
Richard Strauß

Musikalische Leitung: Clemens Krauß

Inszenierung: Rudolf Hartmann   Bühnenbild und Kostüme: Rochus Gliese

Die Gräfin	Viorica Ursuleac
Der Graf, ihr Bruder	Walter Höfermayer
Flamand, ein Musiker	Horst Taubmann
Olivier, ein Dichter	Hans Hotter
La Roche, der Theaterdirektor	Georg Hann
Die Schauspielerin Clairon	Hildegarde Ranczak
Monsieur Taupe	Carl Seydel
Eine italienische Sängerin	Irma Beilke a. G.
Ein italienischer Tenor	Franz Klarwein
Eine junge Tänzerin	Liselotte Schwarz
Der Haushofmeister	Georg Wieter

Acht Diener:
Josef Trojan-Regar
Franz Theo Reuter
Walther Carnuth
Karl Schmidt
Arno Lehner-Schwed
Karl Mücke
Willi Günther
Walter Bracht

Ort der Handlung: Ein Schloß in der Nähe von Paris, zur Zeit als Gluck dort sein Reformwerk der Oper begann. Etwa um 1775.

Einstudierung der Tanz-Szene: Pino Mlakar
Kostümgestaltung und Maske: Alexander C Stenz-Hentze

Anfang 19 Uhr   **Ende gegen 21½ Uhr**

Programm zu ℛ.ℳ 1.—; Textbuch zu ℛ.ℳ 1.— an der Kasse, zu ℛ.ℳ 1.10 bei den Einlaßdienern zu haben

Bayerische Staatsoper, Munich,
1942
A scene from the première taken
from the wings. In foreground,
with his back to the camera,
Horst Taubmann as Flamand;
seated: Viorica Ursuleac as the
Countess and Walter Höfermayer
as the Count; standing, with a
cup in his hand: Georg Hann as
the theatre director, La Roche.
The assembled company has turned its attention to the young
dancer.
Producer: Rudolf Hartmann.
Conductor: Clemens Krauss.
Sets and costumes: Rochus Gliese.

Count has been impatiently awaiting. In a clear allusion to the Countess, Clairon asks her former lover, the poet Olivier, about the final scene of his work which has not yet been written. She and the Count improvise a new scene with impromptu recitative, and for the first time the words of a sonnet dedicated to the Countess are heard. Olivier and Flamand remain behind with the Countess. The poet recites his sonnet again in passionate homage to the honoured lady of the house. Flamand's creative imagination is fired by the words and he retires to the music salon. With some effort the Countess then succeeds in warding off Olivier's declarations of love and breathes a sigh of relief when Flamand returns triumphantly, having set the sonnet to music.

After he has performed the newly composed piece, the Countess is deeply impressed, but now above all by the *words* of the sonnet, which have been given new life by the music. Flamand confesses his love for her and asks for her answer. She promises to come to the library the next

morning at eleven o'clock to give her reply: Olivier or Flamand, *'Wort oder Ton'*.

Because the Countess by nature prefers music to poetry, she subconsciously favours the composer, Flamand. His love for her is expressed in the first instance through his compositions; his personal relationship to her is a secondary factor overshadowed by his artistic creativity.

Olivier's thoughts, on the other hand, are fixed on the woman herself. His masculinity confuses and enchants the Countess. He possesses a superior intellect, and uses it and his poetic talents in the service of his amorous desires.

Symbolically this signifies that thought must always precede word, whereas in music—the most immediate of all the arts—sound springs from an intangible infinity and is both thought and expression at the same time.

The Count returns in a cheerful mood, and talks animatedly of Clairon, who has honoured his 'theatrical talent' with praise. His sister makes affectionate but mocking comments about his burning passion for the actress, but

Bayerische Staatsoper, Munich, 1942
Panorama of the room as the discussion about the primacy in opera of words or music begins. The players *(from left to right):* Hildegarde Ranczak, Viorica Ursuleac, Georg Hann, Horst Taubmann, Walter Höfermayer and Hans Hotter. The ornamental pelmets in the upper windows were removed by the designer after the first performance. The formal atmosphere was relaxed by constantly rearranging the furniture. Producer: Rudolf Hartmann. Conductor: Clemens Krauss. Sets and costumes: Rochus Gliese.

then admits that Flamand and Olivier have caused confusion in her own heart.

The assembled company returns from the theatre. La Roche presents a young female dancer as a surprise foretaste of his festival programme. After a dance, Olivier initiates a lively discussion about music and poetry, *Wort und Ton.* Olivier and the Count agree in rejecting opera as an art form. In an emotional lament La Roche bemoans the 'deafening noise of the orchestra' in 'modern' opera and the imminent demise of the elegant and embellished cantilena of Italian opera. The discussion ends with a duet by two Italian singers in the 'classical manner' so highly valued by La Roche. The Count arranges with Clarion that they should spend the evening together in Paris, and believes that all he has hoped and wished for will now come true.

La Roche, giving in to the general wish of the house guests, then reveals his programme, which has hitherto been kept secret, and presents the first part of 'the festival of homage', a sublime allegory called 'The Birth of Pallas Athene'. This suggestion evokes uncontrollable laughter from both his rivals, Flamand and Olivier, and La Roche feels slighted. The Countess consoles him by asking about the second part of the festival. He develops plans for a production of 'The Fall of Carthage', with every kind of stage-effect. The cheerfulness shown by Olivier and Flamand turns into furious rage.

Unexpectedly La Roche ends the altercation with a convincing and expansive speech. He deploys all the skill of a practical man of the theatre to refute the objections to his scheme, and allows his own genuine artistic passion to be glimpsed beneath the extravagance of his improbable scheme. As a good producer he does not forget to remind mankind of his own services to the theatre and, by improvising the inscription to be placed on his tomb, is greeted by general applause.

Introducing another idea, the Countess commissions a new, joint work from the poet and the composer. Her brother is horrified and mischievously suggests that they should take as their subject the events of that day and all the persons present, dramatizing their conflicts and setting them to music. At first this idea causes general surprise, but is then accepted. The objections raised by La Roche are shouted down. Olivier is ready to begin immediately on the scenario, a decision motivated to a great extent by the thought that the Countess still has to inform him about the end of the opera, namely whether she has decided in favour of himself or Flamand.

After politely taking her leave, Clairon departs for Paris with the Count. Flamand and Olivier watch her go. Each is full of thoughts of the Countess, convinced that he will emerge victor. La Roche urges the two to return to Paris, bombarding the poet with advice about the

Staatsoper, Dresden, 1944
This room in soft pastel shades was designed by Adolf Mahnke in 1944 for the first performance in Dresden. The forward projection of the stage was the result of the producer's previous experience. The object was to increase the intelligibility of the libretto. The casting for the two main female roles was excellent, with Margarethe Teschemacher as the Countess and Martha Rohs as Clairon.
Producer: Rudolf Hartmann.
Conductor: Karl Elmendorff.

draft of his newly commissioned work. He insists on a good exit line in the opera—as he himself makes a weak exit.

The stage is briefly empty before a group of eight servants enter. They quietly comment on the activities and engaging follies of the main characters. They discuss opera from the point of view of those on the other side of the green baize door; one of them wonders whether servants will become the subject for an opera. The others comment wryly on the hectic artistic and personal passions all around them. They provide a further layer of philosophical puzzle, making the audience wonder which is the opera and which the 'opera'. The Major Domo reappears and bids them prepare supper. They leave, happy at the prospect of an evening without guests.

As the Major Domo is preparing the salon he is interrupted by a hidden voice, calling La Roche from a corner of the room. It is Monsieur Taupe, the prompter, another of Krauss's delightful logical ironies. He is an insignificant man, who stumbles in with a huge bound volume under his arm. The prompter, whose job is tireless vigilance, had been asleep throughout the deliberations. Against a muted orchestra he comments eerily on the world of illusion over which he presides. The Major Domo gives him

advice on how to get back to Paris, and he departs, wondering whether everything isn't a dream.

The central question remains unanswered: '*Wort oder Ton?*' The only person who can answer it is the Countess, both theoretically in terms of resolving the discussion, and personally and symbolically in terms of defining her relationship with poet and composer.

She learns from the Major Domo that Olivier has announced he will arrive at eleven o'clock the next morning to learn what the close of the opera is to be. The Countess is taken aback that the two rivals for her affection are once again——as if by fate—linked inseparably to one another. To help herself reach a decision she repeats Flamand's sonnet, but to no avail. 'It is a vain effort to try to separate the two. Words and music fused into one are both bound into a new entity. The secret is that one form of art is redeemed by the other.'

Strauss was not particularly in favour with the authorities after the 'letter affair' of the thirties, when he wrote secretly to Stefan Zweig, and was at times listless and resigned: 'Is there any sense at all in writing this piece while the war is on? Who will be interested, anyway?' However, Krauss persuaded him to start work on a draft

Staatsoper, Vienna, 1944
The Vienna Staatsoper also produced *Capriccio* in 1944. The set is typical Viennese Baroque, representative but a little too heavy. The cast included two newcomers: Maria Cebotari as the Countess and Paul Schöffler as La Roche. Producer: Rudolf Hartmann. Conductor: Karl Böhm. Sets: Robert Kautsky.

Staatsoper, Vienna, 1944
Maria Cebotari as the Countess.
In the long list of successful inter-
preters of this part, Maria Cebotari
has been the most tender and cap-
tivating.
Producer: Rudolf Hartmann.
Conductor: Karl Böhm.
Sets: Robert Kautsky.

ion Joseph Gregor, whom he otherwise valued as a collaborator, was not really up to the task. The composer did not know what to do and mentioned his problem to Clemens Krauss, who said: 'Then write it yourself, Herr Doktor; after all you wrote *Intermezzo* yourself.' Strauss re-plied: 'No, no, I can't do that, I know my limits. *Intermezzo* was a different case altogether—the dialogue and experiences came from my own life and I simply wrote them down. But this work must be built up linguistically; you might say, it must be written as poetry . . .' Then he sudden-ly suggested: 'Krauss, you write it; I think you can do it.' Krauss hesitated, agreed to give it a try, and a few days later was immersed in the project.

The work was written in a relatively short space of time. With the deadline for the pre-mière approaching, new concerns appeared. The air raids each evening were causing increasing disruption of performance schedules and often drove audiences into the shelters. One question was whether there should be an interval or not, i. e. should the opera be divided into two? Orig-inally one had been planned, but later Krauss, as a responsible theatre director, urged that the première be performed without an interval to avoid any irksome interruptions. (Air raids oc-curred fairly regularly between ten and eleven o'clock each evening, which meant that the per-formance had to start at 7 p. m. to be over by ab-out 9.30 p. m.) 'Remember that the first act of *Götterdämmerung* lasts two hours and has several scenes. *We* need two and a half hours for a work with one scene and without "dramatic" events!', Strauss commented. Clemens Krauss acknowledged that he had a point, but ultimate-ly the première was performed with no interval and went off without a hitch. After the war, for the première in Paris, I reverted to the original concept and placed the interval at the point planned for it, which proved successful. The Paris audience was, of course, familiar with Gluck and during the interval lively conversa-tions could be heard about '*Wort oder Ton?*'.

The première was held in October 1942 in ex-traordinary conditions: the composer was out of favour with the Propaganda Minister; the sub-ject matter of the work appeared completely anachronistic, given the spirit of the times; a performance must have seemed utterly ir-relevant. Strauss was increasingly plagued by doubts, and, as with *Die Liebe der Danae,* wanted to hold the work back until after the war. In this situation Krauss showed courage and cunning. With his Austrian diplomatic skill he managed to persuade the angered minister to accept 'pat-

of the new piece which had nevertheless preoc-cupied his thoughts for many years. The period itself was indeed momentous and terrible. 'Per-haps you are right,' Strauss commented pensive-ly, adding with light irony (the undertone of *Capriccio* itself): 'Well, let's write it for ourselves and a few other people who haven't yet lost their reason; let's do it for our own amusement!' But Strauss had miscalculated the opera's impact. Right from the première *Capriccio* captivated opera audiences, who have remained attached to a work that also contains an intellectual chal-lenge.

The question how the libretto should be written preoccupied Strauss for a long time. Hugo von Hofmannsthal and Stefan Zweig were no longer available, and in Strauss's opin-

Opéra-Comique, Paris, 1950
The elegant set of the French pre-
mière. *From left to right:* Michel
Roux as Olivier; Mme Segalla as
the Countess; and Paul Jobin as
Flamand.
Producer: Rudolf Hartmann.
Conductor: Georges Prêtre.

Salzburg Festival, 1950
In the performance at the 1950
Salzburg Festival the singers in-
cluded *(left to right):* Anton Der-
mota as Flamand; Elisabeth Hön-
gen as Clairon; Lisa della Casa as
the Countess; Paul Schöffler as La
Roche; and Hans Braun as
Olivier.
Producer: Rudolf Hartmann.
Conductor: Karl Böhm.
Sets: Gustav Vargo.

ronage' of the première (these efforts took a week and were conducted through secret and tortuous channels); with that the way was clear for the performance, thanks to the flattered vanity of one of the most powerful men of that era.

Capriccio, a work filled with easy grace and light-hearted wisdom, took shape as the farewell of a great master.

Despite the fact that I was present at the première at the Nationaltheater in Munich on the evening of 28 October 1942, it is difficult for me to give a convincing picture of that occasion. Who among the younger generation can really imagine a great city like Munich in total darkness, or theatre-goers picking their way through the blacked-out street with the aid of small torches giving off a dim blue light through a narrow slit? All this for the experience of the *Capriccio* première. They risked being caught in a heavy air raid, yet their yearning to hear Strauss's music, their desire to be part of a festive

occasion and to experience a world of beauty beyond the dangers of war led them to overcome all these material problems.

They were then in Richard Strauss's company for the first performance of his last stage work, which was not an opera in the usual sense but a 'conversation piece for music' about an abstract theme: *'Wort oder Ton?'* The work, performed as a one-act piece lasting two and a half hours, played to a most attentive audience. The première was a success, to an extent hardly anticipated by composer, librettist and all those associated with it. Afterwards it was difficult to relinquish the liberating and uniting atmosphere created by the artistic quality of the new work. But outside the blackened city waited, and one's way homewards was fraught with potential danger... the common feeling of the evening was that *Capriccio* was bound to become popular.

The charm manifested by the various productions of this opera lies in the way the individual

Staatsoper, Hamburg, 1957
Left: Horst Günther as the Count; *centre:* Clara Ebers as the Countess and Gisela Litz as Clairon; *right:* Hermann Prey as Olivier; Toni Blankenheim as La Roche; and Walter Geisler as Flamand. Producer: Rudolf Hartmann. Conductor: Joseph Keilberth. Sets: Alfred Siercke.

Munich Festival
The difficult scene with the Servants in a performance at the Munich Festival. After the war the work was first performed in 1953 at the Gärtnerplatz Theater, and new productions have been frequently mounted.
Producer: Rudolf Hartmann.
Conductor: Robert Heger.
Sets: Rochus Gliese.

Munich Festival, 1964
A scene from the 1964 production with Otto Wiener as La Roche; Richard Holm as Flamand; and Hermann Prey as Olivier. The designer has reinterpreted the idea of pillars, but has created a light and graceful room. The producer used the foreground for the intimate conversation scenes and developed the action in an increasingly free manner. Performances were now held in the small house of the State Opera, the Cuvilliéstheater.
Producer: Rudolf Hartmann.
Conductor: Hans Gierster.
Sets: Herbert Kern.

Cuvilliéstheater, Munich, 1970
The Countess (since 1964 Claire
Watson) and her brother (Hans
Günter Nöcker) in a confidential
conversation. The chess game in
the foreground greatly assisted
comprehension of the libretto.
Producer: Rudolf Hartmann.
Conductor: Ferdinand Leitner;
later Marek Janowski and Gustav
Kuhn.
Sets: Ita Maximowna.

figures are portrayed and developed. They must be finely chiselled and chased, because this is a work where the action consists of no action, and where all the characters, their movements, gestures and little idiosyncrasies, their very appearance, are prominent right from the start, so that each actor produces a new situation and sets a different basic tone. Let us explain this by looking at the character of La Roche, the theatre director. First, its external contours have to be established: director not of a strolling company à la Striese, but the esteemed head of the famous Comédie Française. This in itself sets limits, in the broadest sense, on his appearance, manner and behaviour. A glance at the different performers of the role of La Roche will show the diversity of interpretation that the part is capable of sustaining.

First Georg Hann in the première: stout and pithy, easily upset if he felt himself misunderstood, but entirely taken up with his task. A complete contrast to, say, Paul Schöffler (Vienna), an intelligent actor, whose La Roche is convinced of the value of his ideas, which he vigorously defends, and is always self-assured. Then there was Kurt Böhme (Dresden, Munich), a supreme comic actor, showing La Roche as a man who would gladly have played every part himself, and who fought tenaciously over every detail, making full use of his powerful presence.

Again in contrast there was Otto Wiener (Munich, Vienna), a superior and educated actor, who worked with irony and skilful intellect, quick-witted and full of fun, but never coarse. Or Kieth Engen (Munich), cunning, ironic and very emphatic in his directorial role . . . the list could easily be extended.

Of the female characters, Countess Madeleine (a symbol of the educated, receptive audience) was played among others by: Viorica Ursuleac (première), Margarethe Teschemacher (Dresden), Maria Cebotari (Vienna, Zurich), Lisa della Casa (Vienna, Munich, Salzburg), Claire Watson (Munich), Clara Ebers (Hamburg), Ingrid Bjoner (Düsseldorf) and Lilian Sukis (Munich).

These names indicate the variety and pleasure entailed in producing the work. It is for a producer to cast such diverse personalities in these roles. This point is brought out still more clearly in regard to the casting of Clairon, the Parisian actress: Hildegarde Ranczek (première), Christel Goltz, Elisabeth Höngen, Gisela Litz, Martha Rohs, Ira Malaniuk and Hertha Töpper have been among those who have played this part.

The subsidiary roles of the Major Domo, the Prompter, the Italian singers and the Servants also show the need for sharp characterization. New possibilities of development continually surprise the producer. The variations are inex-

Cuvilliéstheater, Munich, 1978
Since 1978 Lilian Sukis has played
the Countess in the Munich production. The trend has been
towards attaining an impression
of effortless grace.
Producer: Rudolf Hartmann.
Conductor: Gustav Kuhn.
Sets: Ita Maximowna.

haustible (as with *Figaro*), because the relation-
ships that spring up between the members of
each cast develop their own momentum. Logi-
cally enough the size of the theatre where the
opera is shown also matters a great deal. The
greatest impact has been made by performances
in medium-sized theatres such as Theater an der
Wien (Vienna), Cuvilliéstheater (Munich),
Gärtnerplatz Theater (Munich), Opernhaus
(Zurich), Opéra Comique (Paris), because here
circumstances have been ideal for making the libretto clearly audible and intelligible. Of course,
a good conductor remains essential, because
even in a relatively smaller theatre a mediocre
performance by the orchestra will kill the 'conversation', and with it the heart of the piece.

Since the première, the design of the set has
undergone many changes, but happily all those
I have seen have been in keeping with the period
around 1775 in which the work is chronologi-
cally located. There have been no radical 'modern' (and thus, wrong) interpretations. Here
we have to look at how the thoughts of some of
the sensitive set-designers have found expression in these variations. Rochus Gliese, at the
première, constructed a beautifully proportioned and somewhat austere set; a little later, Adolf
Mahnke (Dresden) created a light salon with a
pastel effect; and in Vienna Robert Kautsky produced a pompous Baroque hall. Later designers
concentrated on the presence of the central
character, and the overall effect became more
supple and tender. Some fine examples were
those by Herbert Kern and Ita Maximowa.

With the exception of the Countess, none of
the characters changes costume throughout the
piece; the costume design is therefore more than
usually significant. Some splendid practical solutions have been found, especially for the
Countess and the fashionable Clairon, reflecting
their different personalities. In Vienna and Salzburg the costumes were themselves works of art
in terms of colour and cut. In some instances the
set-designers made the costumes themselves,
but specialists in costume design were also responsible for many beautiful and unforgettable
creations (e. g. Charlotte Flemming).

Capriccio, the testament in music, is Strauss's
superb legacy, a work which captivates everyone
and everything involved it: people, sets, costumes, furniture, instruments, props. *Everything*
clamours to have its say, to make its contribu-
tion to this festive farewell.

Strauss concluded the foreword to *Capriccio*
with these words:

The task facing the conductor and producer in transposing the libretto and score into
the kind of reality intended by the author is
such a major and varied one that—given a
wholly successful performance—it cannot be
valued highly enough by public and critics.
An interpretation true to the music and the
words and a sympathetic imaginative treatment are 'brother and sister, like "*Wort und
Ton*"!'

Vienna, 7 April 1942   Dr. Richard Strauss

17. 6. 48.

MONTREUX-PALACE

TÉLÉGRAMMES
MONTREUPALACE
TÉL. 6 32 31

MONTREUX
SUISSE

Lieber Freund Hartmann!

Vielen Dank für Ihre guten Geburtstagswünsche, denen als überraschendes, prächtiges Geschenk Ihr wunderbarer Artikel in Schuh's Zeitschrift folgte. Ich kann Ihnen nicht beschreiben, welche Freude derselbe bei mir und meiner Frau auslöste, die mit mir begeistert war. Es war letzter schöner Lichtblick in meinem armen Invalidendasein u. ein Hoffnungsstrahl in eine nicht ganz düstere Zukunft, wenn man sein Werk in solchen Händen weiß. Was sind Sie für ein feiner Schriftsteller: als vortragenden Lehrer habe ich Sie schon in Salzburg bewundert. Ich habe einen ganzen Tag jetzt nachgedacht u. gebe Ihnen als Resultat folgenden Rat: es darf nicht sein, daß Ihr Wissen u. Können, um so mehr als Sie als Regisseur später kaum ordentlich verwerten können, wo mehr oder minder talentlosen Schülerchen in den Wind verweht oder mehr oder minder mißverstanden in halbverfallenen Theaterbuden nur mangelhaft zur Darstellung gebracht werden. Das muß Alles schwarz auf weiß niedergelegt werden. Was Sie in Ihren Lehrstunden vortragen, muß Wort für Wort von einem Parlamentsstenographen nachgeschrieben werden als wissenschaftliches Material, aus dem später Rudolf Hartmanns großes Lehrbuch über Opernregie (besonders für Gluck, Mozart-Wagner u. meine Werke) geschaffen wird, wie es noch nicht gibt. Lessing, Göthe, Tieck, auch Hebbel haben ja schon wertvolles Material für Regie u. Schauspielkunst geliefert. Aber das Buch über Opernregie u. Inszenierung muß erst geschrieben werden u. zwar von Rudolf Hartmann, dem Stanislawskij u. Reinhardt

MONTREUX-PALACE

TÉLÉGRAMMES
MONTREUPALACE
TÉL. 6 32 31

MONTREUX
SUISSE

der Oper.

Die Sammlung von peinlich aufgeschriebenen Unterrichtsstunden, wie Sie in dem Buch des großartigen Russen: „Das Geheimnis des schauspielerischen Erfolges" ist nur ein schönes Vorbild.

Ihr Buch muß nicht in 3 Wochen geschrieben, aber morgen der Stenograph bestellt u. angefangen werden, damit auch kein Wort, was Sie den Sängern u. besonders meinem guten Richard predigen, verloren geht u. ich einmal ruhig die Augen schließen kann in dem Bewußtsein, daß mein theatralisches Werk einmal nicht nur von „denkenden" Spielleitern erkannt. Wagner steht auf zu festen Füßen u. wird sogar schlechte Regisseure vertragen, aber meine u. Hofmannsthals Kinder sind zu empfindliche, unreife Geschöpfe, die nicht allzu viel Prügel vertragen!

Also auf ans Werk! Fangt an!

Besprechen Sie diese wichtigste Lebensfrage auch mit meinem Sohne! An den Kosten für den täglichen Stenographen wird er sich in meinem Namen sicher freudig beteiligen. „Opernregie als Wissenschaft" ein ganz neues literarisches Thema: die erste Ergänzung zu 10 (leider zu selten gelesenen) Bänden von Richard Wagner. Auch Hebbels „Mein Wort zum Drama" sehr geistvoll, besser wie seine Nibelungen! Dazu Dr Schuh's Biographie! dann kann es mal nicht gar zu weit fehlen! Mit herzlichsten Grüßen

Ihr

Dr Richard Strauss.

Epilogue

Capriccio brings to a close this study of Richard Strauss's works written for the stage. This large and difficult task could not have been completed without the support I have received from many quarters. In particular I should like to express gratitude to my friend Dr. Willi Schuh for his advice, and my nephew, Fred Hartmann, who was responsible for acquiring the many illustrations from around the world. My warmest thanks also go to my faithful colleague Evelyn Harder for coping with the wearisome task of typing the manuscript. My grateful appreciation and thanks go as well to those in charge of the various libraries and collections, and to the archives of the opera-houses whom I called upon for assistance. (See the list of photo credits on page 279.) I regret to say that I was able to use only a fraction of the illustrations with which I was provided. Had I used them all, this book would have expanded to gigantic proportions. As a result, I was forced to restrict my choice; a painful task, for I doubt very much that it will ever again be possible to assemble such a comprehensive selection of photographs and pictures from home and abroad. If one or two sought-after illustrations were unavailable, this was due to the destruction of many theatre archives during the war. In some cases the details accompanying these illustrations are not quite complete, because, despite intensive research, I was not always able to obtain exact information. Nevertheless, I am confident that the book has done justice to its subject. It has not turned into a specific 'textbook of opera production' of the kind that Richard Strauss once envisaged, but it has fulfilled—in part at least—a personal wish he once expressed to me in a hitherto unpublished letter. These lines signify to me, at one and the same time, his commission and his authorization. The letter reads in part:

My dear friend Hartmann,

Many thanks for your kind birthday greetings, which followed—as a surprising and magnificent present—your wonderful article in Schuh's periodical [*Schweizerische Musikzeitung,* Zurich]. I cannot describe the joy which this brought me and my wife, who is just as excited about it as I am. It cast [one] last beautiful ray of light... and hope on to a not too dismal future to know that one's works will be placed in hands such as these... What you say in your lectures must be taken down word for word by a parliamentary stenographer as scholarly material to be used later in creating Rudolf Hartmann's great textbook on opera production (particularly in regard to Gluck, Mozart, Wagner, and my own works)... Lessing, Goethe, Tieck, even Hebbel have certainly provided the most valuable material for producers and others concerned with the theatre. But the book about directing and staging opera still remains to be written and that must be done by Rudolf Hartmann, the Stanislavsky and the Reinhardt of opera.

... And I shall one day be able to close my eyes calmly in the knowledge that my work for the theatre won't only fall into the hands of over-intellectual producers.

Wagner stands on feet that are too firm, so that he will live on even without a producer, but the children that Hofmannsthal and I have borne are *sensitive, nervous creatures,* which will not withstand too much battering! So, to work! Begin!... and Dr. Schuh's biography as well! *Then things surely can't go too far wrong!*

With the most heartfelt wishes,
Yours,
(signed) Dr. Richard Strauss

Chronological Table of First Performances

Work		Place	Date
1	*Guntram*	Grossherzogliches Hoftheater, Weimar	10 May 1894
2	*Feuersnot*	Königliches Opernhaus, Dresden	21 Nov. 1901
3	*Salome*	Königliches Opernhaus, Dresden	9 Dec. 1905
4	*Elektra*	Königliches Opernhaus, Dresden	25 Jan. 1909
5	*Der Rosenkavalier*	Königliches Opernhaus, Dresden	26 Jan. 1911
6	*Ariadne auf Naxos*	Königliches Hoftheater, Stuttgart	25 Oct. 1912
7	*Josephslegende*	Théâtre National de l'Opéra, Paris	14 May 1914
6a	*Ariadne auf Naxos,* second version	Hofoper, Vienna	4 Oct. 1916
8	*Die Frau ohne Schatten*	Staatsoper, Vienna	10 Oct. 1919
9	*Schlagobers*	Staatsoper, Vienna	9 May 1924
10	*Intermezzo*	Staatsoper (Kleines Haus), Dresden	4 Nov. 1924
11	*Die ägyptische Helena*	Staatsoper, Dresden	6 June 1928
12	*Arabella*	Staatsoper, Dresden	1 July 1933
13	*Die schweigsame Frau*	Staatsoper, Dresden	24 June 1935
14	*Friedenstag*	Bayerische Staatsoper, Munich	24 July 1938
15	*Daphne*	Staatsoper, Dresden	15 Oct. 1938
16	*Die Liebe der Danae*	Festspielhaus, Salzburg	14 Aug. 1952
17	*Capriccio*	Bayerische Staatsoper, Munich	26 Oct. 1942

The cast of the premières is given in each chapter.

Richard Strauss

11 June 1864–8 September 1949

(Death mask owned by the author)

Notes

GUNTRAM

[1] R. Strauss, (ed. Willi Schuh) *Recollections and Reflections*, trans. L. J. Lawrence, London: Boosey and Hawkes, 1953
[2] *Recollections*, p. 146
[3] *Recollections*, p. 141
[4] *Recollections*, p. 140
[5] *Recollections*, p. 148

FEUERSNOT

[1] *Recollections*, p. 149

SALOME

[1] *Recollections*, p. 152
[2] *Recollections*, p. 151
[3] *Recollections*, pp. 151–2

ELEKTRA

[1] *Recollections*, pp. 154–5
[2] *The Correspondence between Richard Strauss and Hugo von Hofmannsthal*, Transl. H. Hammelmann and E. Osers, London: William Collins Sons, 1961, pp. 2–3
[3] *Correspondence*, p. 3
[4] *Correspondence*, p. 4
[5] *Correspondence*, p. 7
[6] *Correspondence*, p. 7
[7] *Correspondence*, p. 14
[8] *Recollections*, pp. 156–7
[9] *Correspondence*, p. 16
[10] *Correspondence*, pp. 16–17
[11] *Correspondence*, p. 12
[12] *Recollections*, p. 155

DER ROSENKAVALIER

[1] *Correspondence*, p. 27
[2] *Correspondence*, p. 55
[3] *Correspondence*, p. 73
[4] *Correspondence*, p. 71

[5] *Recollections*, pp. 157–8
[6] *Correspondence*, p. 69
[7] *Correspondence*, p. 46

ARIADNE AUF NAXOS

[1] *Correspondence*, p. 70
[2] *Correspondence*, pp. 75–6
[3] *Correspondence*, pp. 76–7
[4] *Correspondence*, p. 77
[5] *Correspondence*, p. 78
[6] *Correspondence*, p. 78
[7] *Correspondence*, p. 79
[8] *Correspondence*, p. 81
[9] *Correspondence*, p. 84
[10] *Correspondence*, p. 85
[11] *Correspondence*, p. 85
[12] *Correspondence*, pp. 86–7
[13] *Correspondence*, p. 87
[14] *Correspondence*, p. 93
[15] *Correspondence*, pp. 95–6
[16] *Correspondence*, p. 105
[17] *Correspondence*, p. 105
[18] *Correspondence*, pp. 106–7
[19] *Correspondence*, p. 108
[20] *Correspondence*, p. 109
[21] *Correspondence*, p. 109
[22] *Correspondence*, p. 111
[23] *Correspondence*, p. 113
[24] *Correspondence*, p. 120
[25] *Recollections*, pp. 161–2
[26] *Recollections*, p. 163

JOSEPHSLEGENDE

[1] *Correspondence*, p. 134
[2] *Correspondence*, p. 136
[3] *Correspondence*, p. 142
[4] *Correspondence*, pp. 142–3
[5] *Correspondence*, p. 144
[6] *Correspondence*, p. 172
[7] *Correspondence*, p. 150
[8] *Correspondence*, p. 151

[9] *Recollections*, p. 94
[10] *Recollections*, pp. 164–5

DIE FRAU OHNE SCHATTEN

[1] *Recollections*, p. 166
[2] *Recollections*, pp. 166–7
[3] *Correspondence*, p. 331
[4] *Correspondence*, p. 332
[5] *Correspondence*, pp. 200–1
[6] *Correspondence*, p. 202
[7] *Correspondence*, p. 204
[8] *Correspondence*, pp. 206–7
[9] *Recollections*, p. 166
[10] *Correspondence*, p. 212
[11] *Correspondence*, p. 214
[12] *Correspondence*, p. 217
[13] *Correspondence*, p. 218
[14] *Correspondence*, p. 218
[15] *Correspondence*, p. 216
[16] *Correspondence*, p. 218
[17] *Correspondence*, pp. 219–20
[18] *Correspondence*, p. 229
[19] *Correspondence*, p. 307

INTERMEZZO

[1] *Recollections*, pp. 95–6

[2] *Recollections*, p. 101
[3] *Recollections*, p. 167
[4] *Correspondence*, p. 426
[5] *Correspondence*, p. 511

DIE ÄGYPTISCHE HELENA

[1] *Correspondence*, p. 393
[2] *Correspondence*, p. 394
[3] *Correspondence*, pp. 396–7
[4] *Correspondence*, p. 404
[5] *Correspondence*, p. 405
[6] *Correspondence*, p. 405
[7] *Correspondence*, p. 405
[8] *Correspondence*, p. 410

ARABELLA

[1] *Correspondence*, p. 455
[2] *Correspondence*, p. 460
[3] *Correspondence*, pp. 460–1
[4] *Correspondence*, p. 464
[5] *Correspondence*, p. 482
[6] *Correspondence*, p. 484
[7] *Correspondence*, pp. 486–7
[8] *Correspondence*, pp. 494–5
[9] *Correspondence*, p. 534
[10] *Correspondence*, p. 536

Select Bibliography

Das Bühnenwerk von Richard Strauss in den unter Mitwirkung des Komponisten geschaffenen letzten Münchner Inszenierungen, by Willi Schuh, Zurich, 1954.

Hugo von Hofmannsthal, *Dramen,* vol V: *Operndichtungen,* Frankfurt-am-Main, 1979.

—*Erzählungen, erfundene Gespräche, Briefe, Reisen,* Frankfurt-am-Main, 1979.

Hugo von Hofmannsthal – Richard Strauss, *Der Rosenkavalier, Fassungen, Filmszenarium, Briefe,* ed. by Willi Schuh, Frankfurt-am-Main, 1971.

Richard Strauss, *Recollections and Reflections,* trans. of the above title by L.J. Lawrence, London/New York, 1953.

—*Briefe an die Eltern, 1882–1906,* ed. by Willi Schuh, Zurich/Freiburg i. Br., 1954.

Richard Strauss – Joseph Gregor, *Briefwechsel,* ed. by Roland Tenschert, Salzburg, 1955.

Richard Strauss – Hugo von Hofmannsthal, *The Correspondence Between Richard Strauss and Hugo von Hofmannsthal,* trans. of the above title by Hanns Hammelmann and Ewald Osers, London, 1961, reissued Cambridge/New York, 1980.

Richard Strauss – Clemens Krauss, *Briefwechsel,* ed. by Götz Klaus Kende and Willi Schuh, Munich, 1963, 2nd ed. 1964.

Richard Strauss – Stefan Zweig, *Briefwechsel,* ed. by Willi Schuh, Frankfurt-am-Main, 1957.

Richard Strauss – Stefan Zweig, *A Confidential Matter: The Letters of Richard Strauss and Stefan Zweig, 1931–1935,* trans. of the above title by Max Knight, University of California Press, 1977.

Der Strom der Töne trug mich fort. Die Welt um Richard Strauss in Briefen, in collaboration with Franz und Alice Strauss; ed. by Franz Grasberger, Tutzing, 1967.

Otto Erhardt, *Richard Strauss. Leben, Wirken, Schaffen,* Olten/Freiburg i. Br., 1953.

Oskar Fischel, *Das moderne Bühnenbild,* Berlin, 1923.

Joseph Gregor, *Richard Strauss. Der Meister der Oper,* Munich, 1939.

Günter Haußwald, *Richard Strauss. Ein Beitrag zur Dresdner Operngeschichte,* Dresden, 1953.

Alan Jefferson, *The Operas of Richard Strauss in Britain, 1910–63,* London, 1963.

Götz Klaus Kende, *Richard Strauss und Clemens Krauss. Eine Künstlerfreundschaft und ihre Zusammenarbeit an Capriccio,* Munich, 1960.

Heinrich Kralik, *Richard Strauss. Weltbürger der Musik,* Vienna/Munich/Basle, 1963.

Ernst Krause, *Richard Strauss,* Leipzig, 1963, paperback ed. Munich, 1979.

William Mann, *Richard Strauss: A Critical Study of the Operas,* London, 1964.

Norman Del Mar, *Richard Strauss: A Critical Commentary on his Life and Works,* 3 vols, London, 1962–72.

Richard Strauss-Jahrbuch 1954, ed. by Willi Schuh, Bonn, 1953.

Richard Strauss-Jahrbuch 1959/60, ed. by Willi Schuh, Bonn, 1960.

Richard Strauss und seine Zeit, exhibition catalogue by Signe von Scanzoni, Munich, 1964.

Richard Strauss zum 100. Geburtstag, exhibition catalogue by Franz Grasberger and Franz Hadamowsky, Vienna, 1964.

Willi Schuh, *Über Opern von Richard Strauss, Kritiken und Essays,* vol I, Zurich, 1947.

—*Der Rosenkavalier. Vier Studien,* Olten, 1968.

—'Richard Strauss und seine Libretti', in: *Bericht über den Musikwissenschaftlichen Kongress Bonn 1973,* Kassel/Basle, 1973.

—'Metamorphosen einer Ariette von Richard Strauss', in: *Opernstudien. Anna Amalie Albert zum 65. Geburtstag,* Tutzing, 1973.

—Hofmannsthals Randnotizen für Richard Strauss im 'Ariadne-Libretto', in: *Für Rudolf Hirsch,* Frankfurt-am-Main, 1975.

—*Richard Strauss, Jugend und frühe Meisterjahre, Lebenschronik 1864–1898,* Zurich, 1976.

Karl Schumann, *Das kleine Richard Strauss Buch,* Salzburg, 1970.

Richard Specht, *Richard Strauss und sein Werk,* 2 vols, Leipzig/Vienna/Zurich, 1921.

Franz Trenner, *Richard Strauss. Dokumente seines Lebens und Schaffens,* Munich, 1954.

Stefan Zweig, *Die Welt von gestern. Erinnerungen eines Europäers,* Stockholm, 1944, Frankfurt-am-Main, 1955.

Oskar Fischel, *Das moderne Bühnenbild,* Berlin, 1923.

Eduard Meyer, *Ursprung und Anfänge des Christentums,* vol II, Stuttgart/Berlin, 1924.

Emil Schürer, *Geschichte des jüdischen Volkes im Zeitalter Jesu Christi,* vol I, 4th ed. Leipzig, 1901.

Julius Wellhausen, *Israel und die jüdische Geschichte,* 3rd ed. Berlin, 1897.

Index

Photo Credits

The author and publisher would like to thank all those who have provided the material for the illustrations.

Berlin, Deutsche Staatsoper (Photos Marion Schöne) 193, 234
Boulogne, Colette Masson 63 b., 87 t., 87 b., 135 t., 135 b., 136
Buenos Aires, Teatro Colón 44 b., 60 t., 65, 200, 201, 229 t.
    Photo Miguel Micciche 134
Cologne, Theatermuseum des Instituts für Theaterwissenschaft, Universität Köln 21, 26 t., 26 b., 37 b., 38 t., 41, 42 t., 44 t., 45, 54 t., 54 b., 56, 58 b., 59 t., 59 b., 69 b., 70, 77, 78, 84 t., 84 b., 94 l. and r., 95, 97 t., 97 b., 99, 104 t., 110, 114 r., 127 t., 127 b., 138 l. and r., 139 t., 139 b., 152, 156, 167, 168 t., 168 b., 170, 173 t., 173 b., 180, 181 t., 181 b., 182 t., 182 b., 183, 209 t., 210 b., 211 t., 211 b., 212, 223 b., 228 t., 228 b., 229 b., 243 b., 253, 257
Darmstadt, Peter J. Mosdzen 88
Dresden, Deutsche Fotothek 13
—Staatstheater 20, 32, 52, 53, 67, 68, 124, 154, 166, 178, 196, 222
Florence, Teatro comunale, Maggio musicale 101, 191
Garmisch, Richard-Strauss-Archiv 123 t., 123 b.
Hamburg, Fritz Peyer 61 b., 203 b., 261
London, The Covent Garden Archives, The Royal Opera House 55
—Donald Southern 40
Milan, Teatro alla Scala 100 t., 100 b., 197 t.
Munich, Bayerisches Nationalmuseum 18
—Bayerische Staatsbibliothek, Kartensammlung 30
—Deutsches Museum 194
—Hirmer Bildarchiv 50
—Theatermuseum 27, 33, 37 t., 43, 48, 75, 112, 114 l., 115, 232, 248, 251, 262 t., 262 b.
—Sabine Töpffer 11, 15, 16, 22, 29, 34, 36, 38 b., 46, 47, 58 t., 61 t., 66, 69 l. and r., 71, 81 b., 82, 105 t., 105 b., 118, 120, 122, 129, 131, 132, 143, 145,

155 t., 155 b., 157, 158, 160, 161 t. l. and r., 161 b. l. and r., 169, 174 l. and r., 175, 179, 187, 190 t., 190 b., 192 b., 199, 203 t. l. and r., 208, 213 t., 214, 215, 218, 224, 226 t., 226 b., 227 t., 227 b., 230 l. and r., 231 l. and r., 241, 245 t., 245 b., 246, 247, 249 t l. and r., 249 b l. and r., 263, 264, 269
New York, The Metropolitan Museum of Art, The Collection of Robert L. B.
    Tobin 108
—Metropolitan Opera Archives 35, 60 b., 72, 73, 74 b.
    J. Heffernan 83, 133 b.
    Sedge LeBlang 57 t., 76 b. l., 186, 188
    Louis Mélançon 102, 103, 133 t.
Nuremberg, F. Ulrich 185
Paris, Photo Routhier, Studio Lourmel 64 l. and r., 86, 111, 113 l., 113 r.
Salzburg, Winfried Rabanus 49
—Salzburger Festspiele, Archiv 74 t., 81 t., 104 b., 117, 189 t., 238 l., 238 r., 260 b.
    Photo Ellinger 172, 189 b.
    Photo Madner 197 b.
    Photo Steinmetz 137 t., 137 b.
    Photo Völkel 184
San Francisco, Bill Cogan 130
—Photo Strohmeyer 57 b.
Vienna, Galerie Würthle (Photo Galerie Welz, Salzburg) 236
—Österreichische Nationalbibliothek 24 l. and r., 144, 146, 147 t., 147 b., 148 t., 148 b., 223 t. l. and r.
—Photo Hausmann 159 r.
—Hanny Steffek, Privatarchiv 159 l. (Photo Rudolf Betz, Munich), 192 t.
—Volksoper, Archiv 28 (Photo Paul Macku)
From the private archives of the author 8, 10, 12 t,. 12 b., 39, 63 t., 76 t. r., 76 b., 80 t., 80 b., 98, 116, 150, 151, 164, 195, 209 b., 213 b., 225 t., 225 c., 239, 242 t., 242 b., 252, 255, 256, 258, 259, 260 t.
Illustrations reproduced from original material 79 t., 79 b., 90, 92, 93, 126, 142, 171 l. and r., 176, 206, 240 l. and r., 254, 266

ACKNOWLEDGEMENTS

The extracts from the English translation by L. J. Lawrence of *Richard Strauss: Recollections and Reflections* (© Copyright 1953 by Boosey & Hawkes Ltd.) are reproduced by kind permission of Boosey & Hawkes Music Publishers Ltd., London.

The extracts from the English translation by H. Hammelmann and E. Osers of *The Correspondence between Richard Strauss and Hugo von Hofmannsthal* (© Copyright 1961 by William Collins Sons & Co. Ltd.) are reproduced by kind permission of William Collins Sons & Co. Ltd., London.

Mü 339 Strau (Har)
Th 275 (Vwi)
Th 442   "